Not Many Fathers

Why Othniel Became a Judge

Scripture quotations marked (NKJV) are taken from the New King James Version®. Copyright © 1982 by Thomas Nelson, Inc. Used by permission. All rights reserved.

Scripture quotations marked (NLT) are taken from the Holy Bible, New Living Translation, copyright © 1996, 2004, 2007 by Tyndale House Foundation. Used by permission of Tyndale House Publishers, Inc., Carol Stream, IL 60188. All rights reserved.

Copyright © 2021 by the **Bellbird Trust**

All rights reserved. This book or any portion thereof may not be reproduced, stored in a retrieval system, or transmitted in any form or by any means – electronic, mechanical, photocopy, recording, scanning or other – except for brief quotations in critical reviews or articles, without the prior express written permission of the publisher.

ISBN 978-1-7386150-3-2

Published by: **Bellbird Books**
2 Sabine Drive,
Richmond, 7020
New Zealand.

Special Thanks

To my friend Bruce for his time-consuming efforts in editing this book.

1 Corinthians 4: 14-16 tells us, *"I do not write these things to shame you, but as my beloved children I warn you. For though you might have ten thousand instructors in Christ, yet you do not have many fathers; for in Christ Jesus I have begotten you through the gospel. Therefore I urge you, imitate me."* (NKJV)

This book explores the question, by way of a fictional narrative based on real Biblical events, 'what it means to be a Father and why we need Fathers?'.

Table of Contents

Special Thanks iv

Introduction ix

The Storm 1

Just Kenaz 9

Moses 17

Adoption 25

The Law 36

Blasphemy 46

The Journey Begins 55

Meat to Eat 63

Spies 71

Marriage 83

Children 91

Rebellion 99

Father Caleb 108

No Water 115

Grumblings 122

Snakebite 129

Training 138

Water boy 146

Plague Erupts 156

Second Census 164

War Begins 173

Joshua Takes Over 185

Jordan River	192
Achan's Sin	200
Gibeonites	207
The Longest Day	216
Jabin of Hazor	226
Caleb's Demand	234
The Challenge	243
Gilgal	251
Eastern Tribes	257
Wedding	264
Inheritance	275
Springs of Water	283
New Life	290
Family	297
Time with Caleb	306
Passover	315
Drawing Near	323
Grandchildren	330
Joshua's Summons	335
Caleb Dies	343
Turning Away	351
Cushan-Rishathaim	359
The Call	366
Surprise Attack	382
Spoil and Passover	390
The Judge	397

Death	403
Why Are Fathers Few?	409
Author's Note	418
About the Author	421

Introduction

I began writing this book as a theological discussion and quickly realized that the subject could be explained easier by example rather than theory. I have taken the man called Othniel, mentioned in the book of Joshua as the son of Kenaz, the younger brother of Caleb, and embellished the story of his life demonstrating how the father figures in his life shaped who he became.

What this books intends to shows is that very ordinary people can be shaped throughout their lives by seemingly uneventful events and occurrences to mould them into the person God desires. Such is case for most of us today that only when life is reviewed from old age can you sometimes see a glimpse of all the mundane and often unrelated happenings that have formed you into the person you became. People don't usually set out to be a father; it's only by God creative dealings that men become fathers.   Unfortunately many don't make it.

Othniel was born in the wilderness where the children of Israel wandered for forty years. He grew up in a period during which all the generation that had enrolled in the initial census died off. At the time they crossed the river Jordan to enter the

Promised Land there were only two men aged over sixty – Joshua and Caleb.

Somehow, even though Othniel was born as an outsider, he drew from the experience of the fathers in his life which won him his cherished bride and allowed him to go on and become the first of the Judges of Israel after they had conquered the Land.

The references to Othniel in the Bible are sparse and scattered. However, when these verses are studied collectively and in context a fuller picture emerges. We are told in Joshua Chapter 15 that Othniel was the son of Kenaz, the brother of Caleb (one of the 12 spies). In Judges 3:9 it suggests that Othniel could be Caleb's younger brother, yet it also says that Othniel's father was Kenaz while Caleb's father was Jephunneh. The Bible is not clear on the origin of Kenaz but the Hebrew word here for brother is 'awkh', which also means kin or kinsman, so he may not necessarily have been a blood brother of Caleb. There is also doubt that, in accordance with the Law of Moses, Othniel would not have been allowed to marry Caleb's daughter if indeed they were blood brothers, since she would be a close relative.

Whatever the actual situation I have made a conjecture that Kenaz was a descendant of the Kenites and was simply named Kenaz after his ancestor's heritage. It's interesting to see that Caleb's father Jephunneh is also called a Kenite in Numbers 32:12 and in Joshua 14:6 and 14. For this reason I have assumed the possibility that Kenaz and Jephunneh were both of

Introduction

the Kenite clan from the Midian region and, therefore, Kenizzites.

The Kenites are first mention in Genesis 15:18-21 as living in Canaan in the land God promised to Abraham. They are later mentioned living in the land of Midian as one and the same.

It is assumed that the Kenites where the descendants of Esau's son Reuel (Moses's father-in-law Jethro is also called Reuel). The family of Reuel broke away from Edom (Esau), moved South and lived in the land of Midian. They multiplied to a clan but, while tolerated by the Midians, they never integrated and became known as the Kenites. Reuel remembered Yahweh the God of his ancestor Abraham and taught his offspring in His ways. Jethro followed Yahweh as much as he knew and was known as a priest to Yahweh. This status gave him reverence by the Midians but perhaps not acceptance. They lived east of the Gulf of Aqaba in the north-western regions of the Arabian Desert.

Moses spent 40 years in voluntary exile in Midian after killing an Egyptian. There, he married Zipporah, the daughter of Midianite priest Jethro (also known as Reuel).

During the Baal-Peor episode, when Moabite women seduced Israelite men, Zimri, the son of a Simeonite chief, got involved with a Midianite woman called Cozbi. The couple were speared by Phinehas and war against Midian followed. Perhaps Moses, with forty years of living in Midian, didn't require a lot of persuasion to carry out the Lord's command to destroy the Midianites?

The following are the scriptural references I've based this story on.

Exodus 2:15-21, "When Pharaoh heard of this matter, he sought to kill Moses. But Moses fled from the face of Pharaoh and dwelt in the land of Midian; and he sat down by a well. **Now the priest of Midian had seven daughters**. And they came and drew water, and they filled the troughs to water their father's flock. Then the shepherds came and drove them away; but Moses stood up and helped them, and watered their flock. When **they came to Reuel their father**, he said, "How is it that you have come so soon today?" And they said, "An Egyptian delivered us from the hand of the shepherds, and he also drew enough water for us and watered the flock." So, he said to his daughters, "And where is he? Why is it that you have left the man? Call him, that he may eat bread." Then Moses was content to live with the man, and he gave Zipporah his daughter to Moses." (NKJV) [Emphasis added]

Judges 1:16, "Now **the children of the Kenite, Moses' father-in-law**, went up from the City of Palms with the children of Judah into the Wilderness of Judah, which lies in the South near Arad; and they went and dwelt among the people." (NKJV) [Emphasis added]

Numbers 10:29-33, "Now Moses said to **Hobab the son of Reuel the Midianite, Moses' father-in-law**, "We are setting out for the place of which the Lord said, 'I will give it to you.' Come with us, and we will treat you well; for the Lord has promised good things to Israel." And he said to him, "I will not go, but I will depart to my own land and to my relatives." So, Moses said,

Introduction

"Please do not leave, inasmuch as you know how we are to camp in the wilderness, and you can be our eyes. And it shall be, if you go with us—indeed it shall be—that whatever good the Lord will do to us, the same we will do to you." So, they departed from the mountain of the Lord on a journey of three days;" (NKJV) [Emphasis added]

Joshua 14:6, *"Then the children of Judah came to Joshua in Gilgal. And* **Caleb the son of Jephunneh the Kenizzite** *said to him: "You know the word which the Lord said to Moses the man of God concerning you and me in Kadesh Barnea."* (NKJV) [Emphasis added] Kenizzite here is taken to mean 'of the Kenite people' in the same way as we speak of one of the children of Israel as an Israelite.

Joshua 15:13, *"Now to* **Caleb the son of Jephunneh** *he gave a share among the children of Judah, according to the commandment of the Lord to Joshua, namely, Kirjath Aruba, which is Hebron (Arba was the father of Anak). Caleb drove out the three sons of Anak from there: Sheshai, Ahiman, and Talmai, the children of Anak. Then he went up from there to the inhabitants of Debir (formerly the name of Debir was Kirjath Sepher – the city of Sepher the main person/founder of the city).* (NKJV) [Emphasis added]

And Caleb said, ***"He who attacks Kirjath Sepher and takes it, to him I will give Achsah my daughter as wife." So Othniel the son of Kenaz, the brother of Caleb, took it; and he gave him Achsah his daughter as wife.*** *Now it was so, when she came to him, that she persuaded him to ask her father for a field. So, she dismounted from her donkey, and Caleb said to* her, "What do you wish?" She answered, "Give me a blessing; since you have given me land in the South, give me also springs of water." So, he gave her the upper springs and the lower springs." (NKJV) [Emphasis added]

Judges 3:9, "But when they cried out to the LORD, he raised up for them a deliverer, Othniel son of Kenaz, Caleb's younger brother, who saved them." (NKJV)

Judges 3:10, "The Spirit of the LORD came on him, so that he became Israel's judge and went to war. The LORD gave Cushan-Rishathaim king of Aram into the hands of Othniel, who overpowered him." (NKJV)

Judges 3:11, "So the land had peace for forty years, until Othniel son of Kenaz died." (NKJV)

1 Chronicles 4:13, "The sons of Kenaz: Othniel and Seraiah. The sons of Othniel: Hathath and Meonothai." (NKJV)

Finally, I have used the name Yahweh when referring to God as that was the Hebrew name for God in common use during this time period.

1

The Storm

There it was again; Kenaz leaned over the thicket bush defences and peered into the eerie darkness. He hated this late-night watch, especially when there was no moon, the darkness was all absorbing and nothing could be trusted. Because of the prolonged summer drought Hobab and Kenaz had wandered far from their normal grazing grounds that day while searching for food for their thirty-five goats and fifty-five prized lambs. Arriving near dark they were forced to make camp in the thickets around a faithful watering hole. They'd cut down some of the thicket to shore up the ageing perimeter fence and counted in their prized livestock.

"Lions! I hate those monsters", Kenaz muttered, "always hungry and always ready to nab a cheap lamb meal, if the opportunity presented." Kenaz strained his ears to hear the sound again but he needn't have bothered, the night silence was shattered by the noise of a screaming rider-less camel suddenly not two metres in front of him. "What on Noah's ark is a Camel doing out alone at this time of night?" Kenaz shouted to no one in particular, his heart rate slowly retreating from its dizzying heights. He quickly raced to the fence entrance and prized it open a little and ventured out into the darkness towards the source of the commotion.

Despite its distress the camel seemed pleased to see human company and took no exception to Kenaz approach. Bizarrely it was fully saddled as if someone had just dismounted. He quickly grabbed the reigns and called out to locate its rider. No answer was the firm reply and as the intense darkness made a search impossible Kenaz led the Camel into the safety of the enclosure, firmly closing the entry behind him. "We'll make a search at daybreak," he told himself.

Kenaz led the animal towards the fire to take a better look while he picked up some fresh sticks and built up the fire. "What a magnificent animal," he exclaimed as he surveyed it and the ornately crafted saddle and bridle. Just at that moment the fire burst into life and crackled loudly. The jittery camel spooked; then screaming loudly it raced off into the darkness straight across a sleeping Hobab and ninety slumbering sheep and goats, closely followed by a now very stressed Kenaz. Seconds later the sleeping hoard instantly scattered to ninety-one separate directions, as they too amped up their startle vocals.

Kenaz found himself face to face with a very angry and shaken Hobab. "What the heck are you up to, Boy?" He shouted. Hobab wasn't renowned for his pleasant conversation at the best of times, least of all when he'd just been dragged out of pleasant dreams by a rampant camel. "Where did that animal come from? Get that mongrel out there and herd those sheep back, now! - you crazy idiot." Hobab barked. To emphasize his point, he administered a sharp wallop to Kenaz's head and stormed off into the thicket.

Sometime later order was restored, the flock was accounted for and Hobab and his bleepy friends returned to slumber. As ordered, Kenaz had securely lashed the camel's bridle to the largest tree he could find. He didn't have any experience with camels but he'd seen the traders make them sit by using the command hoosh. Kenaz repeated the term as authoritatively as he dared and miraculously the creature got down from all fours and casually began chewing its cud. With serenity restored he reluctantly went back to his fence watching duty.

Peering into the dark nothingness his thoughts drifted back to childhood. To say the past twenty years had been eventful could be termed an understatement. He would be twenty next spring and, as Hobab told him, seemingly daily, that age brought maturity – Kenaz however believed he was already quite mature. Hobab had spent his entire life tending sheep in deserted places and now at forty-five he had more affinity with his flock than his human counterparts. Even though Kenaz had been his assistant for the past eight years he still treated him more like his sheep dog than a fellow shepherd.

As for his parents, Kenaz's memories were non-existent. He'd been told the story often enough but he had no actual recollection. It was always just referred to as the storm, - a dust storm that is. Although they weren't directly related Hobab and his parents were all Kenites and therefore looked out for each other.

Their ancestors, descendants of Esau's son Reuel, had moved to Midian after a severe drought in Canaan about a century ago. Much of Midian was desert but springs of water and wells were relatively numerous which made sheep herding possible, just. It was a hard life but the choices were sparse. His clan were outsiders although the Midianites tolerated them, simply labelling them as Kenites.

Kenaz parents, so he'd been told, were Shammah and Timna and like him they were nomadic shepherds. Apparently, they had wandered into a particularly volatile region of the Arabian Desert in search of an obscure oasis. Night fell long before their mission was realised so they made camp in an exposed area and quickly built a temporary brush enclosure for their few sheep, pitching their tent at the entrance.

Kenaz was about a year old and as the camp fire burned low he quickly fell asleep secure in the trusty ox skin tent his parents had brought from a trader of Canaan. During the night, as was common in the area, an extreme wind arose. Shammah went out to check the temporary perimeter hedging only to discover much of it missing and all his precious few sheep scampering for the hills away from an advancing sandstorm. Shammah weighted up the situation; the storm was advancing quickly and his sole livelihood was racing for the hills. Timna was summonsed, there was no time to lose. Kenaz was left sleeping securely in the tent.

What happened that night nobody knows for sure? It was Hobab that found their lifeless bodies a couple of days later, both of them partially buried in the sand, overcome by the dust gathered up by the violent wind as it raced across the many miles of proceeding open desert lands. Hobab had found the safety of the watering hole which ironically was only about a couple of hours away and was returning with his flock when he made the grisly discovery.

Recognising them as his kinfolk he'd made a hole on the sand and laid the two to rest, said a few kind words and hurried off not keen to get caught in the area and suffer the same fate. That was when he heard it, a faint cry drifting across the desert now still and scorching in the morning sun. Although tempted to quickly abandon the place something made him go and check the source. To his amazement he discovered a sturdy tent still standing and containing one very thirsty and hot young child.

Every instinct told Hobab to run as fast as he could and leave this child to its fate. The last thing he needed was an infant to care for as he journeyed home. He was old enough to marry but he liked the nomadic carefree lifestyle – no commitments necessary. Whether it was the dry croaky cry or those wide-open tear-filled eyes he wasn't sure but something in his humanity stirred and he scooped up the young child who quickly devoured some water followed by copious gollops of goats' milk.

Kenaz was startled back to the present as a large hand slammed on his shoulder. "You sleeping on your feet, Boy," Hobab bellowed. Kenaz nearly leapt out of the enclosure, he'd been so deep in thought he'd not heard his approach. "Some watchman," Hobab continued sarcastically. "Anyway, it's the end of your shift. You go and get some sleep while I do the job properly. We all know the hungriest hunters come round just before dawn."

It seemed like just minutes that later Kenaz was being woken by a grumpy unloving Hobab. At least he'd made breakfast, Kenaz thought. "We've got to get moving early this morning Boy," Hobab blurted. "On account that we have to find an owner to that lousy camel you stole last night!"

"I didn't steal it, it found me," Kenaz blurted to no avail. Hobab didn't bother to answer but did find the time to begin dismantling their trusty tent despite Kenaz's attempts to finish dressing inside it.

Like a well-oiled machine everything was quickly packed away and lashed onto their faithful donkeys. "We'll leave the sheep in the enclosure for a bit while we search for our camel-less man," Hobab barked. "Unleash the mongrel, we'll take him with us."

"Can't that man ever do anything pleasantly," Kenaz grumbled to himself.

The camel trotted happily along behind Kenaz like he'd been his master all its life as the they set off to search for its owner. It took about an hour but there they found him.

Propped up against a large rock was a well-dressed man devoid of his sandals. Oh, yes and dead as a dodo. The pair rush up to check for any sign of life then quickly retreated repelled by the smell. The camel stood at bay as if saddened by the sight.

"Look at how swollen that leg is," Hobab proclaimed to no one in particular. "I bet he got zapped by a sand viper. Poor sod, what a horrid way to die." Hobab continued in an unusually compassionate mood. "Nothing we could have done for him anyway. Come on, let's see if he's got anything worthwhile on him."

Quickly the two men donned makeshift masks and set to their task of rifling through his belongings. "Can't find anything that says who he is," Hobab finally declared. "Judging by his large gold earring I'd say he was an Ishmaelite." Satisfied they'd left nothing of value the pair hurried off to rescue their flock and lead them to their morning pasture. "You've got to turn that animal loose now, Boy," Hobab demanded. Kenaz began to protest but knew arguing with Hobab was pointless. Reluctantly and sadly, he untied the reins, removed the saddle, and loudly told it to scamper. Strangely the bewilder creature just stood as if saying, "You're the only human within a hundred miles, where on earth do I scamper to?"

Hobab and an unenthusiastic Kenaz rounded up their sheep and set off to their next targeted grazing area and watering hole. Hobab for all his faults knew the desert like the back of his hand and somehow automatically navigated the shortest route to the next stop. Assuming he was now a sheep the lonely camel plodded along aimlessly at the back of the flock. And so it was, at that night's camp that Hobab begrudgingly agreed to Kenaz's eager request to adopt it for his own. "On one condition, Boy," Hobab decreed. "If that thing ever spits at me, I swear I'll cut its throat." Kenaz knew he wasn't joking but for now he didn't care. He had a magnificent animal to take care of. Finally, he had something that he really could call his own. Despite the fact his parents' tent, which Hobab called his own, technically belonged to him, this camel was a living creature capable of loyalty, an emotion Hobab seemed completely incapable of. As for a name, he decided just 'Camel' would do.

2

Just Kenaz

Hobab would've happily stayed in the desert all year, he loved the nomadic lifestyle and saw no real need for human contact or the comforts of home. Kenaz however was delighted to see the small settlement appear and the spritely figure of eighty-five-year-old Jethro marching out to greet them. "Praise Yahweh you've returned," Jethro exclaimed as he hugged his uncaring son. As Kenaz received his welcome Jethro continued excitedly. "Moses left us a couple of months ago. He saw a vision of a burning bush round behind Mt Horeb, over there," and pointed in the direction of the nearby rocky mass. "He claims Yahweh actually spoke to him, telling him to go back to Egypt so he left the very next day taking with him Zipporah and my two grandsons," Jethro concluded almost in tears. "Right at the start of the lambing season too! Thank Yahweh He's bought you two home now to help with the shearing."

Hobab had tolerated Moses as he was about the same age as his father, but as it was with most, he never enjoyed his company. Being the youngest in his family he was strangely quite fond of his oldest sister Zipporah, especially her cooking. Her savoury lamb stew was to die for. Secretly he was quite pleased Moses had gone but knew better than to share that with his father. Right now, there was stew to be eaten and wine to be consumed.

Kenaz lay back in the luxury of his surroundings, he had a full stomach, a skin full of wine and a camel of his own in the yard – life was good.

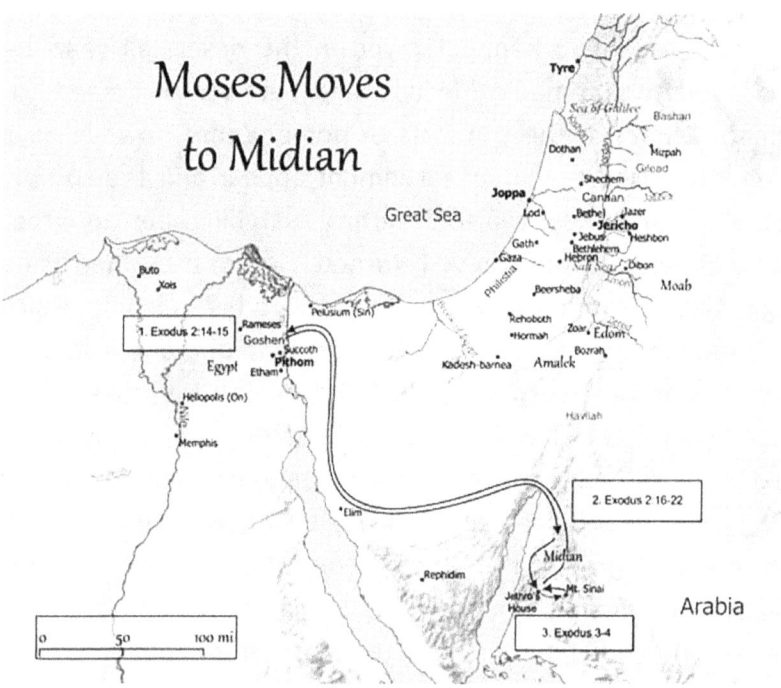

Location of where Jethro lived in Midian

After Hobab had reluctantly rescued that crying baby, nineteen years ago, he had quickly returned home to discharge his unwanted cargo. With seven sisters and only one married surely they'd be keen to take care of this young bundle of nuisance. It was Jael, the second eldest who took up the charge. Jael, while not blessed with the beauty of her elder sister was, however, a very motherly sort and saw the youngster as filling the void of jealousy created by Zipporah's marriage to Moses and the birth of her two sons in quick succession. "What is his name," Jael asked as she lovingly admired her new found charge.

"Dammed if I know," Hobab quickly responded uncaringly, "He didn't have a tag on him when I found him hollowing in that beautiful tent."

The ensuing silence was broken by Moses greeting the family on his return from the flock. "My, my, what have we here? I hear Hobab has found a son to care for? Wonders never cease." Moses exclaimed with a strong hint of sarcasm. He too tolerated Hobab but, as did most others, he found him brash, uncaring and hard to get close to. He was genuinely surprised that Hobab had actually taken the time to save the life of another human being.

"What shall we name him, father?" Jael asked that evening, as the family sat relaxing in the cool of the late evening, their chores done for the day. Jethro had no more knowledge of the child's name than Hobab but since he has the patriarch, he was expected to make a ruling on the matter. Jethro sat contemplating for some time then turned to Hobab. "You found him in the tent of Shammah, did you son?"

"That's right, father. There was some stuff in the tent that seemed to be their belongings. I tell you it was a great tent. Never seen one like it," Hobab replied.

"Never mind the tent, son, that belongs to the child," Jethro stated. "So, you're certain he was Shammah's child?" Jethro concluded in summary.

Hobab didn't reply and the family sat in silence regurgitating various potential family names as the young child played happily on the large sheepskin rug on the ground in front of them. Finally, Jethro broke the thought fest. "Here's what we know." He began slowly and thoughtfully. "His father was Shammah and we know that Shammah was a Kenite of the same clan that we are. He is a male child and he's about one year old, wouldn't you say, Jael." Jael nodded and knew her father's words were a statement not a question – The boy was a year old. "It is certain that Shammah would have already named the boy by this age and declared his name before Yahweh therefore we can't call him something he isn't. This is a quandary," Jethro concluded, rubbing his chin in thought.

Again, silence ensued until Jael desperate to link a name to her new found charge, blurted in excitement, "Since the only thing we know about him is that he's a Kenite, let's just call him Kenite until we hear of the name that Shammah decreed." The family's heads turned in unison to their Patriarch to hear his decision. A prolonged pause followed, then Jethro spoke.

"I have decided that because the only thing we know about the boy is that he is of the clan of the Kenites then he should be known as Kenaz – a person of the Kenite clan." His words were final, any further discussion, pointless.

Jael picked up the child with loving arms from the floor skins and exclaimed proudly, mostly to herself, "I think it's time for Kenaz to go to bed."

Despite asking every member of the Kenite clan they met nobody knew the given name of Shammah's son therefore as the years progressed the title of Kenaz stuck. Kenaz son of Shammah.

Kenaz was awake at first light next morning keen to get his chores done so he could focus on his recently acquired camel. The sheep were released to their pastures near the main watering hole not far from the homestead. He knew the routine well as these had been his chores since he was about five years old. That is until Hobab demanded the boy help him with his wilderness droves. For the past eight years Kenaz and Hobab had wandered the desert for the summer months, leading their few sheep and goats between pastures and watering holes. The four months of winter at home, which always culminated with the shearing time, where a sheer joy. It was a time to relax a little and savor the few small pleasures that life occasionally brought. Chores always first, mind you.

Today that pleasure was Camel. First, I'll ride him, Kenaz decided. He retrieved the saddle and reins which adorned it the night it arrived and quickly set off to untie his prize. Placing the reins, while taking a little more time than expected, was straightforward enough. Mission accomplished, now for the saddle. Kenaz picked up the saddle assuming it would simply slip across its back similar to the way he strapped the donkeys. It was then he noticed, as if for the first time, the large hump smack in the centre of its back right where the saddle should go. Undeterred Kenaz flung the saddle anyway assuming it would somehow find its natural position. Unfortunately, no such position was to be found and the saddle slid ungracefully down the grazing camel's neck and wacked the poor unsuspecting creature hard on the back of the head.

At that point Kenaz's camel knowledge grew a level as he learned first-hand that a camel's expression of displeasure is expressed as a spit. Well actually, more accurately not a spit as we know it but more like a very large open mouth sneeze. A trait that Kenaz discovered, as time progressed, was not uncommon to this particular camel! The fact that the camel had a lovely mouthful of fresh grass at the time of its 'spit' didn't seem to deter it. Moments later a large boisterous laugh rang out from not five metres away. Kenaz covered in copious amounts of saliva and partly chewed grass turned to the direction of the bellow. "Don't you have anything better to do, Hobab," Kenaz yelled.

After a quick clean-up Kenaz figured that for now a saddle may not be a necessity since he only wanted a quick ride. Remembering the hoosh command the animal was quickly at a level Kenaz could easily climb aboard. Effortlessly he scampered into a position of relative comfort just in from of the large hump and the camel, sensing Kenaz's eagerness to ride, sprang to its feet with as much grace as a charging rhino – back legs first. The fickle grip Kenaz had instantly vanished and he found himself thrust through the air at great speed, again much to the delight of a pitiless Hobab. Kenaz landed some distance away, fortunately unhurt and, more importantly, out of spitting range.

Let's say it took time and lots of practice but in due course Kenaz did master the delicate intricacies of camel etiquette together with the ability to mount, dismount and ride with ease. Life was good with a camel.

Hobab observed Kenaz's exploits with his camel and came to the conclusion that judging by size a single camel should be able to carry a substantially greater weight that his humble donkeys. One afternoon while Kenaz was otherwise occupied Hobab led the camel over to a pile of goods and through more good luck than good management finally got the animal to sit. Quickly he began to load the creature with as many objects as he could find a position for. Finally, with the load stacked and lashed Hobab tugged at the reins and began shouting commands he believed the camel would comprehend as, "get up and go."

After some time with zero movement Hobab disappeared into his tent, reappearing with a large staff which he immediately used to first prod, then beat, the hapless animal. Camel for some reason took exception to this and with great care it mustered the largest amount of saliva and regurgitated grass it could and 'spat' with full force all over an unsuspecting Hobab. That action unfortunately did little to calm the situation and Hobab flew into a rage beating the sitting camel with great fury as he angrily brushed aside the partly digested grass and sticky saliva.

Eventually the camel had had enough and while it was unable, or perhaps unwilling, to stand because of its massive load, it could roll. And this it did, quite symmetrically in fact, directly onto a still wildly flailing Hobab, pinning him beneath the load he'd bestowed on the poor creature. Fortunately, the panicked camel bellowed like a trapped tyrannosaurus, almost drowning out Hobab's screams of obscenities which quickly alerted everyone within a few kilometres that something was not right with the world.

After normality was eventually restored Kenaz in no uncertain terms decreed that under no circumstances was Hobab ever to go anywhere near his camel again – ever. Strangely both Hobab and Camel completely agreed. "You might have saved my life nineteen years ago, Hobab but a father to me you have never been," Kenaz shouted back at a limping Hobab, as he led his precious Camel away.

Winter and spring ended all too fast. The rains had passed and the days grew hotter. Soon the grass would wither and the long search for fresh pastures would begin, the single trait that Hobab was very good at.

Exodus 2:11-21, Exodus 3:1-14, Exodus 4:18-20.

3

Moses

It had been Kenaz's task that afternoon to give the animals their afternoon drink at the watering well. He'd taken Camel along, not because it was far but rather to add a spot of amusement to a somewhat menial task. As he closed the well something caught his eye, a small patch of dust far on the horizon. "What in Noah's ark is that," he said aloud despite being alone. Quickly he climbed onto Camel's back and carefully stood to gain a better view. "I swear that's a small group, heading this way. Visitors!" he shouted in excitement. Living in such isolation visitors could be months apart and even if they were only Midian traders, they were a welcome relief. Without hesitation he jumped into his saddle and gave the command for Camel to run.

Camel seemed to sense the excitement and within minutes Kenaz was at the location of the small dust cloud. "Hello Kenaz. How did you manage to obtain such a splendid animal?" Zipporah asked.

"Long story," Kenaz replied. "You came back? Where's Moses?"

"Yes, my long story," Zipporah answered sadly. Kenaz quickly dismounted and demanded his older de facto aunt take his place. Kenaz led her home while her two sons, Gershom and Eliezer, both in their thirties, controlled the pack donkeys.

The celebrations were energetic and colourful as the family reunited around an evening of feasting. "Now Zipporah," Jethro demanded, "tell us all, how was Egypt and where is your husband? Why did he desert you? I thought he was a better man than that!"

"Nothing like that father," Zipporah explained. "He's become a big name in Egypt and through the power of Yahweh he has brought down huge plagues on Pharaoh and the Egyptian people. He told me that Yahweh planned to destroy all the firstborn in Egypt during the night of the fifteenth day of Nisan. He said it would be too dangerous for me and the boys to stay there and I was to return home and stay with you, father."

Jethro stamped his staff on the ground. "This will not do," he decreed. "It is not right for a man to abandon his wife and family even if he is devoting his service to Yahweh. Yahweh will protect His servants and their families. You will have to return," Jethro concluded. "But not tonight, first you must rest."

Sleep evaded Kenaz as he lay in his bed sack that night. "The fifteenth of Nisan, that was about two weeks ago," Kenaz reasoned. "I wonder what happened? Fancy old slow speaking

Moses now a leader of a nation." Kenaz chuckled to himself as he envisaged Moses engaging with a mighty Pharaoh. "Couldn't be a nicer guy," Kenaz recounted, "but eloquent he was not!"

Kenaz didn't have to wait long for his answers. The very next morning a caravan of Midianite traders stopped by the small settlement. They had just come from Horeb not more than a days' journey away and explained that Moses and a vast army of Israelites are camped there. They recounted all the details about what had happened in Egypt. How Pharaoh had virtually pushed the children of Israel out of Egypt only later to chase after them but finally drown in the Red Sea.

The men sat around the fire drinking a refreshing sour liquid called qom. It was a watery by-product left behind in the process of making afiq, a dry type of cheese. Their accounts went on for hours. Finally, Jethro stood bringing the meeting to a close. "I have heard enough. Yahweh is indeed the greatest. I have served Yahweh as a Priest in Midian for more than seventy years and He has never failed me once. He is indeed well able to protect His people. Tomorrow I will take Zipporah and her sons and return them to Moses. Hobab and Kenaz you will accompany me." That one statement was about to change Kenaz's life dramatically.

The small troop rounded the pass that rose above the plains in front of Mount Horeb and there before their eyes appeared a vast mass of people that Yahweh had named the Children of Israel. "Look at that waterfall pouring out of Mt Horeb, Hobab." Jethro exclaimed in amazement. "I never knew there was water in these parts?"

"Well, it certainly wasn't here last year," Hobab answered, "and why is it pouring straight out of sheer rock? Where's it coming from? Look at all those sheep," Hobab continued, clearly distracted by the expansive scene stretching out in front of him.

"How on earth am I going to find Moses among that multitude," Jethro muttered.

He needn't have worried. No sooner had they reached the outskirts of the camp, there was Moses striding out to meet them. "I just got your note from the traders saying you were coming," Moses explained as he greeted his old friend. His greetings continued onto Hobab, Kenaz and his two sons Gershom and Eliezer. Finally, he turned to Zipporah giving her an affectionate pat of the shoulder and with a warm smile said, "You go with my assistant Joshua. He'll show you where to set up your tent."

"Thanks for returning my sons Jethro. Come into my tent and I'll recount all the incredible miracles Yahweh has performed to get us here."

The men sat and listened for hours as Moses explained their dramatic departure from Egypt, their supernatural escape through the parting of the Red Sea which resulted in the destruction of the entire Egyptian army, including Pharaoh himself. Kenaz was enthralled. He'd heard about Yahweh from Jethro but thought He was just a God to be feared. But this description of Yahweh showed Him real, living and active.

Someone who cares and protects. "I'd like to learn more about this God," he decided.

Sometime later Moses called for Kenaz to come to his tent. "Ah Kenaz, there's someone here I want you to meet." A tall, lean, bronzed man of about sixty years stood up and walked over to Kenaz, gave him a great bear hug and kissed him on both cheeks. "Kenaz this is Jephunneh," Moses explained. "He was a Kenite as you are." Kenaz was puzzled, he thought he was among Israelites not members of his father's clan.

"Pleased to meet you Kenaz," Jephunneh said. "This is my son Caleb." A younger man, perhaps in his late thirties, jumped to his feet and rushed over to also bear hug and kiss Kenaz's cheeks. He wasn't as tall as his father but he had a friendly face, a calm voice and a positive air of confidence about him. Kenaz liked him instantly. "Come to our tent Kenaz and eat some bread with us. I think we have much to discuss," Jephunneh requested.

The three men walked off in the direction of their tent quite relaxed, like they'd been best friends forever. "I have a camel," Kenaz blurted excitedly.

"Then you must show us," Caleb responded enthusiastically.

"Here he is," Kenaz announced as the trio rounded the side of his tent.

"What a magnificent animal," Jephunneh remarked as he strode over and slapped it affectionately on its shoulder.

"Ah, be careful not to startle it...," Kenaz began. It seemed Camel didn't appreciate being woken out of a long daydream by a firm pat of the back so Camel turned and delivered a large sticky spit directly into the face of its master's new-found friend. Kenaz secretly hoped the ground would open beneath him and swallow him whole. Sensing Kenaz's embarrassment Caleb quickly threw his father a long cloth he had draped over this shoulder, and changing subject asked, "Where did you get it from?"

"Actually, he found me." Kenaz explained. "His previous master died after being bitten by a sand snake and Camel came to our compound during the night. I've had him ever since."

"You're a blessed man, Kenaz," Jephunneh said as he handed the cloth back to Caleb. "My mistake, son," Jephunneh continue and gave Kenaz a comforting pat on his back. "You see it's a very long time since I've had any dealings with a camel and I quite forgot their reflex is to spit." What a remarkable man Kenaz decided. The contrast to Hobab was night and day. He could get used to being around people like this.

Back in their tent the men sat while the women served drinks and delightful snacks. "In case you're thinking the food measly," Caleb explained, "this isn't the main meal, we'll have that later when we've talked some more." And talk they did.

"So, who was your Kenite father?" Jephunneh asked. "Shammah," Kenaz replied. Jephunneh's face lit up like he'd seen an angel.

"Never! Shammah? Of the sons of Reuel?" Jephunneh's gaze was now transfixed on Kenaz, a tear rolled down his cheeks as his eyes begged for more.

Kenaz replied in the affirmative, "Yes that Shammah, that's my father. I never actually knew him as I was only one when he died."

"He was my very best friend," Jephunneh explained. "We were bought up together in the same village in Midian."

"How old are you Kenaz?" Jephunneh ask. "I was twenty last month," Kenaz replied.

"Ok so I would have been a touch older than you when I was taken," Jephunneh continued. "About forty years ago when Moses fled from Pharaoh, after he'd murdered some obscure Egyptian, that was a tough time in Midian." Kenaz nodded his interest, eager to get the back story on Moses. Moses had told him snippets but never the full story. "Pharaoh didn't take too kindly to Moses's desertion and sent bands of warriors out into Midian where Moses was last reported. Of course, not many of those heathens knew what Moses actually looked like so they just rounded up any young unmarried man that they thought might be about his age. I was captured and dragged back to Egypt in chains. Somehow your father Shammah, managed to elude them, but I never saw him again."

Jephunneh took a moment to compose himself then continued. Back in Egypt Pharaoh's henchmen quickly decided I wasn't Moses but instead of releasing me back to Midian they made me a slave and added me to the Hebrews who were being forced to build the supply city Rameses, in the Goshen region. It was there I met Hezron. He was a descendant of Judah's son Perez; a true nobleman, full of dignity despite being a fellow slave. After a few years I asked him if I could marry his daughter Aria. However, in Israel it's not allowed that a Hebrew daughter could marry a foreigner. There was a solution fortunately. Hezron adopted me as his son therefore I've been gifted his name and heritage and will inherit in the Promised Land when we've arrived. I am now one of the children of Israel as is my son Caleb and his descendants after him. Some still call me a Kenite but that's just a nickname now, it's not my identity," Jephunneh concluded and seemed relieved to have passed on his life's story to his close friend's offspring.

Kenaz had a lot to ponder on that night as he lay in his tent. There was something different about these people and their ways. Jethro had always been kindly to him but Hobab was a monster compared to these people. The affinity he felt with Jephunneh was so comfortable, like he'd known him for years. This wasn't clan, he decided, this was kinship and it felt good.

Exodus 18:2-3, Exodus 1:8-11, Exodus 2:11-15, Joshua 14:6, Exodus 18:1-7, Exodus 17:6.

4

Adoption

Next morning Jethro again sat across from his son-in-law listening to the full account of all that Yahweh had done for His people. Something was stirring in him; he'd served as priest to Yahweh in Midian and now he'd come face to face with those He called His children. This called for a response. Jethro stood and placed his hand on Moses's shoulder. "Blessed is Yahweh, who has rescued you from the Egyptians and from Pharaoh. Yes, He has rescued Israel from the powerful hand of Egypt! Now I know that Yahweh is greater than all the gods; He rescued His people from the oppression of the proud Egyptians." Jethro stood and walked to the tent opening then turned and said, "Moses bring me a lamb so we can make an offering to our mighty God."

Joshua was quickly dispatched to find a perfect lamb while word rapidly spread. What had begun as a small response of worship quickly escalated. Before long Moses's brother Aaron had gathered all the elders of Israel; all those who were the heads of the various tribes and senior members of the larger clans. It was quite an impressive gathering that stood behind Jethro, Moses's father-in-law, who watched as the young men hastily prepared a small stone altar and piled it high with wood.

Joshua appeared proudly leading a fine looking, if not a somewhat reluctant, two-year-old ram. Jethro stepped forward and began to slowly inspect the animal from head to tail. "You have selected well, young man," Jethro declared. As if from nowhere he suddenly pulled a large knife from its sheath beneath his belt and in a well-practiced swipe the animals throat was severed from side to side and it fell to the ground.

Jethro, as he'd done many times before, quickly skinned and dissected the now lifeless ram and carefully placed the various parts on the makeshift altar. "Please bring the fire, now," he demanded and a young man quickly handed him a burning torch. "Great is Yahweh, the God of Israel who does great miracles," Jethro shouted as he ceremoniously lit the corners of the altar with the flaming baton.

Jethro stood back as the blaze took hold and all the assembled patriarchs stood, raised their staffs and cried, "Great is Yahweh the God of Israel."

As the fire crackled and the carcass slowly turned to charcoal, mats were arranged in a large circle and all the men were seated. Moses and Jethro sat on seats behind a table at the head of the group. Then, seemingly choreographed to perfection, women appeared carrying baskets of bread, savouries and nuts and began serving them to the men. As the eating began the crackling fire was drowned-out by the sound of tambourines and singing of countless young women colourfully dressed who energetically danced as they circled the group. The occasion quickly transformed from solemn to festive.

Kenaz, Hobab, Joshua, Caleb and numerous other young men were added as a second tier to the group sitting behind the Elders. This was a time to celebrate and welcome the visitors.

Again, Kenaz found himself deep in ponderous thought, later that night as he lay in his tent. What a welcome! The things that were so different about these people and their ways were easy to accept. Was he really beginning to like it here?

Next day Kenaz spotted Jethro sitting by himself watching a line of people standing outside a small tent over to the side of the main camp. Kenaz wandered over out of curiosity to see what was captivating him. Jethro looked up as Kenaz approached, "I can't find Moses anywhere. Go and find Joshua and ask him why all these people are standing here in this long line all day in the hot sun waiting to get into that tent?"

"You had a question for me Jethro?" Joshua asked as he approached a short time later.

"Is Moses in that tent over there?" Jethro said pointing in the direction of the lone structure. "What's going on with all these people waiting out in the hot sun like this from daylight to dusk?"

"Moses is holding court there," Joshua replied. "He does that most days," he added.

"Didn't he learn anything during his forty years with me? Jethro questioned. "The man is crazy. He'll burn himself out in no time. We can't have that."

As evening approached Joshua cleared the crowds away and as Moses made his way back towards the camp Jethro called him over to where he'd been seated for most of the day. "What is it my father?" Moses asked as he took a seat on the ground beside his father-in-law.

"Why are so many people waiting in the hot sun for so long all day to meet with you, Moses?" Jethro asked. "What are you really accomplishing here? Why are you trying to do all this alone while everyone stands around you from morning till evening?" Jethro continued.

"Okay, one question at a time," Moses began. "You see the people come to me to get a ruling from Yahweh. When a dispute arises, they come to me, and I am the one who settles the case between the quarrelling parties. I inform the people of Yahweh's decrees and give them His instructions," Moses explained.

"This is not good!" Jethro exclaimed. "You're going to wear yourself out—and the people, too. This job is way too heavy a burden for you to handle all by yourself. Now listen to me," Jethro continued, "let me give you a word of advice, and may Yahweh be with you. You should continue to be the people's representative before Yahweh, bringing their disputes to Him. Keep teaching them Yahweh's decrees, and give them His instructions. Show them how to conduct their lives. But please do this also. Select from all the people some capable, honest men who fear Yahweh and hate bribes. Appoint them as leaders over groups of one thousand, one hundred, fifty and ten. They should always be available to solve the people's common disputes, but all the major cases they'll bring to you. Let the leaders decide the smaller matters themselves. They will help you carry the load, making the task easier for you. If you follow this advice, and if Yahweh commands you to do so, then you will be able to endure the pressures, and all these people will go home in peace."

Moses sat for a time quietly considering what his father-in-law had advised. Finally, he said, "It's been a long day and I need food and sleep now. Tomorrow I will hear what Yahweh has to say."

First thing the next morning Moses began to implement his father-in-law's advice and followed his suggestions exactly. He chose capable men from all parts of Israel and appointed them as leaders over the people. He put them in charge of groups of one thousand, one hundred, fifty and ten. He instructed them to always be available to solve the people's common disputes. "You take care of all the smaller matters yourselves," Moses instructed them "but all the major cases, bring them to me."

It took a few days but soon a very ordered hierarchy was in place and Moses found a small resemblance of normality return to his life. "My work here is done, Moses," Jethro advised. I've returned your wife and sons, take good care of them for me? It's time I retraced my steps back to my home and my household."

"What of Kenaz and Hobab?" Moses asked. "Can you please allow them to stay? Hobab has his sheep with him but we have ample pastures. They can return later if they wish."

Kenaz didn't like the thought of leaving. Hobab, however, couldn't wait. "I prefer the company of sheep to crowds of people," he bragged. Kenaz wandered aimlessly through the massive camp contemplating his future. Here, he felt alive and part of something, it was the closest thing to true kinship he'd ever known. Without any particular thought he eventually found himself outside Jephunneh's tent.

The next sound he heard was, "Come on in Kenaz, sit and tell me what's on your mind." Jephunneh listened carefully to Kenaz's personal debate asking questions for clarification but offering no direct advice.

Having unloaded his dilemma, Kenaz felt somewhat pacified but still with no clear answers. "Sleep on it," Jephunneh advised, "things will be clearer in the morning."

Next morning a small group gathered around Jethro as he said his goodbyes. "Hobab?" Jethro asked, not feeling the need to express the question.

"Actually, if I may," Moses answered. "Hobab you're the best desert tracker I've ever seen. You know the lie of the land and where all the watering holes are. We desperately need a man with your skills to point out the way we should travel and where we should rest."

Adoption

Hobab secretly flushed with pride at Moses's glowing description of his skills. He paused momentarily, desperately searching for a nondescript response to mask his true feelings.

"But I'll have to keep my sheep with me here," Hobab stated nonchalantly.

"Well, that's settled then," Moses declared. "You can pitch your tent to the side of the main camp and graze your sheep as you please. But just be ready every time we start to move camp. You're our chief scout."

'Chief Scout,' Hobab repeated to himself, that sounded important. "Okay I'll stay," he answered.

"And you Kenaz?" Jethro asked. Kenaz didn't have time to answer before a voice he didn't even know was there arose from behind him.

"I'll vouch for the boy, Jethro. I'll keep my eye on him," the voice said. Kenaz knew that voice even without looking – Jephunneh. Now it was his turn to fight the glowing pride he felt envelop him. Unlike Hobab, Kenaz didn't try and hide his joy.

"Actually, that will be perfect," Kenaz blurted.

The small group said their long goodbyes, unsure if they'd ever see the old man again. Eventually, as the sun became warmer, Jethro and his faithful pack donkey began the climb over the side of Mt Horeb to his homestead on the other side. He would be home by evening.

Kenaz quickly settled into life in the Israeli camp. Jephunneh insisted Kenaz set up his tent within his family compound among his people of the tribe of Judah. Camel slept out beside his tent and an instant routine evolved, taking the animal each day to find pasture and drink water as needed. Donkeys were plentiful in the camp but camels not so much. Before long Kenaz found he had a nice little camel hire business developing. It seems there was an endless requirement to haul various packages around the camp or pick up supplies that had been delivered by the passing traders. Already he was booked solid for the next several times they moved camp.

As his silver shekels accumulated, he determined a few upgrades were in order. A new tent, a change of wardrobe and new bedding were just a few of the home comforts he indulged in. His transformation from a Hobab trained nomadic shepherd to a tent-dwelling clansman was rapid and dramatic.

Most evenings Kenaz spent sitting with Jephunneh, Caleb and the family listening to the history of their people. How Jacob had come to Egypt with a small clan of sixty-seven souls and how Joseph was second to Pharaoh but after many years the Children of Israel had grown so numerous the Egyptians feared them so, they overpowered them and made them slaves. How Moses, through the power of Yahweh, had with incredible plagues and miracles led the people of Israel out of Egypt with great dignity. And finally, that Yahweh had opened up the mighty Red Sea leading the Tribes of Israel through on dry land but when the Egyptian army followed, He closed the sea over them and destroyed them forever. Kenaz soon knew all the history off by heart but something was missing. He was a Kenite and not of the Children of Israel with no obvious bridge to change that.

"I wished I was an Israelite," Kenaz admitted to the men one evening. Nobody answered Kenaz's musing and the conversation quickly changed to a more uplifting topic. A few mornings later Kenaz was about to lead Camel off to pasture when Jephunneh appeared and asked if he could come with him. Somewhat puzzled at Jephunneh's sudden interest in Camel, Kenaz instantly agreed, welcoming the company. The two sat in the shade as Camel made his fill. Around them vast flocks of sheep and goats grazed on the now lush plain, watered from the tower of water constantly gushing from the rock at Horeb.

The pair sat drinking in the scene that played out in front of them until finally Jephunneh broke the silence. "Kenaz," he said solemnly, "I would like you to become my son and take up an inheritance with me and the tribe of Judah in the Promised Land." His words were a statement, not a question. Kenaz said nothing, he was completely choked up inside, totally unable to speak. All his life he'd been constantly reminded, mostly by Hobab, that he was the outsider, tolerated but never family, never to share an inheritance. Now here was this incredible man whom he'd only know a few weeks that wanted to take him as his son. Finally, Kenaz gained enough composure and simply asked, "Why?"

Jephunneh seemed prepared for the question. "You and I are very similar, Kenaz. I've experienced a little of what your life has been. Remember I came to my people as a Midianite slave so I know exactly what it's like to be an outsider. You have two options in accordance with the traditions passed down from Abraham, either you remain among us as an alien or you become one with us. Remaining a foreigner will restrict who you can marry and certainly it will make it difficult for you to inherit in the Promised Land. Besides all that, Kenaz, I see something in you that is of value, something that will enhance my family and strengthen my inheritance. Caleb is a fine son and has a strong understanding of Yahweh but he is my only son. If something were to befall him then my name could die out."

Kenaz stood, tears rolling down his cheeks, he didn't need time to ponder this offer. Jephunneh stood and the two hugged for what seemed an eternity. Finally, Kenaz uttered the words, "I have never called anyone 'father' but I would be delighted to call you 'my father'!" Kenaz broke free, did a little dance as he let out a very loud "Yippee!" Camel startled by his master's cries of delight reacted in its usual manner by delivering a large grassy spit in the direction of the noise. Despite some of the mass finding its mark, Kenaz didn't care, this was a time of joy.

Later that day Kenaz found himself seated at the head of a large circle of men, all heads of families, senior members of the tribe of Judah. "Brethren and fellow Hebrews,'" Jephunneh began as he rose to his feet. "Today I need you all to witness a momentous event with the addition of a son to my family. From today, this man who is sitting on my left hand here," he continued as he pointed to a beaming young Kenaz, "is to become my son. Just as my firstborn son Caleb, here on my right hand is, so shall Kenaz be. He shall be my son, a son of the mighty tribe of Judah and from today he will be an Israelite, free to live among us and marry a daughter of Israel. He will inherit with Caleb, a possession in the land flowing with milk and honey that we're about to take hold of, just as Yahweh has promised."

Jephunneh bent down and took off one of his sandals and handed it to Kenaz. As he did so he said, "Let all those here now witness that I give my sandal to this man Kenaz who is now my son. Through it he will walk in my steps and walk in my ways and is now part of my family forever as Yahweh is my witness." Kenaz quickly stood and embraced his new father as the rest of the gathered Elders surrounded them, eager to formally kiss the newest member of the tribe of Judah.

The formalities concluded and the celebrations began. Women with food and wine appeared from nearby tents, tambourines began and dancing quickly followed. Kenaz retired to his tent late that night slightly merry from the copious amount of wine he'd consumed but also completely intoxicated with the joy that he was now family – one of the Children of Israel.

Exodus 18:8-12, Exodus 18:14-26, Exodus 18:27, Numbers 10:29-33.

5

The Law

Kenaz was woken a few mornings later by excessive clatter and general busyness outside his tent. "What's going on?" he demanded of a passer-by.

"The Pillar of Cloud has lifted. It's no longer above the Tent of Meeting. This means we're moving camp, you better get moving."

Kenaz looked over toward Moses's meeting tent and sure enough the cloud that hovered above it had moved. It was now much higher and further to the North. His thoughts were interrupted by a caller. "Say Kenaz, does your price still stand for the hire of your camel," the voice asked. "Today's the day." Kenaz acknowledged the contract and like all around him quickly assembled his few belongings, packed them on his camel then headed down the way with Camel to service his new found customer.

The day seemed to drag on forever as the prodigious multitude slowly made their way around the mountains to the edge of the Sinai wilderness. Mt Sinai, a little higher than the surrounding hills stood alone as a striking rocky outcrop. Several small streams flowed from the mountains and Kenaz knew the area as he and Hobab had pastured their few sheep there only last year.

Mt Sinai as it looks today.

The Pillar of Cloud that had gone before the people all day, stopped in front of Mt. Sinai and immediately the throng of wanders scurried to find the best camping spot and, like a well-oiled machine, quickly set to establishing house again. Before long the aroma of the cooking of thousands of evening meals drifted across the camp while animals were watered and settled. By the time darkness fell there was barely a sound heard as the weary occupants of the neatly arrayed tents succumbed to sleep.

Jephunneh strode with purpose to find his family, as a clan meeting had been summoned. Hurriedly, Kenaz ran with his new family to hear the news – clearly something major was afoot. Nahshon, the head Elder of the tribe of Judah stood on a hastily made platform and addressed the gathered tribe. "I have just come from Moses who has a very important message from Yahweh, so listen up." He began solemnly. "We are to prepare ourselves because in two days Yahweh is going to meet with us in person from the top of this mountain here," he continued while pointing towards Mt. Sinai. "That means best clothes, freshly washed, everything neat and tidy and everyone on best behaviour."

"Now about this here mountain," Nahshon continued. "Yahweh is a Holy God and nobody is to go near Sinai because if you do, you'll die – instantly by stoning. This is very serious folks so please hear what I say. Moses was emphatic that even if a sheep or an ox wander there they're to be immediately shot with an arrow. So, is that clear? Everyone be ready on the third day from now to assemble in front of your tents in complete family groups, no one is exempted."

Kenaz stood beside his brother Caleb, together with the entire family of Israel, all dressed in their recently washed, best attire as the first glint of dawn broke to the East. Suddenly a deafening thunder blast shattered the morning dawn as thick cloud poured down from far above and engulfed Mt. Sinai. Thunder and lightning shot out, in rapid succession, as a

The Law

shattering trumpet blast continued. The awesome display was truly terrifying. A deep reverence of Yahweh, the God of Israel, firmly cemented itself into every beating heart as they absorbed the events unfolding before them. Kenaz vowed to never disobey this mighty, awe-inspiring God.

Moses beckoned for the people to move out. Tribe by tribe they quickly marched to their appointed positions in army-like rank and assembled, in stunned silence, directly at the foot of the very mountain which quaked and roared like a smoking furnace. Every soul present, absolutely petrified as they entered the proximity of such explosive power. The multitude quickly found their place then Yahweh came down onto the top of the mountain and called out to Moses to come up the mountain.

No sooner had Moses gone he was back, warning all the people to keep back and not touch the mountain or go too close to it. "Don't try and look to see if you can see Yahweh because if you do you will perish," Moses explained.

All at once the noise stopped but the fire and cloud remain covering the mountain. "I am Yahweh, your God who bought you out of the land of Egypt, out of the house of bondage," declared a clear, distinct but compassionate voice, booming out from the midst of the cloud and fire. The entire mass of people stood transfixed; the absolute reality of Almighty Yahweh cemented by this literal sound their ears now heard.

The voice continued and announced ten commandments of Yahweh that all must strictly adhere to.

- "You shall have no other Gods but me.
- You shall not make for yourself any idol, nor bow down to it or worship it.
- You shall not misuse the name of the Lord your God.
- You shall remember and keep the Sabbath day holy.
- Respect your father and mother.
- You must not commit murder.
- You must not commit adultery.
- You must not steal.
- You must not give false evidence against your neighbour.
- You must not be envious of your neighbour's goods. You shall not be envious of his house nor his wife, nor anything that belongs to your neighbour."

After the statement had ended the people, shaking and trembling, came to Moses and begged him to be the mediator and relay the words of Yahweh to them because they believed they would all die if the Holy voice continued. Moses agreed and a very subdued people returned to their camp that afternoon. Yahweh was no longer a mystery to be spoken of, each one had heard the reality of His voice. Fear and awe filled their hearts.

Days passed quickly. Moses had been up the mountain so long everyone was certain he was dead. The cry went out from the masses for Moses's brother Aaron to take over and make an image of a god that would lead on the way from here. Kenaz watch with shock and amazement as many of the people stripped their golden earrings and Aaron moulded them into an image of an Egyptian calf god. As soon as the people saw it, they danced and shouted, and an impromptu festival broke out.

The celebrations were just warming up when a very loud voice brought things to an abrupt holt. "What, in the name of Yahweh, is going on here?" a very red-faced and intensely angry Moses demanded. Aaron offered the best explanation he could think of on the spur of the moment, but he needn't have bothered. Moses, venting his righteous rage picked up the golden image, ground it to powder, scattered it in the water and made the people drink it.

Moses marched over to his meeting tent and shouted, "Whoever is on the side of Yahweh – come to me now!" Quickly a large number of young men from Moses's tribe, Levi, raced to his side each one brandishing his weapon of choice. "Take your weapon and go from tent to tent and kill your brothers. Do not spare your brother, your friend or your neighbour." Moses demanded.

The young men so charged carried out Moses's orders with gusto until darkness fell that night. A total of three thousand men of the people died that day. Kenaz, although not consenting to Aaron's actions, when he heard the decree from Moses ran to his tent jumped on his camel and rode for the plains. He slept in the open on the outskirts of the camp that night only returning to his tent next morning after hearing the ensuring slaughter had ended.

Moses called the people together and explained that Yahweh was a jealous and holy God and that a cleansing was required because of the golden image that Aaron had made. That was why the slaying of so many was a necessity. He thanked those that stood with him in the name of Yahweh and gave instructions of how they were to gather the bodies of those that died and bury them outside the camp immediately to stop any spread of disease resulting from decaying corpses.

Moses returned up the mountain for another forty days but this time the people were more than happy to await his return. When he did, he was full of plans and commissioned Bezalel and Aholiab to head up a team to build a curtain walled tabernacle where the sin offering could be made and where an inner sanctuary could be so Moses would have a holy place to speak one on one with Yahweh.

Kenaz had briefly met Bezalel because he also was of the tribe of Judah. He remembered that he was an extremely talented and artistic person. He made a very nice living crafting jewellery pieces and selling them to all takers. Kenaz didn't have any such talents but he did have a camel so he offered his services which Bezalel used quite frequently to move heavy objects and relocate things from one place to another. Kenaz enjoyed being useful and was amazed at the beauty of the items crafted as they came into being.

The Law

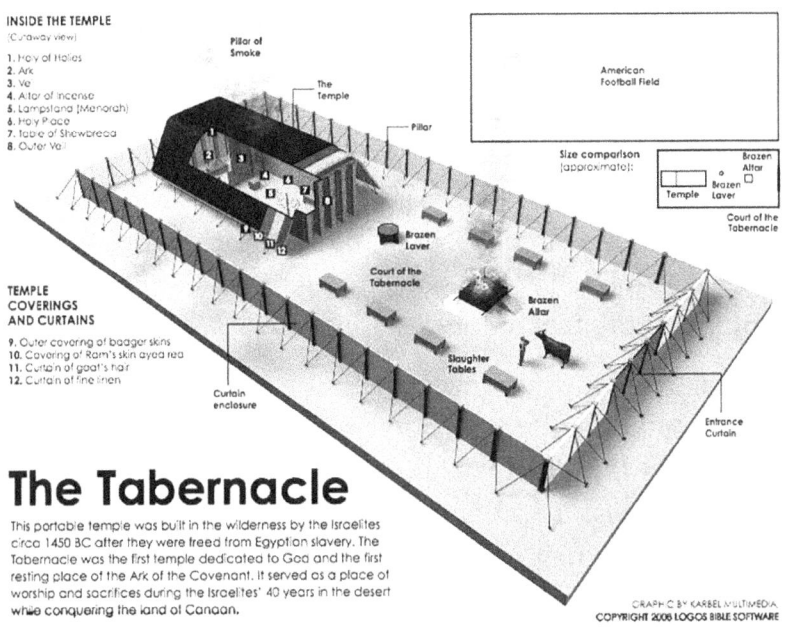

The Tabernacle

This portable temple was built in the wilderness by the Israelites circa 1450 BC after they were freed from Egyptian slavery. The Tabernacle was the first temple dedicated to God and the first resting place of the Ark of the Covenant. It served as a place of worship and sacrifices during the Israelites' 40 years in the desert while conquering the land of Canaan.

Before too long the commission was complete and under the supervision of Moses everything was set up and placed into order. Kenaz and Camel's services were again in frequent demand as the finished, heavy objects, were moved into place. "Just like old times when we worked together for Jethro, isn't it Kenaz?" Moses quipped as he realigned the large bronze altar with the aid of Camel. Kenaz agreed, he liked being around people who knew more than him. He'd learned many new things during those brief weeks of tabernacle building.

Finally, the day had come and the entire congregation of Israel was gathered before the gleaming Tabernacle. Moses displayed his brother Aaron and Aaron's four sons. Each adorned in their newly made stylish priestly garments. A rigorous procedure for cleansing the entire Tabernacle was completed by Aaron and his sons under the very detailed instructions which Moses had received from Yahweh while with Him on the mountain. The cloud that previously had been above Moses's tent of meeting now moved over and stood above the Holy of Holies – the smaller tent enclosure at the West end of the Tabernacle.

While all Israel watched, a bull was sacrificed for the sin offering and a ram for the burnt offering. Aaron and his sons laid the animal parts of the burnt offering onto the altar but the sin offering was burnt outside the camp. Every detail was meticulously carried out in accordance with the strict orders that Moses had received. He was very particular in sprinkling all the atonement blood in the various places as instructed. The basket of unleavened bread was placed in position, the menorah was lit and the wave offering made. Moses and Aaron, having completed everything, stood at the entrance of the tabernacle and blessed the people. At that same moment, fire came down from Yahweh and rapidly consumed the burnt offering. The cloud above The Tabernacle descended over the holy place and the glory of Yahweh enveloped it. The presence of Yahweh was great and the people stood in awe as yet again the reality of their great and mighty God Yahweh was reinforced in their minds.

Aaron's two eldest, sons Nadab and Abihu, each wearing their elegant priestly garments, took their incense censers and without waiting for any instructions from Moses or their father they set them ablaze on the pretence of offering praise to Yahweh. They did this however, in complete disregard to the instruction of order that Yahweh had given. Because The Tabernacle had been atoned by the blood offerings and because the glory cloud of Yahweh was present in the Holy place such blatant disobedience was intolerable to such a holy God therefore fire broke out and consumed the two young men where they stood.

The people stood in shock as they witnessed the dramatic scene. Kenaz again resolved to serve Yahweh the best he could as He sure did mean business when He said things.

Exodus 19:1-2, Exodus 19:10-13, Exodus 19:16-25, Exodus 20:1-17, Exodus 20:18-21, Exodus 32:1-5, Exodus 32:1-30 Exodus 26:1, Exodus 36:1-3, Exodus 40:17-35, Leviticus 8:1-27, Leviticus 10:1-3.

6

Blasphemy

The routine of daily life continued for Kenaz. Camel remained a fantastic money earner being in high demand almost every day, except for the Sabbath, of course. Kenaz had a nice little nest-egg maturing. Most evenings he ate the evening meal with his family following which Jephunneh, Caleb, Kenaz would sit debating current happenings within the vast camp, what the Promised Land would be like, what they were going to plant and enjoy once the land had been conquered. The topic excited Kenaz, He savoured the fact that he had a future, a hope of great things to come. "But first we must fight to gain our inheritance," Jephunneh reminded them. Fighting didn't faze Kenaz if that's what it took to gain an estate.

It had been a year since Kenaz's adoption and being part of family sat well with him. He liked the comradery and the security of relationship. And best of all he didn't have to spend eight months of every year wandering the desert looking for watering holes with Hobab.

Kenaz was woken from a deep slumber at first light one morning to the lingering blast of a shofar. Quickly into his clothes he staggered outside to settle his curiosity only to discover the entire camp trying to do the same. "It's a call to assembly," Jephunneh pronounced as Caleb appeared sleepily from his darkened tent.

The three men hurried along the thoroughfare of tents towards the source of the blasts. They soon found themselves standing outside the tabernacle with a mass of other men mostly unappreciative of the dramatic awakening at such an hour. Moses made his appearance onto a platform with Joshua at his side as a hush fell over the waiting congregation. "Yahweh has decreed we take a census of each individual from every tribe of Israel – except for the tribe of Levi, for now. Every male who is twenty years and above must be registered by reciting their ancestry back as far as our father Israel," Moses decreed. A muffled murmur broke out across the mass of bodies as they each thoughtfully brought to mind their family lines.

"Through this census Yahweh is creating an army, men who can be trained for war so that He can lead us into battle to take the land flowing with milk and honey which is promised to us." Excitement grew in Kenaz as he drank in Moses's words. This was it; they're getting ready to go into the land. Moses continued, "Would the following men from each tribe please come forward." He then listed off twelve names which included two from the double portion tribe of Joseph – one from

Ephraim and one from Manasseh – but he excluded the Tribe of Levi.

As the men joined Moses at the head of the people he explained. "These men are your Generals. They are the leaders of their father's tribe and each of you are to go to them as soon as possible to recite your ancestry by family. They will each record the names then report the totals to Aaron and I. Now, you sons of Levi, don't fret, as Yahweh has other plans for you, which we'll get to shortly," Moses concluded.

Nahshon quickly set up a makeshift registration table outside his tent while his sons prepared scrolls for the Levite scribes to record the names. A long line of eager want-to-be soldiers of the Tribe of Judah rapidly formed as the reciting began. "We'll wait a while," Jephunneh decided as he observed the developing long-winded process.

Kenaz knew his family tree well enough as Jephunneh had made him recount it to him each evening for a whole month after he'd adopted him. Pride welled up in his heart, because he was family and able to prove his lineage. He would now become an integral part of the Army of Israel and would truly earn a right to an inheritance of his own in the land. His life was great thanks to the incredible kindness of his father Jephunneh.

"Jephunneh, I have a question for you," Kenaz said thoughtfully as they finally waited patiently in the registration line. "Since you're also adopted and declared a child of Israel how is it that people still call you a Kenite?"

Jephunneh chuckled as he read Kenaz's concerns, "Nothing derogatory meant by the term, Kenaz," he answered. "In fact, I'm the one who has insisted on it. Despite being fully integrated into Israel I'm very proud of my Kenite upbringing. Yes, we're of the Children of Israel but proudly flavoured by a Kenite culture," Jephunneh concluded. Somehow that made perfect sense to Kenaz, he had a new identity but there was nothing in his past to be ashamed of. He too would also lay claim to his Kenite heritage.

"Next," boomed a loud voice, "step forward and recite your ancestry."

Kenaz took two steps and stood to attention in front of General Nahshon. The scribe to his left refilled the quill ready to record. Kenaz's heart was pounding with excitement. This was his official enrolment into the Army. His reward; an inheritance in the Promised Land. This was it. Slowly he began, "My name is Kenaz, twenty-one years old. I'm a son of Jephunneh, son of Caleb, son of Hezron, son of Perez, son of Judah, son of Israel." Perfect, he thought consolingly.

"And does anyone vouch for this man?" Nahshon asked.

"I do," Jephunneh replied.

"Next," the booming voice rang out. Kenaz was a little disappointed to have been so flippantly dismissed but he didn't care, he was on the scroll, forever etched as a member of the Army of Israel.

As Kenaz made his way back to check on Camel he came across a couple of young men with whom he was acquainted, sitting cross legged staring at the earth and quite distraught. Kenaz, struck with the contrast to his mood, stopped and asked, "Okay, so why the long face? You trying to become a camel?" he joked.

One of the men angrily jumped to his feet and took an aggressive step towards Kenaz. "I'll show you how I can fight, then they'll believe me!" he shouted rather incoherently.

"Slow down my friend," Kenaz quickly replied. "Why would you say that? Nobody's going to fight today."

The young man continued, his militancy still well engaged, "Apparently we're not old enough to fight. Not man enough to die in battle, so that Nahshon says!" he continued sarcastically. "I'll be twenty in three months, you know," he shouted as he stormed off. Kenaz understood now. There were quite a number of nineteen-year somethings around the camp carrying a similar chip on their shoulders. That's their problem he reiterated to himself. I just don't care because at least I'm in the Army he thought and wandered off with a beaming smile.

Over the course of the next few weeks a total of seventy-four thousand six hundred names were recorded from the tribe of Judah alone. From all the twelve tribes the total was six hundred and three thousand five hundred and fifty. "An incredible, formidable Army of Yahweh," Moses stated as he accepted the totals.

Kenaz pondered on his role in the Army. He didn't really like the idea of close combat with blood and all that so perhaps not a spear or a sword. Archery. Yea, I could handle that, he decided. Perhaps a small dagger for my belt like I've seen the Ishmaelite's carry. Kenaz kept a watch out for the frequent trading caravans that passed by almost every day and before long he was the proud owner of a splendid bow, a quiver full of arrows and a razor-sharp dagger complete with its eloquent leather sheath. Kenaz rearranged the dagger beneath his belt a dozen times until he was sure he'd found the perfect position for instant retrieval. With the dagger stowed he squatted to carefully study his bow. "That sure is a beautiful weapon," a voice behind him exclaimed. Kenaz was startled, he thought he was alone. Well, as alone as one can be within the confines of a six hundred thousand strong Army. He quickly turned towards the voice to face his brother, Caleb.

"Do you know how to use that?" Caleb asked. "I used to be a dab hand with a bow in my early days in Egypt," he continued. "Let's go and find a place to practice." The two brothers strode off purposefully towards the nearest rocky backdrop and set up a target. Caleb carefully demonstrated all the fine arts of archery while Kenaz absorbed every word like a sponge.

Kenaz fired off a number of shots and most were well clear of the mark while others, let's just say, were not. "It's only practice over time that'll make you a sure shot," Caleb advised. Kenaz quickly agreed. He had the desire, the enthusiasm and importantly, the time. Every day when he had a little time spare there he was at practice, practice, practice. Before long and several quiver fills of arrows later he too had become a dab hand and practice times quickly turned to competition as he and Caleb fulfilled their brags by nailing their quirkiest shots from ever increasing distances.

Kenaz walked with his head high. Not only was he an Israelite he was a crack archer in Yahweh's Army, the most powerful on the entire earth. Life was good.

Some weeks passed when late one afternoon Kenaz heard a great commotion coming from the direction of the Tabernacle. Hoping to see a panicked young bull running amuck after escaping a sacrifice he was rather surprised to see a very angry looking man restrained in a secure enclosure with several nearby people shouting loudly at a very concerned looking Moses. "What's going on?" Kenaz asked a bystander.

"He was caught fighting another guy in the middle of the camp. Apparently, he really lost it and started cursing and blaspheming Yahweh. It took six guys to restrain him. They brought him to Moses to make judgement on his fate." The bystander explained, "He's from the tribe of Dan but his father was an Egyptian," he added gratuitously.

"The man will be held here overnight until I hear his fate from Yahweh," Moses shouted to the group of onlookers.

Next morning the shofar sounded loudly and a large number of people, Kenaz among them, gathered outside the Tabernacle to hear the man's fate. Kenaz glanced over to the man whose expression of anger the previous day had now morphed into one of grave dismay. Moses strode over and began speaking to the gathered crowd. "Yahweh has spoken regarding this man who has blatantly blasphemed the Holy name of Yahweh," Moses announced. "In accordance with the law the penalty is death by stoning." Kenaz watched as the confined man visibly winced. "He is to be taken outside the camp and every one present here must throw a stone at him until he is dead," Moses concluded.

The idea of him contributing to the stoning didn't appeal to Kenaz until righteous indignation stirred within. This man certainly can't be allowed to speak of his Yahweh that way, he reasoned. The man was led outside the camp against a large rocky outcrop, below which conveniently lay an abundance of fallen rock. All those that had heard the cursing were encourage to lay their hands on the head of the condemned man's head and return to the crowd. The man was then released from his bonds and those restraining him rapidly vanished.

"This will be done to all those that blaspheme the name of Yahweh; the mighty God of Israel," Moses declared and he picked up a nearby stone and hurled it at the man who immediately attempted to make a rapid ascent up the confining rock face. No sooner had Moses's rock left his hand than thousands of rocks, Kenaz's included, hurtled towards the defenceless convict, many finding their exact mark. The man fell to his knees and within seconds his lifeless body lay covered in a great pile of stones.

Kenaz pondered on the events later that day and decided that yes, he would certainly fear Yahweh and do all he could to follow His law. He was a Holy God indeed.

Numbers 1:1-4, Numbers 1:27, Numbers 1:45-46, Leviticus 24:10-23.

7

The Journey Begins

A bleary eyed Kenaz trundled through the camp towards the sound of yet another shofar blast. "If he could just get his hands on that thing...."

"You shall not kill," rang out from a familiar voice who had well surmised Kenaz's early awakened mood.

"No Caleb, I heard that rule isn't in effect before 5am," Kenaz joked.

The two brothers stood together within the immense army that spread out before the Tabernacle at the edge of the camp. Moses stood on his platform and began to speak. "I know it's early but we've all got a lot to do today. Yahweh has told me of the layout He wants for this camp. From now on, this Tabernacle is to be the very centre of our camp. This is the holy place of Yahweh. All the people of the tribe of Levi will plant their tents encircling this structure because they are the ones that have been sanctified and are dedicated to the service of the Tabernacle. When we move, they all have their specific jobs and are the ones who will dismantle it and move it to our next resting place. Nobody, and I mean nobody, from any other tribe is to come near or even look at the holy object because if they do, that person will die – instantly." Moses paused to let his point sink home. Kenaz gulped and made a strong mental note. He was quickly learning that Yahweh was a very Holy God.

"Now, as for the rest of you," Moses continued, "each tribe is to camp together and each family within their tribe is to dwell together under their clan's banner. All the tribes will be separate from each other, arrayed around this tabernacle like the spokes of a chariot wheel. Don't forget that the Levites will be living closest around it so each General is to set their standard some distance back from Levi, spreading outward from there in a V-shape. Is that clear?" he asked.

Without waiting for any questions Moses continued. "The order of tribes is also set by Yahweh. On the East side, over here," he said pointing toward the sun which was just beginning to make its appearance on the horizon, "will be the army of Judah under General Nahshon. Their quadrant will include the armies of Issachar and Zebulun – each tribe by themselves, of course. These tribes will break camp first when we move out.

"Next quarter to the South will be Reuben, Simeon and Gad who will move out next. Once these tribes are on the move then the Levites will move out with the Tabernacle components. They'll go under their standard, secure in the middle as we travel.

The Journey Begins

"The next section on the West side is Ephraim, Manasseh and Benjamin. They will follow next after the Levites. On the North side is Dan together with Asher, then Naphtali. These will break camp last and travel under their standard." Moses paused to allow the understanding to cement, then continued.

"Just to be clear, we're not moving out today as you can see the cloud is still firmly over the holy place of the Tabernacle. However, today I want every tribe to reorganise, before nightfall, under the standard of each tribe in strict accordance with the layout I have just described. This is an ordnance from Yahweh and therefore it's not optional. You know who your tribe General is so report to him for guidance of where to set up your tents and I will direct each General to their designated portion. Remember this Tabernacle will remain where it is right now and we'll form our circle around it." As Moses began descending from his platform he shouted, "Get to it."

For many hours that day extreme chaos reigned as more than a million people moved position. Points of the compass seemingly moved hourly as orders were barked from all-in-sundry. Tribe standards were held high then ripped down by an exasperated pointing mob. Eventually a resemblance of calm ensued as the sound of securing tents finally gave way to the mixed aroma of ten thousand evening meals being roasted or boiled.

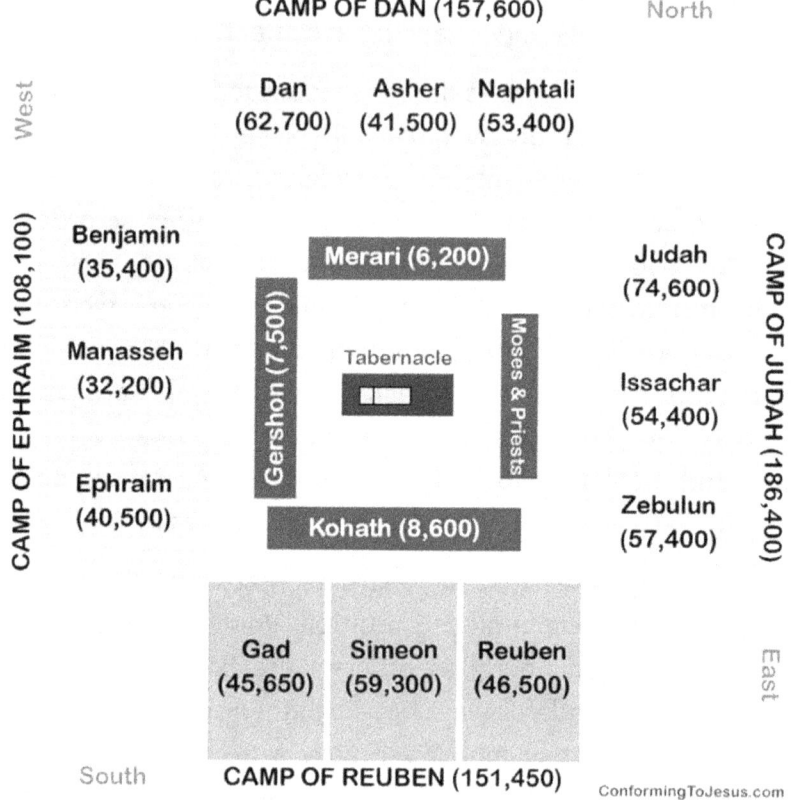

Diagrammatic Layout of the Camp.

Next morning Kenaz was woken early by someone from a neighbouring tribe securing the hire of his camel services for the day. As he made his way past the hoard of sleeping tents the logic of the layout struck him. It was now possible to describe an address for almost anyone in the makeshift and very portable camp. His client described his as they walked. "The eighth tent in the fourteenth circular row within the tribe of Dan." What simple genius Kenaz mused as he decided that not only was Yahweh a Holy God to be feared and obeyed, He also was a wise God, one too of order. Would he ever understand Yahweh, he pondered?

Kenaz had only experienced one Passover and while he understood fully the facts surrounding the original one in Egypt he struggled with the concept. Why did Yahweh have to kill so many seemingly innocent Egyptians to get His people out of there, couldn't He have just got rid of Pharaoh and his cronies, he reasoned. Perhaps he'd bring it up during the meal tonight.

The order had gone out from Moses for each family group to take a lamb and slaughter it at twilight on the fourteenth day of the first month of the year. Jephunneh return from the Tabernacle where one of the Levites had done the honours of slaughtering the animal, sprinkling its blood and burning its offal. Caleb, Kenaz and Jephunneh, after having skinned it, set to roasting the lamb over the fire on their improvised rotisserie. Kenaz drank in the aroma of the sizzling carcass. He enjoyed a good feed of lamb and tonight would be a feast.

The women had prepared unleavened bread, bitter herbs and copious savoury morsels and dips. The extended family sat together as the evening gave way to night and the reflective repast began. Jephunneh, as the head of the family, led the occasion by recounting the event of just three years ago when they'd all encountered the mighty power of Yahweh delivering them in such dramatic fashion. The wine flowed and abundant servings were consumed. "Everything has to be eaten tonight," Jephunneh reminded his family encouragingly. "And remember, no breaking of the lamb's bones."

Kenaz, the only one not present at the original Passover encounter, was keen to expand his understanding. His earlier ponderings weighed in on him as the discourse transitioned from the anxieties of eating that initiatory meal to the thrill of witnessing their Egyptians slave masters begging them to leave, showering them with gifts and blessings while they did so. Kenaz realised he'd have to ask his question now or the moment would pass. "Why did Yahweh have to kill so many seemingly innocent Egyptians to get His people out of Egypt, couldn't He have just killed off Pharaoh and his cronies?" Kenaz blurted, bringing the festivities to a temporary screeching holt as all eyes turned upon him.

Finally, Caleb broke the silence, "You had to be there to understand, my brother. There was no such thing as an innocent Egyptian. Even those who were slaves with us treated us with utter contempt," he explained.

"What Caleb says is so true," Jephunneh added. "For us, however, it wasn't about the killing of the Egyptians, it was the power of the blood that saved us. That's what we celebrate; that simple act of painting the lamb's blood on our door lintel was enough to move our Almighty Yahweh so He passed over our house, sparing our firstborn. Not only is He powerful, He's also gracious to those He cares for, those that obey Him," he concluded.

The Journey Begins

Kenaz, alone that night, regurgitated Jephunneh's words. This was yet another side of Yahweh to comprehend. Not only must He be obeyed but there was more than fear causing the obedience. Yahweh also protected those who obeyed Him. Suddenly all the laws, the order and the ritual made a little more sense. Yahweh was indeed a Holy and powerful God but if we did everything He told us, then His protection was assured. Kenaz tucked this new realization securely into his 'understanding Yahweh' thought compartment.

Kenaz was giving Camel a quick brush-down ready for another day when he heard the commotion. "The cloud is lifting. The cloud is lifting," echoed around the camp. He looked up and sure enough the Pillar of Cloud that had hovered above the holy place in the Tabernacle was now high in the sky.

"Looks like we've got ourselves a trek today, Camel," he declared.

They had been under the shadow of Mt Sinai for nearly twenty-two months and stuff had accumulated. Camel was well-laden as Kenaz gave him the command to rise. "No room for customers today," he added cheerfully. He was excited to be on the move as were most others he met. Not that they didn't have most things they needed in Sinai, it was where they were headed – they were off to the Promised Land.

Just as Moses had instructed, the tribe of Judah peeled off first with General Nahshon leading the way, holding his banner high. Kenaz could just make it out above the maze of heads in front of him. Camel set his own pace which, it seemed, was slightly faster than the general procession and Kenaz soon found himself near the front with Camel breathing down General Nahshon's neck. Much to his amazement the man walking in step with the General was his old shepherd-mate Hobab.

Kenaz ran up and slapped Hobab on the shoulder, "I thought you must have gone home? I haven't seen you since Jethro left." Kenaz said.

"Can't talk now Kenaz, can't you see I'm tracking:, Hobab barked. "That's what I stayed for and that's what I do. And keep that lousy camel well clear of me!" he added.

"Nice to see you too, Hobab," Kenaz commented sarcastically as he quickly retreated. He certainly hadn't mellowed any.

They trundled on all day and as dusk approached the Pillar of Cloud leading them stopped but didn't descend. "We rest for the night and do the same thing tomorrow," Moses announced.

It was to be three days before the cloud finally settled and normal camp life resumed.

Numbers 1:49-53, Numbers 2:1-34, Numbers 9:1-5.

8

Meat to Eat

Kenaz sat outside his tent looking up at the moonless night sky. The night was warm and he couldn't sleep. This new physical location felt much the same as the previous one. His eyes wandered over to the Pillar of Cloud hovering over the Tabernacle. By day it was just a puffy white cloud but at night the thing lit up the night sky like a great ball of fire. Not a heat fire mind you, but one that gave a warm glow across the sprawling hoard of tents. Kenaz felt the comfort and protection that the Fire Pillar provided.

As Kenaz watched, suddenly a massive bout of fire shot out across the camp to the far outer reaches where the mixed races rested. In addition to the twelve tribes of Israel, there was a large number of people of various races that chose to travel with Israel when they saw the might, the power of Yahweh, that His presence was tangible and wanted to share in His blessings. Unfortunately, that was the limit of their understanding of the Mighty God of Israel, they were only in it for the blessings, only for what they could get out of it.

Unfortunately, this led to much grumbling and the usual source of any form of trouble. While most in Israel had a better understanding of Yahweh the frequent mutterings of complaint resonated with many like a yeast infesting the dough.

Kenaz quickly jumped onto his camel and yelled at the dozing animal to "Stand, stand." From his new vantage point, atop a two-metre camel, Kenaz had a pretty good view of the unfolding situation. Upon reaching the camp outskirts the fire had descended to the ground and was now dashing around the camp in a circular motion with licks of fire shooting out consuming some of the people there. Dozens of tents were ablaze, women and children screamed as they dashed tearfully towards the perceived safety of the centre ground. The men rushed about in a state of absolute terror doing what they could to save their animals and belongings.

Within minutes the vast city of tents erupted into mass panic. Awakened from, slumber many saw the fire and screaming then assumed the worst as they collectively scampered towards the Tabernacle, all the while screaming, "Moses, help Moses!"

Moses stood at the front of a shaking crowd and lifted his hands up to Heaven and prayed to Yahweh asking Him to stop the fire and save His people. His voice was heeded and within minutes the fireball retreated into the pillar above the Tabernacle and order assumed as a rattled horde retreated to their allotted sector.

Meat to Eat

Next morning almost the entire camp ambled out to the edge of the tent city to gawk at the scorched surrounds. The inhabitants of the region however were not slow to voice their displeasure at Yahweh's actions. They explained to the people they weren't complaining against Yahweh. "How would we dare to speak against the mighty God of Israel," they clarified. "We were talking about food. This manna stuff that falls every day is okay for a bit, but it's been months now. Before we left Egypt, we had an abundance of fresh produce. We had lovely vegetables and fish but best of all we had meat! We have a craving for meat, meat – give us meat!"

Any consideration of Yahweh's actions the previous night vanished as the onlookers thinking aligned with the outcasts and they quickly took ownership of the grumbling. Before long the entire multitude repeated the cry from every tent door in mock weeping as they wailed, "Where is my meat? Who will give me meat? We had it much better in Egypt."

To say Moses was angry was an understatement. After hearing the angry chant of the people growing louder and more militant by the minute, he rushed into the Tent of Meeting.

Hours later a much calmer Moses reappeared and called the people together. "Yahweh has heard your grumblings and He is very angry with you all, mostly because of what you said about being better off in Egypt. May I remind you; you were slaves there, with terrible taskmasters. How dare you complain before Yahweh in this way," Moses admonished.

"That said," Moses continued, "Yahweh has decreed that you will all eat meat." A collective joyous cheer arose from the listening mass. "The thing is," Moses explained, "you're not going to eat meat for one day or two, or for five or ten or even twenty. You going eat it for a whole month until you gag and are sick of it. Why, because you have rejected Yahweh, who is here among you, and you have whined to Him, saying, 'Why did we ever leave Egypt?'"

Comments of contempt popped out from the crowd, "Fine with me."

"No problems."

"Only *one* month!"

Moses ignored the unsolicited feedback and continued. "So, prepare yourselves and be ready for the feast. I have no idea how He's going to do this, it's beyond my imagination and I did question Him on it. All He said in reply was, "Has my arm lost its power? Tomorrow you'll see whether or not my word comes true!""

That night a strong wind encircled the camp and Kenaz worried if he'd be able to find the manna that always fell to the ground in the wee hours. Manna gathering was his first task at sunrise and it didn't take long as there was always plenty. He'd devised an ingenious device that captured much of the manna that fell onto his tent by manufacturing a large flysheet that was pinned at the top but spread out down the side of the tent. Along the bottom he'd crafted a small wooden trough to fit under it that sloped down to a good-sized bowl at one end. As the manna fell, and Kenaz slept, it would gently slide down the flysheet roll along the trough and into the bowl. That was Camel's portion and surprisingly there was always enough for a very appreciative camel.

As for Kenaz he enjoyed the manna, it was a golden dark brownie colour in the shape of a coriander seed. Most people ground it then cooked it in pans. It tasted like pastry wafers mixed with honey. However, as much as he savoured manna the thought of eating meat for a whole month certainly would bring a welcome change.

As Kenaz emerged from his boudoir he brushed his fingers back through his long darks locks then stopped in his tracks. On every side of the camp there were birds. The entire sky seemed darkened by them. Strangely however they weren't flying, they fluttered, hovering just above the ground, held down by that strong wind that blew all night.

"Come on man, don't just stand there. We've got birds to catch., Caleb's voice rang out as Kenaz was jolted out of his trance. The two gathered up the largest sacks they could find, loaded Camel and were off.

The distance was a little further than it looked and catching them not as easy as imagined. Soon enough though a reasonable technique was devised and before long the sacks were bulging. "Let's gut and pluck these outside the camp to minimise the mess when we get back?" Caleb suggested. As the hours passed the pile of carcasses grew as the pair became more professional by the minute. All around them thousands of excited hands grabbed for quail or devised increasingly dramatic methods of whacking them out of the air. Amazingly, despite literally millions of birds being caught and slaughtered the sky was still just as full of them.

Very early the next morning the pair arrived back at home base and the cooking began. The strong aroma of moist roasting quail permeated every atom of that desert city as every family excitedly cooked to preserve their catch. A feast was prepared and the families sat round eager to finally satisfy their cravings.

Jephunneh recited a thanks to their provider Yahweh and the family set to the task of demolishing the massive spread. As they finished the distant sound of a woman wailing trailed their thoughts. Before too long however, the sound grew stronger, quickly transforming into screaming.

Kenaz ventured out onto the thoroughfare and came face to face with a young woman standing and squealing hysterically. After a few minutes of Kenaz's flustering consolation, the young women finally calmed enough to tell him that all the men in her family had just died of a strange plague before returning to full scream again. The same account was coming from all over the camp. Thousands had died.

An anxious Kenaz desperately pressed Jephunneh and Caleb for ideas on how to escape the unfolding disaster. "I would bet good money that this is the hand of Yahweh," Jephunneh replied after thoughtful consideration. "If it is, the only safe place is the Tabernacle. Let's all go, NOW." At Jephunneh's final statement the entire family sprang into action and ran together to the place of Yahweh's dwelling. "It's better to be closer to His mercy than far from it," he instructed his family as they assembled along with a myriad of others outside the Tabernacle.

They'd no sooner arrived when Kenaz caught sight of a distraught Moses standing alone at the side of the Tabernacle door. He strode up to him and asked, "What's going on with all the death, Moses?"

Moses looked straight into the eyes of his once shepherd-hand and with a sad voice said, "This is the hand of Yahweh. He told me this would happen. Those that complained and instigated things are now all dead. There's a lot of them I'm afraid. I'm waiting to hear what Yahweh wants to do next, Kenaz, but you might as well go home as the plague has already ended."

Kenaz wandered back thoughtfully to his family and relayed the news. As the group silently made their way home, Caleb, bursting with curiosity, said to Kenaz, "How come you can just bowl up to Moses like that? That took guts, my brother!" Kenaz was a little surprised at his older brother's question but decided to answer it graciously anyway.

"Don't forget I did live in the same house with him at Jethro's for about twenty years," Kenaz answered.

The answer seemed to satisfy Caleb who just answered, "I'm very glad you asked. It's far more comforting to hear that sort of thing direct."

That night Kenaz reflected on this Yahweh, the God of Israel. Yes, He was very kind to provide His people with meat when they complained. But to then turn around and kill thousands before they'd even finished eating? Kenaz wasn't sure he liked that aspect of Him. Sometimes, he reasoned, I've got a perfect right to complain if I feel hard done by. Finally, not sure what to think he tucked the debate away for another day.

The birds did hang around for the whole month but with meat every day Kenaz decided a diet of manna wasn't so bad after all. It also took days to burry all the dead from that devastating afternoon.

Kenaz often wondered about the young girl he'd clumsily consoled that night. He never saw her again but did feel compassion for her, losing all the men in her family in one instant. That definitely would be devastating.

The people nicknamed the place 'The Graves of Craving' which Kenaz agreed was very appropriate. Next morning was the start of the next month. At first light the trumpet blew, the Pillar of Cloud lifted; the thought of moving on was very exhilarating. A good place to leave behind he decided as the Army of Israel, led by the Pillar of Cloud of the mighty Yahweh, turned and began marching directly towards the Promised Land.

Numbers 11:1-35.

9

Spies

Kenaz found himself traipsing past the Tabernacle early one morning on his way with Camel to earn some cash for the day. Suddenly he was stopped in his tracks by a mature but very beautiful woman coming out of Moses's tent followed by the man himself smiling, content with the world. A million thoughts flooded Kenaz's mind but the most prominent was a familiar phase from his old charge Hobab, – "Moses, you old dog, what have you been up to?"

As Kenaz gazed an older woman, also staring at Moses, smacked straight into the side of Camel. Why she hadn't seen a nearly seven-foot creature directly in front of her soon became apparent as Kenaz rushed to help her to her feet. The woman, who when he took a closer look was Moses's older sister Miriam. He'd seen her around but had never actually met her.

As she brushed off the dust, she continued muttering to herself and then in a voice clearly intended for Moses's hearing said, "Adulterer, adulterer. Just because Yahweh talks to you all the time that doesn't mean you can do what you like." Moses simply smiled back at his sister politely and walked on. Obviously, some sort of family dispute, Kenaz decided. Time to high-tail it out of here! Too late, a hand grabbed his arm firmly and drew him round to face her directly. Clearly with Moses gone she had to vent here anger somehow and, unfortunately for Kenaz, he was closest."

Confused and unsure of how to calm the situation Kenaz foolishly asked, "Who is that beautiful women in Moses's tent?" still focused on his initial sighting. Miriam turned to Kenaz as if he was the underlying cause of every worldly problem.

Then with clinched teeth she muttered deliberately, "That my boy is the Ethiopian beauty tramp that Pharaoh gave to Moses as his wife when he lived in his palace as the son of his daughter!" With barely a pause for breath she continued, "Now after forty years she thinks she can just march back into his life and take up from where she left off. What about Jethro's daughter and her two boys? Who does he think he is?"

"That's enough, Miriam, release that young man," a voice announced. As Miriam unhanded him Kenaz took several quick clearance steps then turned to see whose voice had made the angry woman respond so well. Kenaz's heart leapt a few beats as he observed Aaron the High Priest of Israel, dressed in his full priestly garb with a firm grip on the arm of his somewhat reluctant brother Moses, striding towards them. Blimey, he thought, I'm right in the thick of it here. Way above my pay grade, let's go, he reasoned. This thought was immediately followed by an overwhelming curiosity to see what happens next, so he took a few further steps back and observed.

The siblings stood together and 'conversation' was brutal. Aaron instead of calming his sister, took her side with poor Moses unable to get a word in edgeways. Miriam words were particularly venom-filled and clearly demonstrated her fluent mastery of the fringes of the Hebrew language as Aaron chipped in occasionally to stoke the flames. Not content to confine the subject to the returned Ethiopian wife the pair turned on Moses about his relationship with Yahweh. "Yahweh doesn't just speak to you, He talks to us too, you know," they shouted.

As Moses stood meekly absorbing the verbal blows his angry siblings delivered, suddenly a voice boomed out of the Pillar of Cloud above the Tabernacle. Kenaz was terrified, he wanted to run as far away as he could but his legs just froze in place.

"Moses is my faithful servant. Unlike with others, where I've used visions and dreams to speak, I speak to Moses face to face, in my very presence. Why then were you not afraid to rage against MY servant?" the voice of Yahweh Himself questioned.

Aaron shrugged and said, "He's right Moses, I'm very sorry we spoke to you that way, right Miriam?" As he turned for confirmation from his sister he abruptly yelled, "Oh no, not that." Kenaz watching from what he considered a safe distance observed Miriam as she became covered in mature white leprosy from top to toe. "Please Moses," they both begged. "We've sinned horrendously, forgive us. Please don't let our sister be consumed, eaten alive by this horrible disease?"

Moses didn't reply, instead he cried out to Yahweh, "Please heal her, oh God, I pray?"

Yahweh replied from the Pillar of Cloud and said, "Okay but she must suffer this for seven days and, in accordance with my law, be shut outside the camp in the common place for lepers. After that she'll be healed and can return." Miriam, alone and untouchable, hastily made her way to the outer regions, desperate to comply with Yahweh's word.

Kenaz unfroze and hurried off. The whistle in his heart that morning had been replaced by trembling. He had just witnessed first-hand the operational hand of Mighty Yahweh, the God of Israel. He made a mental note to be far more respectful to his old friend and shepherd-mate, Moses. Kenaz's relationship with Yahweh had rapidly morphed into one of obedience by fear. He wasn't sure he liked that.

After the seven days were ended Kenaz woke to the trumpet blast and seeing the Pillar of Cloud lifted he quickly set about breaking camp and marching onward with the army of Judah. They marched on until they reached the wilderness of Paran, directly opposite the Promised Land. Kenaz felt his excitement grow, very soon they would enter the Land. After two years in Israel the good-life was about to flourish!

Spies

"Okay, spit it out Caleb. Why are you grinning like a dog that's just found a fresh carcass?" Kenaz queried as his older brother strode merrily into the family compound.

Caleb beaming from ear to ear making no attempt to conceal his pride, said, "In a minute! Father, gather the family. I have news."

A bunch of expectant eyes sat around the family circle as Caleb began. "I was called to a meeting with Moses this morning," he said, pausing for impressive effect. "Yahweh has instructed him to spy out the land of Canaan ready for our invasion," he continued.

Excitement overwhelmed Kenaz and he leapt to his feet, punched the air and exclaimed, "Yesssss."

"Ah, but that's not the best bit," Caleb continued ignoring his brother's excitement. "I've been selected as one of the spies, to represent the tribe of Judah. Together with eleven others from the rest of the tribes."

The family cheered and congratulated Caleb as he sat. "We leave in the morning," Caleb added.

"May Yahweh go with you my son," Jephunneh said. Then after a short pause added, "And you be very careful too, Caleb. I hear there are giants in that land. Massive men that can wipe you out with one slap of their hand."

"Yahweh is far greater than any man giant, Father. He will go with us," Caleb answered assuredly.

"You can take my camel with you, brother," Kenaz proffered.

"Actually, that's an excellent idea, it'll enhance my disguise as a trader."

Early next morning the family said their goodbyes as Caleb walked over to join the other eleven as they received their final instructions from Moses. "See what the land is like, what parts are good and what parts are bad. See their cities if they're strongly defended or not and bring us back some fruit," Moses instructed.

The twelve men and one camel led by Caleb set off to the cheers and encouragement of thousands of weary desert wanderers. "May Yahweh be with you," Moses shouted as the men retreated from view. "See you in forty days."

With his camel gone Kenaz had time on his hands, lots of time. Some days he took his bow and headed to the outskirts and practiced. But mostly he just lay in his tent and imagined. What would his estate look like? Perhaps he would get himself a vineyard – now there's an idea he mused. His thoughts then began to drift towards the current owners of his vineyard. Perhaps it's one belonging to a giant. Perhaps all the vineyards belong to the giants? This negative thought troubled him. He'd always envisaged a bit of a scrap, he'd win and hey presto, his new vineyard. But how could he fight a giant? Na, they're only a figment of the pessimists' imagination, he decided. No such things as giants and he return to planning his first vintage.

Spies

The forty days seemed like an eternity but finally the shout went out, "The spies have returned." Each one was laden with fruit and produce, as was Camel. "Thanks for Camel, Kenaz," Caleb said as he handed him back to his owner. " Camel's cameo saved my life more than once."

Next morning all the tribes gathered excitedly to hear their full account of this promised land. The twelve spies entered the platform with Moses leading them in. Each of them carrying copious portions of fruit and vegetables, produce from the land.

The biggest applause went up for the Eschol grapes whose cluster was so large it took two men to carry it on a pole between them.

Each one recounted their experiences in detail, confirming it was certainly a great land. They'd been all through it and truly it is a land flowing with milk and honey as can be seen from the abundance and varieties of fruits.

"And what of the people?" Moses asked.

Ten of the spies quickly jumped forward and blocked out Caleb and Joshua. Almost as one the ten began shouting about the giants they saw. "Massive. We were like grasshoppers to them. Their cities are strong and extremely well-fortified – and we saw the descendants of Anak there," they exclaimed. An instant hush ascended on the crowd as the name Anak was absorbed into their minds. Anak, that massive, dangerous and most renowned giant that ever lived. His descendants lived there! The hush was quickly replaced by a rapidly growing mutter as each recounted their own magnified appraisal of this Anak. "I'm sorry guys," the ten spies continued, "we won't be able to fight these people. They're way too strong and powerful for us. We'd not last ten minutes."

Finally, Caleb was able to break through the mob of ten sowing fear and dread into the crowd. "That is so not true," Caleb shouted in his strongest voice.

"I agree totally," Joshua confirmed. "Just be quiet and listen for a minute," Caleb cautioned the other ten. The crowd became very quiet and listened intently as Caleb spoke, desperate for hope they still had a land to go to.

"Yes, it is true that the descendants of Anak live there," Caleb confirmed," but don't forget we have Yahweh who fights for us. Remember the incredible things He did for us against the Egyptians. Remember the parting of the Red Sea and how when it closed, the entire Egyptian army was wiped out. Remember the water He provided for us from that rock in Horeb and the manna we eat every day." Moses clapped heartily as Caleb finished with Joshua shouting his full agreement.

The ten however, weren't about to be outdone. "This man's been nothing but a troublemaker for every one of the past forty days, "they shouted to the crowd. "Incredibly optimistic, dismissing every negative thing we saw. The man's a liar. Do you know, he even drew his sword on us at one point to try and force us to accept his story." The crowd went wild at this report hurling abuse at Caleb, defending the ten.

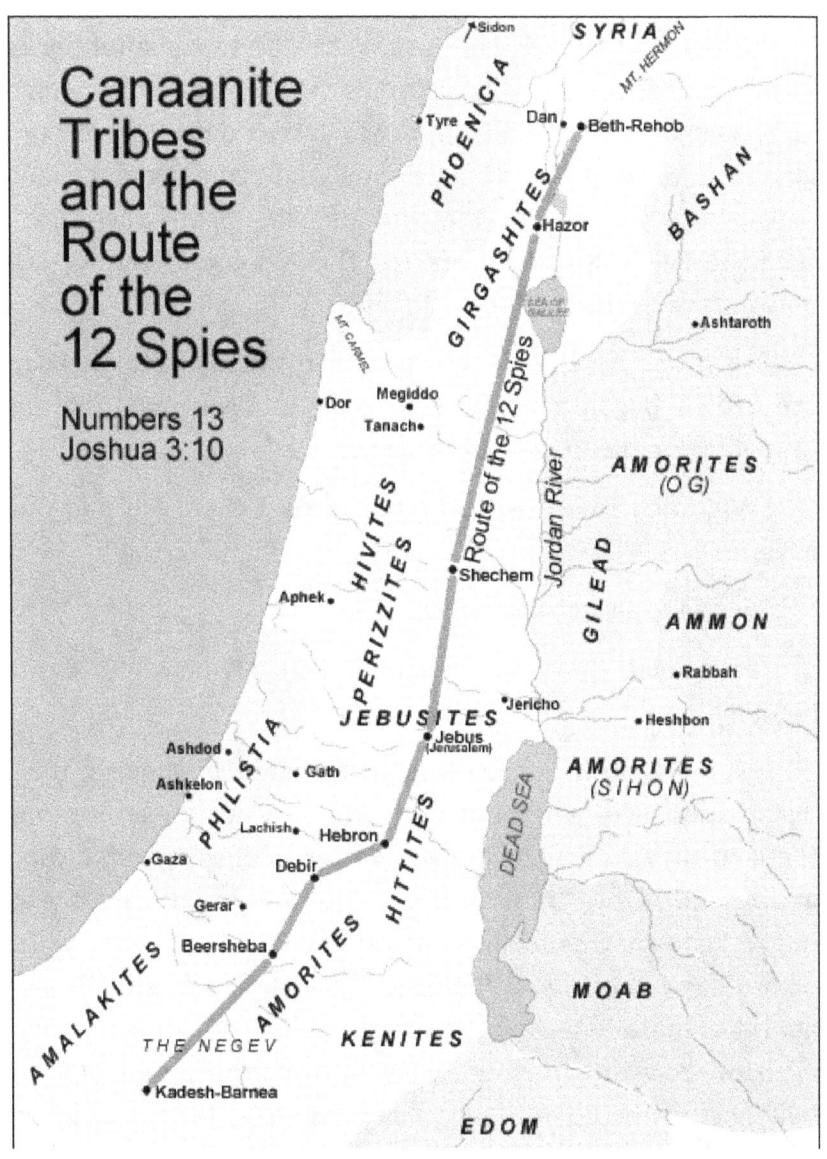

The Journey of the Twelve Spies.

Joshua attempted to shout above the noise and after finally gaining some hearing said, "I confess the bit about the sword does have an element of truth but in Caleb's defence these ten guys here were so timid. They jumped at everything and it was only by Caleb's cunning that any of us came through alive. Listen to Caleb, his report is true. This is a great land we are able to take it with the help of Yahweh."

Sadly, the voice of the ten prevailed the loudest. Voices in the crowd began to join the negative. "Why has Yahweh brought us to this land just to die in battle."

"Why didn't we stay in Egypt, at least there we had our lives."

"Yes, let's all go back to Egypt."

"Let's elect a new leader and head back to Egypt immediately."

Caleb and Joshua ripped at their clothes in anguish, their desperation increasing as they tried to convince the crowd that the land they'd passed through, was exceedingly good. Moses and Aaron lay prostrate on the platform, weeping and crying out to Yahweh. Eventually some rebel makers pushed forward with a bag full of rocks. "Come on guys, let's stone them and get rid of these two trouble makers and let's do our own thing. A mighty roar of agreement went up from the crowd as each quickly scurried to find a suitable nearby rock. Instead of a hail of rocks however, a deafening trumpet blast emanated from the Pillar of Cloud above the Tabernacle. Every person in the entire camp froze in their tracks and stood to attention at the mighty blast.

Moses shouted to the people as he rose to leave the platform, "Wait here until I'm back, then I'll tell you exactly what Yahweh thinks of this morning's fiasco." Moses and Aaron disappeared into the Tabernacle and surprisingly the crowd kept their peace, most totally expectant of a full Godly justification of their thinking.

Before long the duo reappeared looking very stern-faced. I'll get straight to it," Moses began. "Yahweh says: These ten spies and all of you children of Abraham have seen my glory and all the signs I did in Egypt and in the wilderness yet you have put me to the test ten times now over the past two years and have not heeded my voice. Enough is enough. Therefore, none of you will see this land which I promised your fathers Abraham, Isaac and Jacob to give to you. The only exceptions are Caleb and Joshua because they bought back a good report.

"Your little ones that you said would be the victims, Yahweh will bring in and they will possess the Land that you have rejected today. For the next forty years you are going to be shepherds in this desert while the next generation grows. That's one year for each day these spies spent in the land. Every person who was twenty years old when they registered for the Army will die, except my two servants here." Moses concluded his words and beckoned to Caleb and Joshua to quickly leave the platform with him.

No sooner had their feet touch the ground than the ten spies remaining on the stage dropped dead. Horror and dread fell over the crowd as they rapidly retreated to their tents wailing loudly from Moses's news.

Kenaz didn't want to eat that night, nor the next day. His future and dreams were in tatters. He lay on his bed and wept utterly distraught. He relived his excitement at being eligible to join the Army and the callous distain he held for those nineteen-year-olds that he saw on his return. If only he could turn back the clock and be one of them now. "Forty years," he wailed.

Numbers 12:1-16, Numbers 13:1-2, Numbers 13:6, Numbers 13:25-33, Numbers 14:1-10, Numbers 14:28-39,

10

Marriage

___

"Come sit for a while, Kenaz," Jephunneh requested. Kenaz understood that a request from his father to sit for a while was not exactly optional so he quickly took a seat on the ground beside him. "Ah there you are, Carmi," Jephunneh exclaimed as a rather short and slightly overweight bearded man in his fifties entered the family compound. Kenaz knew Carmi as he was also of the tribe of Judah but only as an acquaintance. He wasn't a close friend of either him or Jephunneh. Kenaz's curiosity flourished as the man took a seat opposite him and Jephunneh.

The three men made polite conversation as the women served them sweet savoury cakes. Okay, Kenaz reasoned to himself, this is a conference, not a casual chat. Perhaps Carmi has a business proposal for his camel services, he reasoned.

It'd been eight years now since the forty-year delay declaration had been made because of those evil spies. Kenaz had mostly come to terms with his disappointments and had ambled on with life. The tribes had moved back from the fringes of Canaan moving through various locations in the surrounding wilderness, wherever water could be found. Hobab had proven a valuable asset to the budding nation in this regard.

Kenaz's despair of knowing he would not inherit his vineyard had diminished. He realised that while he was going to die before the end of forty years it wasn't necessarily imminent so he made a conscious effort to continue with life, but it's fair to say the spark of that life had diminished somewhat. Kenaz wasn't alone in his attitude as every person he knew, with the exception of Caleb and Joshua, were in exactly the same situation.

Kenaz was jolted back to the present as Jephunneh's tone suddenly turned authoritative. "Kenaz," he began, "I've invited Carmi here today because we have a proposition to put to you. How old are you now, Kenaz?" Jephunneh asked. Strange question to ask when discussing a business deal but what the heck, he was proud of his youthfulness.

"I turned thirty just a few weeks ago, father", Kenaz answered. "I'm sure you recall the festivities," he added.

"I certainly do, my son, but I asked the question for Carmi's benefit, not mine," Jephunneh stated. "Kenaz also has a camel," Jephunneh added. "He earns a very good living from it too."

"What do you say, Carmi?" Jephunneh asked. Carmi sat thoughtful for a minute or two as he consumed yet another savoury. "You see Kenaz, Yahweh has blessed me with five daughters and only one son. I'm sure He knows what He's doing but my preference would have been for the opposite. My son Achan is still young but my eldest daughter Charna, at nineteen, is of age," Carmi continued, choosing his words carefully. Kenaz felt himself blush, slightly awkward as he began to comprehend the likely reason for the meeting. He recomposed himself and braced for what may be coming next.

"Jephunneh and I have been talking and we have decided you will take my Charna to be your wife. We wanted to discuss with you the matter of the dowry," Carmi stated. "She is a virgin, of course," he added quickly. Kenaz well knew virgin status increased the dowry price, this man knew how to extract value.

Kenaz sat for a while as he contemplated the idea of parting with his sliver coinage in return for a wife. It wasn't something that was on his mind that morning but Jephunneh had reminded him several times during the past year that it was time he considered the continuance of his name. He needed to produce a son, an heir, to take up an inheritance in the Promised Land when the time finally came. Finally, Kenaz broke the silence, "Okay, I'll pay the dowry for your Charna," Kenaz advised.

Carmi, quick to conclude the deal broke into a smile and said, "Jephunneh and I have agreed thirty shekels of silver." As Kenaz got up to retrieve the necessary silver from his tent Carmi miraculously produced a set of scales seemingly out of thin air and eagerly set them up as Kenaz returned. Thirty shekels of silver were carefully weighed out. Kenaz handed the precious metal to his father who weighed it again then handed it to Carmi.

"As Yahweh is our witness, my son Kenaz has paid you, Carmi, the full dowry price for your eldest daughter Charna. The wedding ceremony will be in one month from now," Jephunneh confirmed as the exchange was concluded.

The three men sat in contemplative silence and drank qom to cement their now common bond. Carmi contemplated the spending of his new-found fortune. Kenaz's emotions oscillated rapidly between the excitement of becoming a married man to the fear of how he could possibly share his tent with a woman! Jephunneh thoughts focused on his son, joy welling in his heart at the thought of even more grandchildren. The fact that Charna, the sole reason for the contemplative fest, was totally unaware of the concluded transaction, was seemingly irrelevant.

Caleb who at forty-five had married Mishael eight years ago, was full of advice to his brother about all things married. He insisted his sisters, most of whom had been married for the best part of twenty years, go through poor Kenaz's tent and remove everything smelly, alive or growing. Kenaz protested but deep down he didn't mind. The place was to be shared with his bride and laying aside many years of bachelorhood could do no harm. This was a time of new beginnings.

The month of preparations passed, in what seemed to Kenaz, like a single day. He had washed his clothes, several times, and although they weren't at all worn out, he splashed out on some new sandals. Caleb insisted they arrive at the ceremony early and it was with much trepidation that Kenaz stood, waiting to lay eyes on a bride he'd never met, the woman he was scheduled to spend the rest of his life with.

He slowly drank in the scene around him. The outdoor area was swept clean without a rock or stick to be seen. A large canopy stood in the middle with a myriad of colourful mats arrayed around it. Tables stood to one side awaiting the arrival of the feast components. Any reason for a feast, what else was there to do while spending forty years in a wilderness. Over to one side, almost as an afterthought, stood a single tent – the bridal chamber – decoratively garnished with colourful streamers. Kenaz blushed at the thought of his very public first encounter.

His thoughts were interrupted by an approaching grand procession. Young women danced to symbols and swirled large streamers at arm's length. Behind was his bride covered from head to toe, born aloft by her brother Achan and his three friends. Behind her walked all the invited guests clapping, singing and swaying to the musical rhythm.

Kenaz quickly took his place under the canopy as the young men gently lowered his bride to her feet beside him. With her face completely covered he still had no idea what she looked like but she sure smelt wonderful. Just then a very calming voice beside him said, "Hello, nice to finally meet you, Kenaz."

"Very nice to meet you too, Charna," Kenaz replied to his cloaked bride.

Jephunneh and Carmi stood together in front of the very nervous couple. Carmi bursting with pride said, "We've managed to get one of your oldest friends to officiate today, Kenaz." Oh, please Yahweh, not Hobab, Kenaz begged within himself. His fears rapidly evaporated as he saw his old friend Moses, the leader of all the tribes of Israel, the friend of Mighty Yahweh step out of nowhere and take both their hands in his.

"Kenaz and Charna we are all gathered today to witness the joining of you both in marriage in plain view of Yahweh," Moses began. "First we break bread together." Moses took a small loaf from one of the young girls standing near and broke the loaf in two passing a portion to Kenaz. "Each of you are to take and eat a small portion of this loaf which symbolises the fellowship of eating and doing things together as one," Moses said. Kenaz broke a piece off and passed it towards his bride. A slender hand reached out from under the layers of light clothing, broke off a piece and quickly poked it up under her veil.

"And with this cup we agree to share in all life's burdens," Moses continued as he handed a small wooden goblet first to Kenaz then to Charna. Kenaz marvelled how anyone could eat or drink anything in that garb, let alone so delicately. Moses handed the empty goblet back to Kenaz. "You must now stomp on, and shatter this goblet, which will represent the breaking away from all of your previous life. You and your bride will walk a different life together from now on," Moses reiterated. Kenaz obligingly took the goblet, dropped it to the ground and stomped firmly. The wooden vessel shattered into a dozen small pieces and a loud cheer went up from the chosen observers.

"What Yahweh has joined together, let no man separate," Moses decreed. "A man must leave his father and mother and be joined to his wife, and they shall become one flesh." As Moses spoke his final words he turned, raised his arm guiding the couple towards the bridal chamber. A nervous Kenaz reached out to take the hand of his young bride, which trembled lightly in his as they walked slowly towards the waiting tent.

Inside the tent an abundance of candles lit the place as bright as day. Finally alone Kenaz turned to his wife and asked if he could please see her face for the very first time. Carefully Charna lifted her veil as Kenaz stood transfixed gazing into the two most beautiful hazel eyes he'd ever seen. The form of her face sheer beauty, enhanced by her long jet-black hair. Every ounce of anxiety vanished from his mind as he exclaimed, "My, you're absolutely, stunningly beautiful. And you're all mine," he added as he reached out excitedly and embraced his prize.

Sometime later a very contented couple lay together chatting like they'd been together all their lives. "Oh, I guess we better throw this out to the waiting hordes," Kenaz suggested. Charna didn't reply but giggled happily as Kenaz picked up the stained virginity sheet, reached a hand through the tent door and placed it carefully over the side of the tent, the symbol plain for all to see. His bride was who she said she was. A loud cheer went up from the invited guests as the festivities got under way in earnest.

Kenaz and Charna eventually forced themselves to leave their sanctuary chamber and join the celebrations. For the first time in eight years, he was truly happy again. He had a wife and a real stunner at that.

"I just have one question for you, my Kenaz?" Charna asked lovingly. "How on earth did they get Moses to officiate at our wedding?"

"Ha, ha," Kenaz laughed. "I was bought up in Jethro's house for about twenty years before I became Jephunneh's son. Jethro lives in Midian and is Moses's father-in-law. We worked together for Jethro," Kenaz explained. "I've got a camel too, you know," he added as an afterthought.

"Never!" exclaimed Charna.

11

Children

Kenaz tied up Camel and fed him the last of his remaining manna for that day. Wearied from a day of carrying supplies for various customers from the Midianite traders that frequently passed by. Since they were never allowed to bring their camel trains into the camp all purchases had to be transferred by other means to the tent door. This provided steady work for Kenaz but it involved a lot of walking, through and beyond the vast camp. Today had been such a day.

As he trudged across the compound his wife bubbling with joy ran across the compound to meet him. Grabbing him by the arm she led him lovingly over to their small enclave area across from their main tent. Married life agreed with Kenaz even though many things had changed during the three years since that day. Instead of his single tent inside Jephunneh's compound he had established his own area which adjoined Jephunneh's and neighboured with Caleb's. Mostly each family followed their individual routines within their own compounds but extended family get-togethers were frequently convened under the slightest of pretexts.

Kenaz found that because the tribes moved to a new location about once each year that rearranging his compound was only a matter of time. Each time he claimed a little more space and made the new additions he'd dreamed of. His latest layout included a stall for Camel, a conclave area, a covered cooking area to shade from the hot sun, the main sleeping tent with an adjoining tent for a child, or two. The child's tent however stood empty even though three years of married bliss had passed. For some reason Charna was unable to conceive. While Kenaz was blasé on the subject, Charna's maternal instinct raged, frequently bringing her to tears. Kenaz unsure of what to do ignored the problem. Jephunneh on the other hand was most concerned at the lack of grandsons apparent and recently pulled his son aside to discuss techniques, much to Kenaz's extreme embarrassment.

Tonight, however Charna's mood was joyful and much to Kenaz's surprise she led him to a mat, sat him down, poured some water into a bowel and began washing his feet. "I've even cooked you a special meal my husband, the father of our child," Charna mentioned casually.

"Great, I'm starving... Say what?" Kenaz answered, as Charna's words finally reached his brain. "Seriously, you're finally pregnant?" Kenaz asked with urgency.

"Yes, seems I am." Charna answered with the broadest smile imaginable.

Kenaz leapt to his feet, gave his wife a massive bear hug then rushed towards the door exclaiming, "Yippee, I'm going to have a son. I'm off to tell Jephunneh. He'll be so pleased."

A slightly bewildered Charna stood watching her husband disappear across the compound. "That didn't quite go as I'd envisaged it. Men!" she said quietly to herself.

Over the next few months Kenaz told everyone he met, regardless of their interest, his wife was finally giving him a son! Life had thrown him another cherry and he was determined to savour every moment of it. Charna, on the other hand received copious advice from every woman she met. Everyone, it seemed, had a horror story or a great list of do's or don'ts. Even the advice of her own mother, who now lived nearby, only instilled alarm. Caleb's wife Mishael had given birth to a son, Mesha and two daughters. And despite being several years older, upon seeing the horror building within her sister-in-law she took charge of the situation by explaining the real facts to Charna. The pair becoming close friends as a result.

The day finally arrived when Charna woke early one morning, her body racked with initial contractions. "Please make it stop, Kenaz?" Charna begged. "Oh, get out of here and go, get the midwife," she ordered. With the midwife retrieved Kenaz was given strict orders to, well, 'just disappear' this was woman's work.

The contractions went for all that day but near evening time the midwife repositioned Charna so she squatted on top of the birthing stone; essentially just a large flat, smooth rock that

Kenaz was ordered to find and haul into the tent a few weeks ago. Bending forward with her thighs pressing hard against her groin she pushed with all her might, while under strong 'encouragement' from the midwife who sat behind ready to catch. Just when she felt she could do no more she heard a shout of delight from the midwife, "It's a girl." Charna didn't hear or care – the pain had stopped!

The midwife quickly set to work on the infant. First cutting its umbilical cord, rubbing its little body all over with salt; to harden the skin. She then swaddled it to straighten out its limbs after the trauma of the delivery. Next, she worked manipulating the head to form a proper shape. She was particularly proud of her head work as none of her births were left with round heads like many Egyptian children she knew.

In the meantime, Charna was left to clear the placenta and wash herself as best she could. Regardless of how well she scrubbed she would be unclean and untouchable for eighty days. Secretly she was quite glad it was a girl as the other women had told her that the days of isolation after childbirth were the most wonderful gift – no cooking, cleaning or caring for anyone else except getting to know her new child. Had it been a boy she would only be unclean for forty days.

"It's a what?" exclaimed Kenaz. "My firstborn has to be a son," he wailed. The tiny infant was carried out by the midwife and paraded past the line of curious onlookers. Kenaz able only to look and not touch gazed at his new daughter with mixed emotions. He so wanted a son but never-the-less this little bundle was all his. Perhaps next time, he decided.

Children

The weeks went by and the frequent evening conversations turned to names for the little daughter. Jephunneh, Caleb and Kenaz sat discussing various family names and discarded many. "As the father, Kenaz, it's your obligation to name the child, regardless of what we advise," Jephunneh stated.

After some considerable silence Kenaz announced, "Her name will be Edna. I'll tell Charna in the morning".

Time progressed and Edna grew and much to his surprise he found he thoroughly enjoyed having a little daughter around and she quickly became his pride and joy. Contrary to her mother's wishes riding an aging Camel, under her father's leading, became a particularly favourite pastime.

As the years progressed more pregnancies ensued resulting in yet more daughters. In addition to Edna, he now had Jael, Adina and Tamar. Finally, after ten years of marriage and just over twenty years living with the tribes of Israel, Charna gave birth to a son.

Finally, Kenaz, now at forty years of age, felt like a real man. He had a son, an heir. Someone to take up his inheritance in the Promised Land and savour that first vintage from a prized vineyard.

This time there was no debate nor discussion, Kenaz immediately announced, "His name would be Othniel. He will be a lion of a man using the strength of Yahweh," he added. As soon as the forty days of purification were complete Kenaz arranged for his wife and son to go to the Tabernacle with him for the required purification in accordance with the law Moses had received from Yahweh. The requirement for Charna was a young ram less than a year old and a young pigeon. Even though Othniel wasn't the first child he was, however, the firstborn son and heir. A firstborn male was required to be dedicated to Yahweh through the offering of two young pigeons or doves. Kenaz's was very insistent that his son be treated as if he was his firstborn child.

The family set off together with seven-year-old Edna being tasked with leading the somewhat reluctant ram. Jael carried the small cage containing the three birds who sat cooing contentedly totally oblivious to their pending fate. Camel remained confined to his stall.

On arrival at the gate of the Tabernacle, it was early morning rush hour. In addition to the regular morning sacrifices there were several other families waiting their turn for similar reasons. Kenaz held Othniel, Charna took charge of the four girls and the animals as they waited in line for their turn.

Eventually they made it to the front of the line as a Levite priest came up to inquire of their offerings. He led the family over to the side of the entrance. Beyond was a large bronze altar which was well ablaze from the morning's work. The man took the ram from a reluctant Edna and quickly whipped out a knife slitting its throat while another priest held a bowel to catch the blood. The sight of the dying animal and the smell of the blood instantly overwhelmed Edna as she turned and vomited on the ground against the exterior fence of the tabernacle. "Don't worry," a young priest assured her, as he hurried up with a bucket of dirt and threw it over the evidence. "It's quite a common occurrence around here."

His consoling was interrupted by a very excited Jael, "Wow, that was so cool. Did you see how quickly all the blood came out," she exclaimed loudly to nobody in particular.

The lamb was expertly skinned and gutted. Aaron the High Priest was ushered over. He put his hands on the remains of the ram then sprinkled some of the blood onto Charna. He then poured the rest on the burning altar. He quickly took one of the pigeons and in a well-practiced move broke its neck and again sprinkled a little of its blood on Charna. He then placed the bird into the middle of the altar fire with a large bronze fork. "With these offerings you're now cleansed and your purification is complete," Aaron advised. The first priest picked up the ram carcass and carried it off to the boiling pot.

"That's holy food now, for the priest to eat," Kenaz instructed his attentive family.

Aaron was about to walk off as Kenaz spoke up. "We've also brought my son to dedicate him to Yahweh."

Aaron took a slightly bemused look at the now four rather subdued young children standing beside him and said, "So none of these are sons?"

"Absolutely not," replied an indigent Kenaz; who could possibly mistake his beautiful daughters as sons. "This is Othniel, he's my firstborn son. I want to dedicate him to Yahweh."

"Oh, so sorry girls," Aaron replied, "yes of course, such a dedication is required." He then took the two pigeons, broke their necks and again sprinkled a little blood on Othniel, Kenaz and Charna. After instructing one of the nearby priests to place the dead birds into the altar fire he picked up a sleeping Othniel and held him aloft. After confirming his name, he declared loudly, "Yahweh, in accordance with his parents' desire, we dedicate young Othniel to you. May his days be many and may they all be blessed." He handed him back to Kenaz who made no effort to conceal his joy.

"Thank you," was all he could utter.

It was a contented and reunited family that walked happily back to their compound later that morning. Kenaz was determined his son would be taught everything, starting as soon as he could walk. He didn't want him frittering away his youth the way that he had.

Four years after the birth of Othniel, Charna gave birth again. This time to another son, which did please Kenaz, but not to the extent of his firstborn. "This son will be called Seraiah," Kenaz decreed.

Leviticus 12:1-8, Exodus 22:29, 1 Chronicles 4:13.

12

Rebellion

It was the Sabbath, a day of no work and a time for one to rest. Kenaz had taken the family for a walk past the edge of the camp to a tree shaded, grassy area beside a small stream – a true oasis in the desert. He'd found the spot recently while working a now very old Camel and the place quickly became a Sabbath day refuge away from the bustle of daily camp life.

And so the family lay relaxing, listening to the soothing trickle of the stream while nibbling on the contents of the pre-packed lunch Charna had prepared the day before. Othniel, who would be five in a week, sat with his feet in the stream exploring the creek-bed for any tiny crustacean inhabitants. As he played, he noticed a man casually walk by with a donkey laden with wood. "That guy's having a restful Sabbath," Kenaz joke aloud.

"Shouldn't he be resting like us, Father," Othniel asked.

"Not everyone is respectful to Yahweh's laws," Kenaz answered. Othniel, satisfied with the answer and now tired of the subject, went back to his crustacean search.

As dusk began to fall the family began their stroll home. The moment they left their oasis they suddenly encountered a large crowd striding purposefully towards them. At the head was Moses leading a man tied with a rope – the very man Othniel had seen much earlier in the day. Behind Moses were literally thousands of people marching with deliberate intent. Othniel and his family, overcome with curiosity, hurriedly turned tracks and followed among the crowd. "What's going on?" Kenaz asked a nearby marcher.

"The man broke the Sabbath by gathering firewood for cooking," the marcher replied.

Reaching a rocky outcrop Moses stopped and called for silence. "This man was found gathering sticks, working on the Sabbath day," Moses declared. "I put him under guard while I waited to hear from Yahweh, and He has now decreed His judgement. This man is to be stoned to death because he broke the laws of Yahweh. Now that the Sabbath is ended at this twelfth hour, each of you is to pick up a stone and carry out the judgement."

Moses quickly abandoned his charge and as he did so a barrage of stones and rocks hurtled towards the defenceless man. Othniel keen to participate picked up a small rock and threw it with all his might and even though it fell wide of its mark he was convinced it was his stone that had delivered the final lethal blow. Within minutes the lifeless man was covered in a mountain of rock and Moses dismissed the crowd.

At just five years of age empathy was an unknown emotion for Othniel. The finality of the judgement for such a seemingly small offence, however, was clearly understood. "He wasn't stoned just because he picked up a few sticks on the Sabbath," Kenaz explained to his son, as they walked home in the fading light. "He was killed because he broke the laws of Yahweh. He disobeyed the Mighty Yahweh. It doesn't matter which law you break; murder is as serious as working on the Sabbath in His eyes." Kenaz concluded. Othniel, despite his age, now clearly understood. The law of Yahweh was not to be trifled with. He determined there and then to get to know all those Laws thoroughly.

A few weeks later, his fifth birthday celebrated in style, Othniel set off exploring within the camp accompanied by Caleb's third son Elah. Caleb's wife Mishael, after having produced one son and two daughters, stopped producing. Because of Caleb's celebrity type status in the camp he had an endless string of female admirers. He was assured of making it to the Promised Land, which made him irresistible to almost every father of young daughters in the camp. A few years ago Caleb had taken a second wife Ephah who quickly gave him three more sons, Iru, Elah and Naam. Elah was about the same age as Othniel and the pair frequently went exploring together. Not yet satisfied with the abundance of his offspring, Caleb took yet another wife who gave him a daughter he named Achsah who immediately became his pride and joy. She was followed in quick succession by brothers Sheber, Tirhanah, Shaaph and Sheva.

With Caleb's growing clan Othniel was never short of a playmate or three. Today he headed off with Elah as they made their way towards the Tabernacle to explore something on the West side. Approaching the Tabernacle the sight of a large gathering of men shouting at Moses distracted them from their mission. "Cool, there's going to be a big fight," Elah exclaimed with eager excitement.

"Na, I don't think so," Othniel replied, "Moses won't fight them but Yahweh might do something. My dad's told me stories of all the things that Moses has done and I wouldn't try and fight with him," Othniel replied wisely.

The two boys sidled up beside the group to listen. "You take on way too much Moses and Aaron," the group shouted. "All the congregation of Israel is holy and Yahweh is among them too. Why do you make yourself so high and mighty above all the rest of the assembly of Yahweh?" they demanded.

Moses fell flat to the ground when he heard their hurtful words. "Alright," he announced, "we'll let Yahweh choose who will come near Him. Do this: Each one of you take a golden censer and put fire and incense in them and come back first thing tomorrow morning. At that time Yahweh will choose His man," Moses concluded.

That option seemed to pacify the angry crowd and, as they began to disburse and ready their censers, Moses suddenly shouted, "Where are Dathan and Abiram? They're part of the leadership. Why are they not here?"

Joshua stepped forward and said, "Sorry Moses. I tried to get them here but they refused. They said for me to tell you that they reckon, you Moses, act like a prince over us! That You bought us up out of a very pleasant land to kill us all in this wilderness. Moreover, you haven't bought us into a land flowing with milk and honey, nor given us an inheritance of fields and vineyards. They finished by saying, "We will not come up and stand before you.""

When Moses heard that he got very angry. He shouted out to Yahweh, "Do not respect the offerings of the men of Korah. I have not taken one donkey from them, nor have I hurt any one of them in any way." Then turning to the surrounding crowd, he shouted, "Meet back here tomorrow morning, all two hundred and fifty of you to present yourselves before Yahweh with your censers filled with fire and incense."

Othniel and Elah looked at each other in excitement. "Wow, how cool," Elah exclaimed. "We've got to be here tomorrow!"

"Yep, totally agree," Othniel confirmed. "We're going to see Yahweh do something ourselves."

Next morning the boys were at the Tabernacle bright and early. Word had spread widely in the camp and the number of on-lookers quickly swelled into the thousands. All two hundred and fifty of the leaders of the rebellion stood along from the entrance of the Tabernacle with Moses and Aaron standing at the door. Each held their censer with a smoking swirl of incense rising from it. Suddenly the cloud above the Holy Place glowed brightly and a booming voice said. "Moses and Aaron separate yourselves from this congregation and I'll consume them in a moment. The words suddenly hit home to young Othniel as he was struck with fear by the physical voice of the mighty Yahweh. He wanted to run but his legs froze.

Moses fell on his face at the voice of Yahweh and cried out, "Oh Yahweh, the God of the spirit of all flesh. Shall one man sin and you be angry with the whole congregation?" Good thinking, Moses, Othniel reasoned to himself.

The voice of Yahweh spoke in reply, "Then you must tell the people to keep well clear of the compounds of Dathan and Abiram."

Moses jumped up and quickly ran to the compounds of Dathan and Abiram who lived side by side among the tribe of Levi surrounding the Tabernacle. Othniel and Elah snuck through the crowd and arrived about the same time as Moses, securing a front row view. As he arrived, he found the two men and their families sitting calmly drinking qom completely secure in their own importance. "Get away from these men and their families," Moses roared to all in close proximity. One look at the seriousness and urgency of Moses convinced everyone and a clearance of several meters rapidly formed.

Moses then said to Dathan and Abiram, "This is how you'll know that Yahweh has sent me to do all these things and that it was not my idea: If these men die a natural death and suffer the fate of all mankind, then Yahweh has not sent me. But if the Lord brings about something totally new, and the earth opens its mouth and swallows them, with everything that belongs to them, and they go down alive into the realm of the dead, then you will know that these men have treated Yahweh with contempt." Peels of contemptuous laughter broke out from the two men.

No sooner had he finished speaking all this than the ground under them split apart and the earth opened its mouth and swallowed them and their households, and all those associated with Korah, together with their possessions. They went down alive into the pit, with everything they owned; the earth closed over them, and they perished and were gone from the community.

At their cries, all the Israelites around them fled, shouting, "The earth is going to swallow us too!" Othniel and Elah screamed in terror at all they'd seen and ran for their lives.

"My Dad told me to always run for the Tabernacle when anything like this happened," Othniel shouted to his friend.

"Let's go," Elah replied hastily.

At the very moment the boys arrived back near the Tabernacle a massive fire ball broke out from Yahweh and consumed the two hundred and fifty men who were offering their incense. The sight of the fireball, the screaming and yelling as the men were consumed, shook the two boys to the core. This was not the excitement they had envisaged for the day. "Let's go home," Othniel said. Elah took very little persuasion and the boys ran like startled deer back to their respective lodgings.

Othniel didn't sleep much that night. Suddenly he'd seen a lot of the physical presence of Yahweh. Even at his young age he knew he had two choices. Either he could live in constant fear of Yahweh or he could learn to obey Him. The one big thing he remembered from the day was that Yahweh was faithful to those who were faithful to Him. He remembered now the words of his Uncle Caleb telling him exactly that.

Next morning two very subdued young boys walked off together, going nowhere in particular, wanting to explore but lacking the desire. As they neared the Tabernacle, they found a huge mob standing round Moses shouting at him. "Do these people never learn," Othniel said, mostly to himself. As they got closer it was clear they were very displeased with Moses.

"You've killed the people of Yahweh," they shouted.

Suddenly the cloud above the Holy Place lit up and a voice spoke to Moses. "Get away from this assembly so I can put an end to them at once." And both Moses and Aaron fell facedown before Yahweh.

Then Moses said to Aaron, "Take your censer and put incense in it, along with burning coals from the altar, and hurry to the assembly to make atonement for them. Wrath has already come out from Yahweh; the plague has started." So, Aaron did as Moses said, and ran into the midst of the assembly. A plague had already started among the people, but Aaron offered the incense and made atonement for them. He stood between the living and the dead, and the plague stopped. Again, Othniel and Elah found themselves running for home as fast as their legs would carry them. Running loose around the camp was no place for a pair of five-year-olds they decided.

A few days later Kenaz announced to the family over dinner that evening that he'd heard the official count of the dead from the plague. The total was fourteen thousand seven hundred killed, in addition to those who had died because of the rebellion the day before.

There was a mass burial and it seemed most in the camp had lost somebody they knew. A few days later the Pillar of Cloud lifted, the trumpet blew and the very sombre tribes of Israel moved out to a new wilderness location at the direction of The Cloud.

Numbers 16:1-50, 1 Chronicles 2:42, 48-49, 1 Chronicles 4:14.

13

Father Caleb

"Come quick, Dad, it's Camel," Othniel shouted. A very concerned Kenaz rushed after his twelve-year-old son to Camel's stall. "I tried commanding Camel to stand but he wouldn't budge," Othniel reported. Kenaz stood by Camel's head and looked into his blank eyes.

"Come on Camel just give it one more shot," Kenaz encouraged consolingly to his old charge. After several false starts the endearing words of Kenaz finally worked and Camel slowly rose to its feet, to the sound of much groaning and creaking of bones.

"There'll be no work for you today," Kenaz assured him. "Come on Othniel, let's take Camel for a walk." Othniel understood his father's meaning, this would be Camel's last day in the camp. Removing the remains of a deceased camel from the middle of a city of more than a million people in a very hot wilderness was not an option. In addition, there would be all the cleansing ritual they'd all have to go through. The trio plodded out, each engaged in their own thoughts. "Thirty-two years I've had him, Othniel," Kenaz reminisced aloud.

"Really Dad," Othniel exclaimed, genuinely surprised. "How long do Camels usually live for?" "I've been told about forty years," Kenaz replied. I have no idea how old Camel was when I got him but I always imagined he was about ten years old, for some reason.

Upon reaching the edge of the camp the trio headed off into the scorching desert to a rocky outcrop in the distance. Othniel suggested they should've brought a packed lunch but Kenaz wasn't interested in food, his thoughts were on his old friend. It seemed forever but finally they rounded the corner of the peak they'd seen in the distance. "I think this will do," Kenaz stated as he walked to the front of Camel and removed the reins. "Goodbye old friend," Kenaz said as he slapped his only means of income on its hump. Camel took the signal and slowly wandered off across the seemingly endless barren land. As he did so he turned his head for one long last look at his kind master.

"It's as if he knows," Othniel stated, confirming the obvious. The two watched for some time as the old animal plodded on to nothingness then they turned and made for home.

As they walked Kenaz was desperate to talk of any subject except camels. "Tell me, son," Kenaz asked, "when you get to the Promised Land, what will you claim for an inheritance?" Othniel was well versed with how the conversation should go as his father had repeated his dream of having a vineyard for as long as he could remember. If Kenaz was to be believed, the entire land of Canaan was covered in grape vines all producing bunches identical to the one the spies had brought back from Eschol.

Othniel, however, had never seen a vineyard nor a bunch of Eschol grapes. He had however tasted olive oil, which Kenaz frequently obtained from the Midianite traders. He also knew a bit about sheep and goats which were very common about the camp. "Please don't take this the wrong way Father but I'm not so sure if I'm cut out to make wine. I like the idea of growing olives," Othniel blurted, glad for the opportunity to finally broach the subject.

"Oh, I see," Kenaz replied.

The two marched on in silence for some time then Kenaz opened up on his apparently unlimited knowledge of growing and pressing olives. That had been one of his chores as a young boy in Jethro's house, he explained.

As the weeks went by Kenaz found he had an abundance of time on his hands without the work of his trusted Camel so he focused purposefully on instructing his firstborn son, his heir apparent, on all the wonders and splendours he'd heard about the Promised Land. The more Othniel heard the more his excitement grew. Since the day he began to talk he'd heard about this Land and that his generation would inherit it, but hearing his father talk about it with such passion instilled a realisation that his inheritance was real – he was actually going to inherit.

The forty-year penalty was frequently mentioned within the Kenaz household. Othniel calculated since his father had been in the camp for thirty-two years and he arrived about a year and a half before the spies returned with their bad report, then he must have only another nine years left. A sudden reality dawned on him, he was now twelve but in nine more years, he'd be twenty-one. Old enough to join the army, old enough to fight, old enough to inherit. No longer was his father's talk of the Promised Land the ramblings of a deprived old man. No, he now hung on every word his father spoke, this was his land and he would physically be there, doing everything his father spoke of. He was truly thankful his father had lived this long since the rebellion to carry this realisation home to him.

Jephunneh had died about a year ago, which had knocked Kenaz hard. Jephunneh was ninety-one when he passed and Kenaz argued that was a reasonable innings. The decree meant he would die before the end of the forty years, therefore he calculated he would be less than sixty when he died. "Damn those spies," Kenaz exclaimed each time the subject came to mind.

Caleb on the other hand, despite already being in his seventies, didn't look a day over forty. Since the day he'd returned from the spying mission he hadn't aged one day more. He still held the looks, strength, physique and stamina of a forty-year-old.

Because of his close friendship with Caleb's son Elah, Othniel spent a lot of time in Caleb's house. Not that he preferred him to his own father but there was something about

Caleb and he had no idea why. While listening to his father regurgitating his knowledge of the Promised Land the difference suddenly hit home to him like a camel train. Despite how much his father spoke about the Land he would never be able to take him there. Caleb on the other hand had been promised by Yahweh that he would possess the Land. Caleb could actually help him to physically inherit. That was the difference.

From that day forward Othniel resolved to turn the words he'd learnt from such a young age, about the Promised Land, into a living reality through someone who had actually been there and was certain to return.

Caleb was quick to pick on the change in his twelve-year-old nephew. One evening after a combined family meal Caleb walked over to Othniel who was quietly amusing himself scratching doodles on the dirt floor. Caleb sat on the floor beside him attempting to decipher the somewhat recognisable artwork. "What are you drawing, Othniel?" Caleb asked.

Othniel dropped his drawing stick, his interest focused elsewhere. "Tell me about the Promised Land," he begged. "You and Joshua are the only two people in the whole camp who have ever been there."

Caleb brightened instantly. Despite it being thirty-two years ago, he remembered it like yesterday. "What do you think of life in this Camp," Caleb asked.

"It's the only thing I've ever known," Othniel answered slightly puzzled at the question in response to his.

"Not for me", Caleb replied. "See, I grew up as a slave in Egypt. Until Moses came along that was the only life I ever knew. The drudgery and boredom of doing the same tasks day after day was my life. If I didn't complete my quota, I got a whipping. By your age I worked twelve hours every day of the week.

"Then Moses showed up and I saw the faithfulness of Yahweh. What He'd promised our Father Abraham, that we, his descendants, would be strangers in a land that was not ours, and that we'd serve them, that they'd afflict us for four hundred years. True to His word He took us out of that Land, not as defeated but as a mighty, respected army with our oppressors decimated. I experienced the physical presence of Yahweh at Mount Sinai when He gave us the Law. I know, that I know that I know, that if our Yahweh has promised to take us to the Promised Land, then regardless of how many giants lived there, He would most definitely do it. But not just get us there but do so with His awesome power."

Othniel could feel his passion soar as he listened intently to his uncle recount his living experience of the Yahweh he knew personally. "Please, do keep going, I want to know everything", Othniel begged.

The two chatted for hours that night and a strong bond formed between them. Caleb had tried to instruct his own sons with a measure of success, but this young Othniel had a hunger to know about the Land and he was determined to feed it.

During the weeks that followed, Othniel spent every possible hour with Caleb. Every day seemed to bring a new revelation. He could get used to this.

14

No Water

With Camel gone Kenaz decided he had plenty of shekels accumulated to see him through the next nine years of wilderness living and still leave plenty to pass on to his sons. He did however need a means to transport his accumulated household trappings, each time they moved. Donkey breeding had become a big thing in the camp resulting in a massive exploding donkey population. His brother Caleb had recently seen the birth of three colts and it took very little persuasion to make him give Kenaz two of them.

Othniel was delighted as colts were good runners. Donkey racing had recently become a popular pastime among the young in particular. Mostly, it seemed, because everyone had easy access to one. Caleb's only daughter Achsah, while only eight showed, and frequently demonstrated, an extremely competitive streak. Othniel had little time for girls, they were useless at everything, especially fighting – in his opinion.

So it was that when Achsah challenged him to a donkey race to the edge of the camp he instantly accepted. "Easy pickings," Othniel exclaimed. "Girls have no idea how to ride."

"Prove it," Achsah responded. "Go get your colt, we'll race now."

Colts were frisky at the best of times, let alone when they'd never been ridden. When it came to riding colts essentially there was no technique. The primary and sole objective was to stay on. Saddles and reins were pointless on the baby donkeys. Therefore, the only way to stay attached was to lay forward, wrap your arms tightly around its neck and cling on round its midriff with both your legs. Each competitor rehearsed the mounting method in their minds. Riding an old donkey was one thing but a fresh colt was anyone's guess.

Achsah's brother Sheber stood as the starter while a hoard of young children raced to the finish line about a kilometre away at the camp's fringe. Some of the older boys exchanged a quick wager with surprisingly the girl being the odds-on favourite. "Go!" shouted Sheber and both contenders leapt onto their charges only for both colts to buck up in instant alarm flinging their riders to the ground. Undeterred, Achsah grabbed a nearby cloth and threw it across the donkey's eyes. Unable to see, the donkey calmed instantly and she clambered expertly aboard. Safely clenched she gave the command to remove the covering. The hapless unsuspecting animal's sudden sole vision was of a long open pathway ahead and something just behind its ears screamed in words it had no concept of. Without a thought it did what any startled animal would do, it bolted.

Not to be outdone by a girl Othniel mimicked her method exactly and he too clung to a bolting donkey colt racing towards it knew not where. Side by side they raced on, each one taking turns to push the other into a passing obstacle, but to no avail. Othniel, however, being older was quite a bit bigger than the slender framed Achsah which made holding on that much more difficult. Had the animal run straight he would not have slipped to the side and slowed the colt down. No matter how much he yelled it just wouldn't go any faster and in due course he crossed the line at a forty-five-degree incline, but attached, only to see a very cocky looking Achsah standing ahead of him holding a now calm but somewhat exhausted young donkey.

"Let that be a lesson to you Othniel," Achsah screamed, as she danced with delight. "You will never win against me!"

"We'll see," Othniel replied. He'd been well and truly beaten and by a girl at that! As they walked back to the start the two chatted as if for the first time. Much to Othniel's surprise they found they had a number of similar likes and dislikes. Their two families had done things together since before they were born and of course they knew each other well. This, however, was the first time Othniel had actually considered a girl as some sort of an equal even though she was four years younger than him. Othniel added his new found understanding of the female world to his growing life experiences. Perhaps there was a lot more to girls than just being mothers, cooks and cleaners, he reasoned.

Next day the Pillar of Cloud lifted, the trumpet blew and the entire camp was rapidly dismantled and carried off to a new location. Hobab had disappeared some weeks back and nobody knew exactly when or why. Had he run away or had he wandered out into the desert and died? Whatever the reason he was sorely missed for his water finding skills. The Pillar of Cloud directed the Tribes to where they should camp but Hobab always helped find extra sources of water. At today's campsite however, no Hobab equated to almost zero water.

Othniel walked with his father who was under strict instructions from Charna to return that evening with water. It had been two days and her last container was well and truly dry. As they walked past the Tabernacle, they couldn't help but notice a very angry mob tearing into an equally distraught Moses. All the usual voices rang loud. "Why did you bring us out of Egypt just to die here?"

"If only we had died at the rebellion."

"You lied to us, this isn't the land of grain, figs, vines or pomegranates!"

"We want water, NOW!"

Moses and Aaron somehow extracted themselves, ran to the Tabernacle entrance and fell down prostrate towards the Holy Place. Almost immediately the Cloud above it lit up and the voice of Yahweh spoke. Othniel froze, he'd never actually heard the voice of Yahweh before. "Moses," His voice said, "you and Aaron take your rod and gather everyone together,

No Water

speak to the rock in front of them and then there'll be an abundance of water for every person and animal."

The rock was a very large outcrop just outside the camp. In fact, the only outcrop for kilometres in any direction. All the congregation hastily gathered at Moses's command, desperate for fresh water. Moses, unlike his usual calm self, was hopping mad at all the abuse that had recently been dumped on him. He marched up to the rock and without uttering a word, wacked the rock hard, twice, with his trusted staff. Instantly, a vast fountain of water gushed out of the rock and thousands of parched mouths pushed forward to claim their share. What started as a trickle across the desert floor quickly became a raging torrent and even the distant stragglers gained their fill.

No sooner had the filling began than the voice of Yahweh boomed out from the camp for all to hear. "Moses, I told you and Aaron to speak to the rock, so that I would be magnified in the eyes of the people. You, however, chose to disobey me and have stuck the rock with your staff. For this reason, you will die in this wilderness and another will lead my people into the land." Moses hung his head and quietly made his way back toward the Tabernacle. Othniel, however, was astounded. This was another side of Yahweh. He demanded absolute adherence to His word. If he was to get to the Promised Land then adherence it must be.

A few days later while chatting to Caleb, Othniel asked, "How can I be certain of doing everything that Yahweh asked of me?"

"The starting point is knowing His Law," Caleb replied.

"Will you please teach me then?" Othniel asked.

"Actually," Caleb replied, "I can do much better than that. The young Levites hold lessons each morning outside the Tabernacle, if you want to attend."

Next morning twelve-year-old Othniel was up at the break of day and with chores completed at break-neck speed he was off to Torah lessons. Moses had written down all the Law and words which Yahweh had told him and over the course of each week these were read aloud for all to hear by young Levites (those of the tribes of Levi who were assigned solely to the Tabernacle and the things of Yahweh).

Othniel attended every day for months, where he listened intently and asked questions. In time he befriended one of the young men who, sensing Othniel's eagerness to learn, offered to teach him how to read. Over the next two years, whenever he had the time, he sat under his tutor and his reading skills blossomed.

During this period Othniel got to understand the workings of daily life within the Tabernacle, what the various offerings where and why. Although he was never allowed to actually participate, he often stood by and watched as the priests went about their tasks. The precise order and detail were impressed upon him. Yahweh was a God of great detail and when He said something He seriously meant it. "Obedience, obedience, obedience," was his tutor's common phase.

No Water

The day after his seventeenth birthday their location was abandon and they moved out to camp at the foot of Mount Hor. After only a few days there, the trumpets blew early one morning, but this time not for moving but for assembly. The entire camp stood gathered and Moses addressed the massive throng.

"Yahweh has declared that my brother Aaron is to climb this mountain and die there today because he too disobeyed Yahweh with that whole speaking to the rock thing. Today his son Eleazar will become High Priest before Yahweh. Aaron, myself and Eleazar are now going to climb this mountain for that purpose."

The three men strode off, with Aaron the least enthusiastic of the trio, and began the climb to the summit. Despite Moses nearing one hundred and twenty years of age and Aaron being three years older, neither man showed the slightest sign of their age. They both possessed the strength and vigour of a forty-year-old.

Late that day, two men returned down the mountain to the waiting crowd. Eleazar was now fully dressed in the ornate High Priest's garments that had adorned his father only hours earlier.

"There will be a period of thirty days of mourning for our High Priest, my brother," Moses decreed.

Numbers 20:1-13, Numbers 20:22-29.

15

Grumblings

"Attack, attack, attack." Eighteen-year-old Othniel turned in his bed woken from a very pleasant dream, something to do with Eschol grapes, young maidens and other things, as his thoughts quickly vaporised. "Hooligans," he muttered as he desperately searched for slumber and the continuation of his respite. The shouting however, didn't fade. It was quickly followed by much screaming, bellowing and genuine panic and now rapid blasts of a shofar. Giving up any hope for further rest Othniel began to dress, "This better be worth it," he muttered. "It's the very middle of the night."

As Othniel emerged from his tent he was joined by a myriad of other sleep deprived bodies overcome with curiosity. "What is it?" Othniel begged of his father.

"No idea yet but it doesn't sound good". Kenaz rustled through his stuff to retrieve his long-deserted bow and arrows. It suddenly struck Othniel this could be war. One with a real enemy, killing people! He'd always envisaged his side would be doing the attacking.

His father emerged from a newly created pile of rubble, tuning his bow and dusting off the arrows. "The noise is coming from the outskirts, it seems," Kenaz said, trying to make some sense of the situation. "You stay put here, Othniel and take care of our family," he ordered as he strode off towards the noise. As he did, the Pillar of Fire glowing warmly above the Tabernacle suddenly broke off and instantly formed a bright fiery circle which raced around the outskirts of the camp.

Before too long Kenaz return unscathed to his distressed family who had been fed a constant barrage of alarming reports – massive enemy attack, thousands are dead, we're all going to die! "Well?" ask Charna as Kenaz quietly packed away his bow and unused pack of arrows.

"We were attacked," Kenaz answered as he took a seat with his wife and two sons, his four daughters now all married. "As far as I can determine, it was some sort of raiding party whose main objective seemed to be to take captives," Kenaz explained. "Doesn't sound like many of us were killed, only a few injured defending their families. I arrived there just as the Pillar of Fire arrived. Man, you should have seen those bandits run when that showed up. They raced off on their camels like a ram escaping a sacrifice. Unfortunately, it sounds like they've taken a few hundred captives though," Kenaz concluded.

Next morning the trumpets blared early for a call to assembly. Moses advised, "That Yahweh had allowed us to capture one of the raiders and who'd sung like a canary. He'd told us the raid was a coordinated attack by the Canaanite King Arad. His people live in the South near the road we're now passing through. Arad believed he could stop the people of Yahweh reaching the Promised Land."

"We must get our people back," Moses continued as the massive Army of Israel cheered loudly. "Let's all now make a vow to Yahweh for His help," Moses continued. "Yahweh. If you will give us a clear victory over this evil King Arad then we'll utterly annihilate every city of theirs." All of Israel enthusiastically shouted their agreement.

An army of ten thousand from each tribe was quickly assembled and forty-eight hours later not a man of the kingdom of Arad remained alive. Every building burnt to the ground, everything of any permanence dismantled and thrown to waste. Any evidence of human habitation was totally eradicated leaving a very clear message for all to see. 'Don't mess with Israel, whose God is Yahweh.' Every person that Arad took captive was returned alive and in turn the Army of Israel took away all Arad's young women and children as their own captives plus much livestock.

Othniel, too young to go to battle, pestered his Uncle Caleb for every detail of the war. His confidence in the power of Yahweh multiplied with every description Caleb gave.

"You shouldn't talk like that, Kenaz," Caleb warned some days later.

Grumblings

"Well then, explain to me, my wise brother. Why are we heading deep into this lousy desert again?" Kenaz replied. It had been several weeks now since the swift and miraculous victory against King Arad and most in Israel shared Kenaz's view that since they'd had a taste of victory nothing should stop them now.

"Who cares about the Edomite," Kenaz continued. "So what, if they won't let us march across their land. We'll wipe them out just like Arad."

"Quite enough," scolded older brother Caleb. "Don't speak against Yahweh who directed us to go around Edom instead of going through it."

This was now their third week of marching. A day on the move, settle for two days then pack up everything and move again. Kenaz wasn't alone in his reasoning. After wandering in the wilderness now for just over thirty-eight years most folks were over it. Not so the younger generation, they had known no other life other than wilderness life. What's more they were all children of promise. They were the ones who would inherit and they knew when.

Finally the camp rested for the night and in an exceptionally well-rehearsed performance the camp was re-established and normal life resumed. That day had been particularly hot which accelerated the grumblings. Very early next morning a well discussed mutiny was perpetrated. A group of several thousand, Kenaz among them, ambushed poor Moses as he left the Tabernacle.

"Why have you brought us up out of Egypt to die in this stinking wilderness? There is no food, no water, and we all absolutely loathe this worthless manna bread." The accusations flew thick and fast but Moses didn't answer a single word. Just at that moment a yell broke out from the middle of the mob,

"Snake!" he yelped, "I've been bitten." Very soon the whole crowd began yelling, with many others being bitten too. It seemed the area they'd chosen to hold their little outburst on was directly above a massive sand viper mating convention. Their presence underground undetectable, until they moved.

Kenaz escaped and retreated to his compound. Othniel's younger brother Seraiah desperately pressed his father for all the gory details. "Did they die, dad?" he begged.

"Yes, of course they died," Kenaz replied. "A sand viper is one of the deadliest creatures in this desert. They ambush their prey by hiding beneath the sand and strike as soon as it's in range. People aren't prey but unfortunately sand vipers, for some strange reason, don't like being trodden on so the mad creature strikes back."

It turned out that the nest under the crowd at the Tabernacle wasn't an isolated one. Reports quickly emerged of bites and deaths all over the camp. Rapidly a new crowd again gathered outside the Tabernacle, after first cautiously turning over the sandy ground to check for slithery occupants.

"Moses, Moses," they cried. "We've sinned. We spoke against Yahweh and against you; please pray to Yahweh that He will take away these deadly snakes."

Grumblings

Moses turned towards the Holy Place in the Tabernacle and prayed to Yahweh for the people. Almost at once Yahweh answered Moses saying, "Make a snake of bronze, set it on a high pole so everyone can see it. From now on everyone who is bitten, when he looks at it, shall live."

Moses set a team to work immediately and before nightfall a large bronze snake stood entwined around a long bronze pole, in centre place, right in the middle of the camp near the entrance to the Tabernacle. The snake bites didn't stop but the deaths slowed dramatically. Anyone who was bitten, when he looked at the bronze serpent, felt no harm.

"Why couldn't Yahweh wave His hand and get rid of these deadly pests?" Kenaz exclaimed to his family over the evening meal that night. 'Instead, we all have to look up to this mythical saviour, high on a pole. Doesn't stop you getting bitten," he continued.

"Father," Othniel replied cautiously, "I don't like it when you talk about Yahweh like that. He's done so much for us and at the end of the forty years He is going to lead us into the Promised Land.

Kenaz flew into a rage, "Promised Land, Promised Land. I don't want to hear that word in this house. For thirty-eight years I've heard of nothing else. But what have we done about it? Nothing but wander back and forth aimlessly in this barren forsaken desert with just enough water and food to keep us alive!" The two boys watched the anguish boiling within their father and quietly left the compound.

Othniel and his brother Seraiah were the only ones living at home after their youngest sister Tamar had married last summer. They squatted together on the pathway outside their compound. "I don't know what's got into father," Seraiah said sadly. Othniel had a fair idea but how to put it into words for his younger brother to understand.

"Dad," Othniel began "wasn't bought up as a slave in Egypt as most others of his generation were. He arrived as an outsider and became a child of Israel. There's so much missing from his upbringing compared to others. He has only known the good, never the bad. He knows he's going to die before the end of the forty-year penalty and he doesn't like it. Each year which ticks by the angrier he gets. I'm mean he's only fifty-eight which is very young to die compared to Grandpa Jephunneh who died in his nineties."

The sudden realisation of what Othniel had said hit home to both boys. Their father would be gone within the next one or two years. Othniel wished he possessed some form of magical power that could see into his father's mind and extract all his life experiences and the knowledge and lessons he'd learned along the way. He was only eighteen but yet he was about to become the oldest male in his family line. "Least Uncle Caleb is not going to die," fourteen-year-old Seraiah chipped in innocently. "He'll be able to tell us what to do." Othniel didn't reply but the thought struck a chord with him. Despite the increasing dearth of fathers in the camp, at least he'd still have one.

Numbers 21:1-3, Numbers 21:4-9.

16

Snakebite

It had been a whole week without moving camp and the travel respite sat well with most. Even Kenaz had calmed somewhat, not having seen a snake in all that time. The journey around Edom was long but at least now they were at the furthest eastern point and would soon be turning again towards the Promised Land.

Othniel had gone with his father to collect water from the nearby stream. The day was pleasant, Kenaz felt relaxed so he sat with his son to absorb the ambiance. "You know, I've probably got less than two years left, my son, if the forty years penalty is to be believed," Kenaz said, reflectively.

"I know father," Othniel replied caringly, not keen to stir that emotional pot too deeply.

"You see son," Kenaz continued, "I came to Israel as a Kenite but through the generosity of my father Jephunneh I became one of the people of God. I quickly found I had a lot to learn. I knew about Yahweh before I came because Jethro was a priest of His. But I never knew He was real until I heard His actual voice thunder out from Mt. Sinai." Othniel was suddenly attentive, this subject was dear to his heart.

Kenaz continued with his discourse, determined to pass what he could to his son and heir. "It was so awe inspiring to hear Him spell out the laws we must all keep and not sin. They sound easy, Othniel, but I tell you they're very hard to keep. During the many years since I've managed to keep some but unfortunately not all of them." Othniel, had to agree., He'd seen his father's failings on more than one occasion. "Yea, I guess I've done my share of sin offerings," Kenaz reflected.

"I saw men stoned more than once for disobedience; you were with me once, I recall?" Othniel nodded sober agreement and Kenaz continued. "But I also saw His provision, many, many times during our journeys. I mean every day He showered us with that manna stuff. Regardless of what people say about it being monotonous, it tastes great and I've never felt hungry. He even fed us with an overabundance of quails once. But most of all my boy, He demands obedience. We all discovered that the hard way after those spies came back with their evil report." Othniel agreed, that was his greatest takeaway for the lessons he'd received from the young Levite.

"Othniel, you're my heir," Kenaz continued. "I had expected to inherit a lovely vineyard in the Promised Land and pass it on to you in my old age. However, that's not to be. Yahweh has included me in those that will end their days in this forsaken wilderness. Please learn from my mistakes. Yahweh has decreed that His people will inherit the Promised Land and I assure you they most definitely will. Why? Because He said so. That's the one thing that I have so strongly learned in my short life. If Yahweh says He'll do something then as sure as the sun will come up tomorrow, He will do it.

"So, my son, stick close to Yahweh. Do whatever He says and learn to trust Him regardless of circumstances. If there is a giant in the path of your promises, He will remove it. Do that and for certain you will have your vineyard."

"Actually, it's an olive yard," Othniel corrected.

"Oh, come on son, you can't drink olive oil," Kenaz joked.

"Oh, there's one other thing," Kenaz said. "I want you to have this. I bought it off a trader years ago but haven't used it much but perhaps you will." He handed Othniel his prized dagger neatly ensconced in its brown leather sheath.

Othniel was genuinely pleased. "Thanks father, I will certainly cherish it," he said and tucked it firmly beneath his waist belt.

The sermon over, Kenaz seemed relieved and jumped to his feet, picked up the water pitcher and said, "Come on, let's get this liquid back to you mother."

The very next day chaos prevailed as once again the Tribes broke camp and set off toward the unknown. Judah, just as had been decreed all those years ago, moved out first. General Nahshon had long since died and Caleb, now the father of Judah took his place. With the Pillar of Cloud just ahead Kenaz and his family marched at the very front of the Tribes alongside his brother General Caleb and his large clan.

Kenaz led his favourite donkey which today was far from such. Cantankerous was one description but Kenaz preferred outright stubborn. Not only did it believe it shouldn't have to walk today it also believed that if it did then it should be able to continually wander off to the left, away from the main throng. Kenaz quickly tired of its tricks tied its rein to the other donkey's pack causing it to follow in train. Seemingly that was all it wanted so Kenaz left the now contented creature and assumed his step beside his General brother.

Kenaz's brotherly chat was soon disrupted by a shout from behind, "Your donkey's off!" Kenaz turned to see his donkey happily trotting off to the left again. He instantly took chase and was genuinely surprised at the distance a loaded donkey can cover in such a short time. Kenaz was almost in reach of it when a small protruding rock tripped his foot and he stumbled and fell flat on his face – straight onto a sand viper. The startled, trapped snake reacted instantly by latching onto the nearest part of its perceived attacker. In Kenaz case, his neck. Paralysed with fear Kenaz was unable even to scream. All thoughts of his wayward donkey vanished as he slowly gained composure and he grabbed the snake around its neck and began to pull. Desperately the viper held tight pumping copious quantities of deadly venom directly into Kenaz's neck.

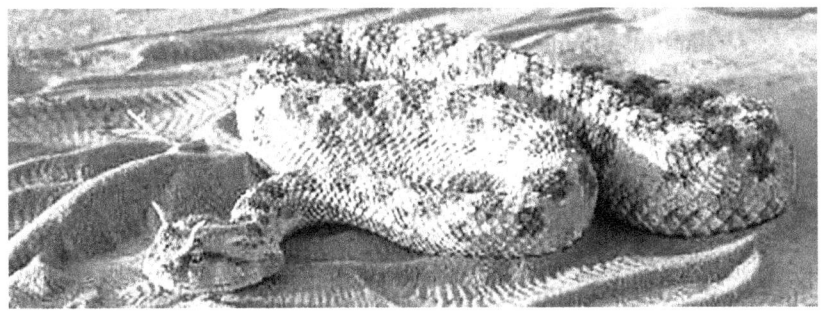

An Arabian Sand Viper.

Within seconds Othniel, Seraiah and their mother were at the scene. Othniel took charge sliding the attached fangs back out the way they came. Safely removed, he grabbed his father's recent gift – a small dagger in its leather sheath – and severed the animal's head, tossing it far to the side.

Kenaz recovered from the initial shock and now sat quietly while Charna washed the two tiny puncture marks using water from her precious reserves. "The bronze serpent," Othniel exclaimed, "we need it but where is it?" Kenaz nodded his agreement as best he could as Othniel dashed off to find the symbol.

Back through the hoard of travellers he rushed, asking all and sundry if they'd seen the standard. None had. He ran over to a small rocky outcrop to gain some height and look above the crowd. For as far he could see, kilometres back along the lines, there were people, people, people but no sign of a protruding serpent on a pole. The general of each tribe held their tribal banner but none were a bronze serpent. "Where's the Levi tribe," he questioned as he counted back the banners. "It's their job to carry that snake," he reasoned.

Suddenly a vision of his father sitting on the sand with excess venom oozing from his neck, flashed through his mind. The situation was urgent. Being at the front of twelve tribes with Levi in two parts among the tribes meant a distance of several kilometres in the mass of well over a million people. He'd have to run.

Othniel race on, past the banner of Issachar, past Zebulun and finally to the first group of Levi, the son of Gershon. Othniel rush up to their standard bearer at their head. "Who's got the bronze serpent?" he begged.

"None of us," the holder replied," we carry the tabernacle. Try the sons of Kohath, three tribes down."

Othniel raced on past Reuben, Simeon and Gad and then finally the sons of Kohath. Desperation now unfettered, he rushed up to their leader demanding to know who had the bronze serpent. There'd been a bite and it was urgent. "I'm sorry," the leader replied, "we only carry the holy things, those that are dedicated to Yahweh."

"Is there another group?" Othniel questioned.

"Well of course, the sons of Gershon, they're up ahead. They carry those things," the leader replied. "I can assure you, it's definitely not with us!"

Othniel was devastated. All the time wasted and now it seems he passed the thing about an hour ago. Without wasting further breath, he ran off back the way he came. As he ran, he comforted himself with the thought that death from a viper bite usually wasn't instant. He'd known some that had lingered on for days before they succumbed. The pain, however was incredible, so he'd heard. That thought spurred him on and eventually he arrived at the head of the tribe of Reuben. The tail of the first Levi pack were right ahead. He wouldn't take anyone's word for it this time.

Othniel raced into the back of the pack screaming for the bronze serpent. "Who's carrying the serpent?" Othniel repeated as loud as he could above the clatter of ten thousand feet and the mutter of the crowd.

Finally, he heard a response. "See that young boy over there, his name is Joah. I'm sure I saw him take it down." Overjoyed at the acknowledgement, Othniel rushed over to two young boys carrying a large bronze pole on their shoulders, nicely concealed by a large ox skin mat!

"Why on earth would you want to cover it!?" Othniel demanded as he approached. "The people are supposed to see it, aren't they?"

"True," Joah answered, "but you see the mat got wet when we were packing up so we hung it here to dry as we walked. Clever, don't you think?" Joah continued proudly.

Othniel didn't have time for small talk. The serpent was found, he'd get it to his father and he'd be saved. The urgency in his explanations spurred Joah into action. Leaving the younger to carry the now discarded mat he set off with Othniel balancing the other end of the large pole. Othniel was surprised how heavy it was; and how long!

After what seemed forever the pair arrived at the spot of his father's accident. His four sisters, their husband's together with their children had been advised and now stood around Kenaz. Caleb was there and Charna sat cradling her husband tight as she cried aloud and unrestrained. Othniel and Joah push through the small group as he shouted excitedly, "I've got the bronze serpent. You're going to live, father." Nobody replied, nor seemed to care.

It was then that Othniel caught sight of his father's lifeless body, his face purple and grotesquely swollen to twice it's normal size. Every emotion drained from Othniel as he dropped to his knees and wailed to his lung's capacity. He was too late; his mission had failed. "Why, why couldn't you hold on?" he questioned.

Edna, his older sister, came over and embraced Othniel as he wept. "It wasn't your fault, Othniel," she said calmly. "Because the bite was on his neck it swelled up so much that he couldn't breathe. It wasn't the poison; he just couldn't get any air. He only died a short time ago."

The family wrapped Kenaz's lifeless body carefully in a large skin that someone had produced from among their belongings and his body was carefully placed into a recently dug hole. They then gathered around him in the middle of nowhere, the searing heat of the midday sun in full effect as a million people plodded past not more than a hundred metres away.

So it was that his family mourned and cried at the loss of a husband, brother, father, father-in-law and grandfather.

Kenaz had come to Israel as a Kenite, a young single man, had been adopted into Israel through the generous heart of his father Jephunneh who taught him the ways of Yahweh, a God he'd learned how to serve and obey. This man, his spirit now departed thirty-eight years later, was surrounded by his faithful wife, his caring brother and thirty-nine offspring – his children, sons-in-law and grandchildren. In his own imperfect way he had been a father to many. Othniel, in his reflecting heart, prayed to Yahweh, "Please help me to finish what my father has already achieved and realise his inheritance for this family in the Promised Land."

It was with sad hearts that the family left the man Kenaz buried deep in that sandy forsaken desert that afternoon and slowly made their way on to the next camp stop.

Numbers 21:4, Numbers 21:8-13

17

Training

"Come on, son, you can't laze here all afternoon," Caleb said as he approached. Othniel was startled, lost in his own thoughts. He'd gone out to the desert again, to mourn his loss. It had been over a month since his father had passed but for Othniel it seemed like yesterday. If only, was his motto. If only I'd found that bronze serpent quicker. If only I'd ran after that donkey. If only he'd spent more time with him. In the desert, outside the camp, he felt a connection to his father. He was out there somewhere.

They'd moved camp at least a dozen times since the death and were now poised on the top of Pisgah which is a large flat plateau overlooking a large swathe of desert to the East and the border of the land of the Amorites. Caleb sat down beside his nephew on the top of the mountain but said nothing. The pair remained deep in their own thoughts for some time and surprisingly it was Othniel who broke the silence.

Training

"Dumb desert," Othniel said abruptly. "Why'd we have to spend so much time in it? Why couldn't we have parked in a nice place to wait out the forty years?" Caleb knew that Othniel understood the answer to his own question. His father would still have died, perhaps just not of a snake bite. "I miss him so much," Othniel continued. "He was teaching me everything, about Yahweh and about the Promised Land. I've got so much more to learn," he wailed.

Caleb waited silently until the outburst had finished then said brightly, "You know, I'm told you can actually see the Promised Land from this very spot on a nice day. Come, Othniel, walk with me, I'll show you something." Othniel reluctantly got to his feet and walked some distance along the top of the plateau ridge to its North-Western corner. Caleb stood peering through the dense heat haze then said, "Look over there, Othniel. See that faint patch of green over there," pointing to some growth just visible through the dense atmosphere. Othniel strained his eyes and yes there it was, a distinct green patch right at the edge of the barren plain beneath them. "Those trees," Caleb said with excitement in his voice, "mark the edge of the Jorden River. Immediately across that river is the Promised Land. Believe it or not, the river is less than five kilometres in a straight line from this very spot."

"Never," Othniel replied.

"As Yahweh is my witness," Caleb responded. "We are so close, my son. Question is, are you ready? One thing I'll always remember about your father," Caleb continued, "was his excitement for the Land. He talked about it endlessly, even when he knew he wasn't going to inherit." Othniel had to agree, that was always a faithful subject to bring up if you ever had an hour or two to kill.

Slowly but surely Othniel felt something stirring within him. After almost thirty-nine years they were now so close. Perhaps another eighteen months at most. It was then that Caleb's question struck home, 'Are you ready?'

"What did you mean, are you ready?" Othniel asked.

"To fight," Caleb answered abruptly. "The Promised Land is ours; Yahweh has made that clear," Caleb explained. "However, we have to take it from the present occupiers and I'm fairly certain they won't want us to do that. You'll have to fight for it. You need to be ready; you need to learn how to fight."

Othniel looked across at the glimpse bunch of green in the distance that gave way to the Promised Land. All the words of his father came flooding back to him. 'You're the heir, you'll have to take the vineyard for me! No father, an 'olive' yard – Oh, come on son, you can't drink olive oil!' A smile broke out across Othniel's face for the first time in weeks.

"What's your weapon of choice?" Caleb asked.

"I have a dagger," Othniel replied, his mood brightening. "Hmm, you might need something a little bigger than that. Okay, let's go and let's start training in the morning. Always better to do it early before the sun gets hot."

Training

The two walked back to camp in a contemplative mood. Othniel felt rejuvenated, seeing just how close they finally were to the Promised Land sparked something in him. "Thanks for rescuing me this afternoon Uncle," Othniel said.

"No problem, that's what father's do," Caleb replied smiling.

"One more thing," Othniel asked, "how did you know that you could see the Promised Land from that spot?"

"Moses sent Joshua and I up here a couple of days ago to see if there was a way around the Amorite's land. It was much clearer that day and we could easily make out the Jordan River," Caleb answered.

Next morning Othniel was dragged out of bed early by his good friend and Caleb's son, Elah. "Dad demands we report to him at the plateau you were at yesterday. He's starting our training. Come on man, you have to show me where that is."

Othniel stirred. He liked the idea of a competition but not at this hour. "It's still dark out," he complained.

Fifteen minutes later two nineteen-year-olds stood on the mountain ridge in the cool morning air as the sky glowed a warm red announcing the heat to come. Caleb threw an assortment of weapons at their feet. "Where did all those come from?" Elah asked as he surveyed the pile of swords, spears, knives and bows that lay at his feet.

"These were 'gifted' to us when we annihilated King Arad last year. They're good weapons but they sure didn't help him," Caleb replied recalling the short battle.

"Right," Caleb started, "I'm going to teach you boys how to fight in war. We do have Yahweh on our side but His job is to go before us and strike terror into our enemies. He usually leaves it to us to do the killing, therefore it's very important you know how to do that. For some strange reason our opponents don't want to die and they fight back. Unless you know how to fight then it's you who might succumb. Oh, and one other thing. I am your father or Uncle but I'm also the elder and leader of your Tribe, the Tribe of Judah. When we're training or whenever we're in battle I'm General – my word stands, you obey."

The transformation from Father to General was blatantly obvious to the young men as an air of authority enveloped Caleb. "Yes Sir," Othniel replied.

Caleb picked up a sword and waved it towards the boys. "In battle," he began, "there are only two positions, Offensive and Defensive. If we attack, (offensive) then you can assume the enemy will defend, vigorously. In other words, they'll try to attack us, at which point you have to defend yourself.

"To make things real we're going to use real weapons – lethal weapons – and you will fight each other. Not to the death, obviously, and I'll be deducting points if I see blood," he concluded. He handed a bow and arrows to Elah and a large shield to Othniel. He paced out about thirty strides and placed one of the boys at each end. "Elah, you're to fire off as many

Training

arrows as you can at Othniel while he tries to protect himself." Both boys gulped, this was not their idea of friendly training.

Never having handled a bow before, Elah's first dozen shots fell well short of the mark. Enjoying the lack of danger Othniel began to relax and chided his friend, telling him he fired like a girl. Caleb sat on the ground nearby enjoying the entertainment. Othniel rested his shield against his knee for a moment while he removed a small stone from his sandal as arrows fell harmlessly around him. Stone removed, he bent to repossess his shield when a random arrow hit the side of his belt and stuck fast. The reality jolted Othniel, this was no game. It might have been a lucky shot but that wayward arrow could have ended his life. "Never let your guard down, Othniel," Caleb scolded. "Now run towards him and take his bow," Caleb ordered.

Watching Othniel's approach Elah fired as rapidly as he could. Suddenly Othniel dropped his heavy shield, roared dramatically and rushed forward. At close range a bow was next to useless so Elah discarded his weapon and dived at his opponent shouting loudly as he did so. The two boys clashed, weapons and friendship totally abandoned and a tussle of strength took charge. They wrestled wildly sensing their very life depended on it. Now on the ground, the two evenly matched rivals fought on, each desperate to inflict a fatal blow. Othniel suddenly recalled his father's dagger lodged in his belt as he loosened one hand and made a grab for it. "Okay, stop!" the General ordered. Both young men froze their positions not trusting of the others action. Othniel had managed to free his dagger but Elah had noticed. Both his hands were strained holding back Othniel's knife just an arm's length above his heart.

The boys released and jumped to their feet, adrenalin surging through their veins. Immediately the General shouted, "Othniel, you take the arrows and Elah the shield. Let's see more of that raw aggression," he barked.

With the roles reversed, both young men found their tasks much easier. No longer was this a contest between friends, this was enemy combat, life or death. The arrows were no longer aimed at a friendly target but were fired with lethal intent. The defence likewise was rapid and effective.

The morning flew by as the General traded arrows for spears, then swords with a trusted shield as their only defence. As the day grew longer the two boy's transformation to fearless warrior slowly began to take shape.

The heat of the day had fully matured as Caleb called time. Both boys, drenched in sweat, threw down their weapons, utterly exhausted. "In real time," Caleb warned, "intense battles can rage on all day. You guys need to sharpen up your fitness."

Othniel and Elah exchanged a weary grin. What they wanted to say was, 'are you kidding; what could be more intense than that?" Instead, they both simply stated, "Yes General."

Every day, except for Sabbath, for the next three months Caleb trained his boys. The result was two fearless warriors ready and willing to engage in battle with a clear understanding of how to win. "If you can fight like this between yourselves," Caleb encouraged, "imagine what you can do when Yahweh fights with you."

Numbers 21:20.

18

Water boy

The camp had moved again, this time down onto the plain below the plateau of Pisgah. "We're waiting to hear from Sihon, the King of the Amorites," Caleb advised. "We need to take the track through his territory to the plains of Moab which will bring us right beside the Jorden River."

"He's sure taking his time in replying," Othniel answered.

Since his father had died Othniel, while still living with his mother and younger brother Seraiah, spent most days accompanying his uncle, General Caleb. Caleb was also close to Joshua, the only other remaining spy, and therefore he was always in the know. Othniel, eager to learn, was forever asking questions. "What happens if this great Sihon says no?" Othniel asked.

"Let's wait and see," Caleb replied, "but I'm sure Yahweh knows exactly what to do."

The very next day Othniel went early to the Tabernacle to place himself among those listening to the reading of the Torah;

the Law. Just as things were about to get underway, he noticed a young boy run up to Moses and demand his urgent attention. "Sir, my dad was outside the camp tending his sheep when he noticed a lot of men riding camels heading our way fast." The boy reported. Moses thanked the lad and sent a bunch of other young boys off in different directions with a summons for the General of each tribe to assemble before him, immediately.

Caleb dropped what he was doing in response to the unusual call. Elah, curious to know, also tagged along and soon met up with an excited Othniel who filled in some detail. Before long twelve warrior Generals sat on the ground around Moses as he relayed the news. "It seems we have a reply from the Amorite king. He's sent his troops out to meet us. It seems they've stopped to regroup near Jahaz which is close by," Moses explained. "I want each of you to urgently select ten thousand of your best men, of military age, and we'll go out in the name of Yahweh to tell him what we think of his reply."

"No, you lads may not be included," Caleb scolded later. "Moses particularly stated that all our soldiers have to be of military age – over twenty years old." After some robust discussion it was decided that they could tag along but not to fight, their role was to provide water as required, whenever a warrior called for it. "Support is as important as fighting," Caleb reiterated.

Word spread quickly in the camp and within no time at least ten thousand men, each with their weapon of choice, marched out of the division of Judah with Caleb at their head. Bringing up the rear were two young men each proudly leading a donkey with a large pitcher, filled with water, lashed on each side.

Outside the camp all the troops assembled together and quickly organised themselves into their divisions and platoons in accordance with the ordinance Jethro had suggested almost forty years prior. There were captains of thousands, captains of hundreds and captains of tens. Every man knew his place and who to report to. Most importantly was the understanding of obedience. Forty years of living under the Laws of Yahweh had taught this next generation of men one major lesson – obedience, obedience, obedience.

The twelve Generals, with Joshua at their head, quickly hatched a plan of attack. Speed and surprise formed its backbone. Those with swords and spears first, followed by archers who, when in range, were to fire from behind the leading fighters to rain down a mass of arrows on the attacking hoard. While they protected their heads from the onslaught above those with hand weapons would rush in and strike their unprotected regions.

With the plan clearly relayed to every soldier they quickly formed into the required format. And with the Generals in the lead, like a choreographed dance troop, one hundred and twenty thousand freshly minted warriors raced at full speed across the plain to encounter their enemy, all the while shouting, "In the name of Yahweh." Two young men at the rear, leading their laden donkey's, found the pace impossible to match.

To say Sihon's army of several hundred thousand hadn't heard them coming would be a gross understatement. They were ready for these foreign desert wanderers – or so they thought. At the desired position, without pausing the Generals gave the command, "FIRE." Within seconds twenty thousand archers rained volley after volley of razor-sharp arrows onto Sihon and his men. As they cowered under their broad shields the leading Israelites smashed into the mass of unprotected bodies, inflicting lethal wounds as they went. Within minutes the ferocity of the attack filled every heart of Sihon's people with sheer terror and they instantly abandoned all thought of counter-attack, opting instead for an unrehearsed mass panic retreat, screaming at the top of their voices as they did so.

Unfortunately, the retreat occurred so spontaneously that those at the rear of Sihon army had no knowledge of it and pushed forward eager to inflict their own damage on the foreign invaders, who had dared to ask if they could march across their land. As the rear pushers met the forward retreaters chaos ensued. In the confusion those pushing forward mistook their own men as the attacking army and did exactly what they'd been trained for, they fought back – as did the retreating forces desperate for a clear path. The result was that the vast bulk of Sihon's army killed each other. The tribes of Israel, the army of Yahweh pushed on stimulating the panic and chaos, their task now confined to clearing up the tail.

Two groups of no more than one hundred men each from the tribe of Gad, had been instructed to skirt around each side of Sihon's camp with the goal of surprising and capturing the command post, safely ensconced at the rear. They arrived to find an extremely angry Sihon barking loudly at his troops and waving his sword towards his Generals in a vain attempt to coax them into reordering the unfolding chaos.

A group of camels stood at the ready nearby in case a quick retreat became necessary. The ambush participants quietly untied the innocent camels and set them to flight. With stage one completed they rushed the unsuspecting command post from all sides and within minutes Sihon and all his Generals lay dead.

The battle lasted no more than about an hour at which point the entire army of Sihon had been decimated with most dead or dying from their injuries. No more than a dozen swift runners had escaped but Joshua had forbidden their pursuit, "Let them spread the horrifying details of their mass slaughter at the hand of Yahweh," he decreed.

The battle had been raging for some time before two very disappointed young men arrived, their laden donkeys well outpaced by the swift running troops of Israel. The screams, the curses, the groans of agony, the smell of sweaty dead and dying men lying in pools of their own blood often accompanied by an involuntary discharge of excrement or urine, was overwhelming. The smell and sound of battle instantly became forever imprinted on Othniel's mind. "So this is what it looks like when Yahweh fights for us," Othniel declared mostly to himself.

"Wow, what a mess and so quick," Elah exclaimed, again mostly to himself.

With no Israelite screaming for water Othniel and Elah started walking among the dead and dying picking up their weapons and laying them in a pile. "There's some great weapons here," Elah shouted above the noise as he held up an engraved polished spear.

"Too bad he never got to use it," Othniel commented. "You know," he continued, "I don't see any of the tribes of Israel lying here, do you?"

"Actually, you're right, I can't see any," Elah replied.

The two boys walked on picking their way across the mass of bodies. A sound at Othniel's feet suddenly caught his attention. He looked down to see the face of a young fighter perhaps a couple of years younger than him. He had an arrow protruding from the top of his left shoulder and a massive gash in his right leg. As he lay in obvious agony his begging eyes looked straight into Othniel's and he spoke slowly. The language was one Othniel had no concept of but regardless he knew the boy was asking desperately for his help. His thoughts drifted to his own younger brother, Seraiah; that could be him lying there. The dilemma overwhelmed him, what to do? – he was the enemy but he could be his brother. Without a further thought he said, "I'll get you some water," at least that may ease him a little in his final moments.

Othniel turned to walk back to his donkey but found his path blocked by bodies, in every direction. As he stood mapping out the best path Elah suddenly shouted, "Lookout behind you." Othniel spun around to see his young charge now sitting upright using the last his remaining energy to try and thrust a large dagger into Othniel's thigh. He'd obviously mistaken Othniel's kind Hebrew words about getting him some water as something akin to 'I'm going to leave you to die, you filthy scum.' Instinct from his months of training surged through Othniel's brain. He jumped high from harm's way grabbing a nearby disused spear, then like a coiled cobra he twisted mid-air and slammed the pointy end directly into the head of his injured foe. He threw it with such force that the spear when right through the boy's head pinning him to the ground on the other side. Death was instant. Othniel was shaken but roiled up. He grabbed the nearest sword and went about finishing off all injured and dying in his path. Mercy was out of the question. The training words of General Caleb ringing loudly in his ears, 'Never trust your enemy – EVER' How could he have been so stupid. He tucked the lesson away to hold him in good stead for the future.

With the annihilation complete, the troops of Israel were counted and amazingly despite some minor cuts and bruises not one single man of all the tribes of Israel was missing. "Praise Yahweh – Hallelujah," they shouted triumphantly.

The men quickly searched the dead for weapons and spoil which they laid on the former Amorite donkeys to send back to the camp. Meanwhile Joshua conferred with the generals and it was decided that not a man in the land of Sihon should be left alive. Within a week of setting out that day every town and village within his territory had been invaded right up to the fortified border of Ammon. Not one soul was spared except for the young virgins which the men took as captives.

Instead of moving all the animals into the camp, many from the tribe of Gad and Reuben moved into the now deserted cities of Heshbon and Jazer together with their surrounding villages so that they could care for the large flocks they'd inherited; their passion was for tending sheep and goats. The remaining tribes set up camp in their usual pattern around the Tabernacle adjacent to the cities.

A few weeks later the camp set out and settled at Edrei. This time it was Og the Amorite King of Bashan that, despite all he'd heard regarding what had been done to King Sihon, decided that since he was a giant of a man then he could easily defeat these dog intruders.

Yahweh told Moses, "Do not fear Og, because I've given him into your hand, together with all his people and all his land. You will do to him as you did to Sihon king of the Amorites, who dwelt at Heshbon."

So that's exactly what they did. In a matter of only a few weeks they'd destroyed Og, his sons, and all his people, until there were no survivors left. Israel again took possession of his land and all his spoil.

Othniel went with Caleb after the fighting had ceased to take a look over the city of Bashan and soon found the impressive deserted residence of King Og. It was Othniel's first time in a city and he wasn't sure he'd like it. Tent dwelling was all he had known and that was good enough for him.

The pair wandered around the multi-roomed complex and discovered the sleeping quarters of the giant king. In the centre of the large room was a massive bed; fit for a mammoth, literally. Completely made of iron four metres long and two metres wide. "This was just for one man!" Caleb exclaimed. "I could fit my entire family in it."

"Hmm," Othniel answered laughing, "It's been a while since you've seen you family isn't it General?"

"Last count," Caleb answered, "Three wives, ten children and I believe sixteen grandchildren."

Numbers 21:21-35, Deuteronomy 3:11.

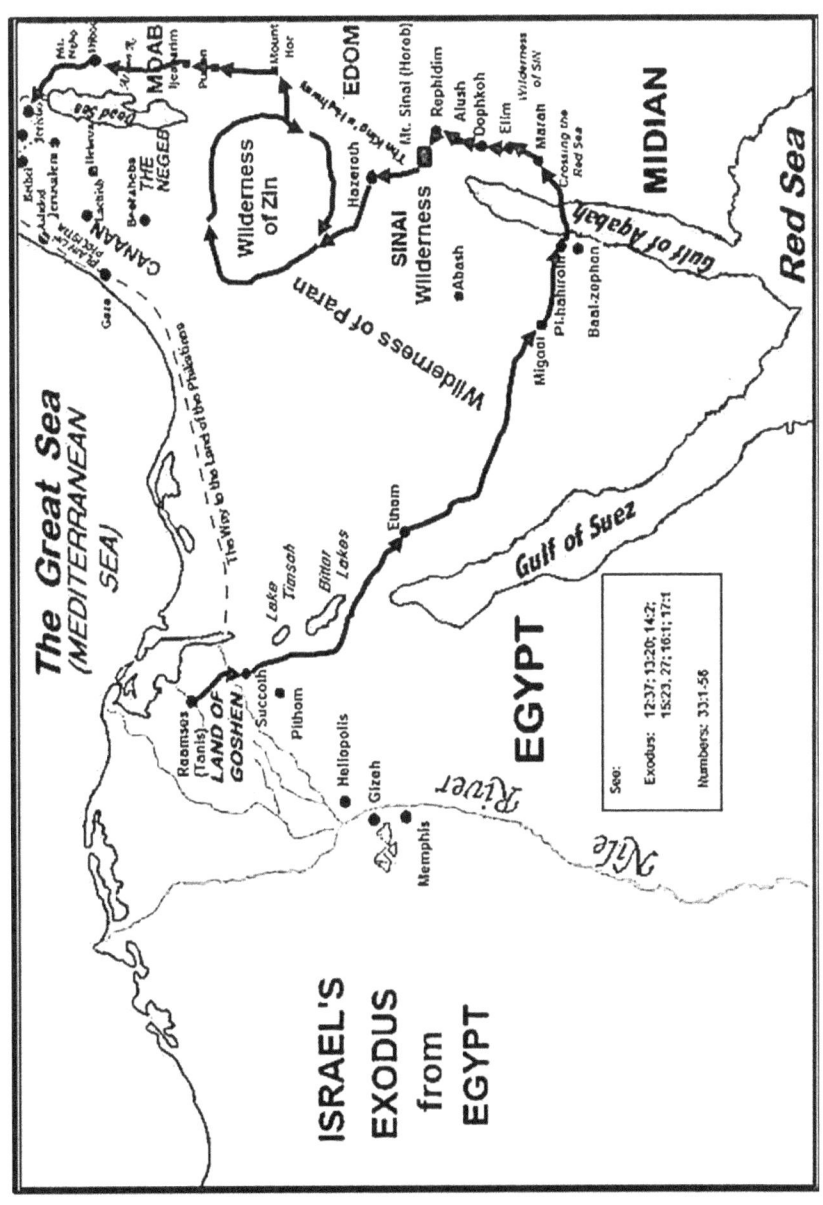

The forty-year Journey of the Tribes of Israel.

19

Plague Erupts

The trumpet blast sounded, the Cloud lifted and a million followers of Yahweh expertly dismantled their camp to march off following a cloud. This time the Cloud descended on the grassy plains of Moab at a place called Acacia Grove. Right on the edge of the River Jordan beyond which was the Promised Land with the city of Jericho in plain view. "I reckon that'll be our first target," Caleb advised. Othniel, like many others within the camp, could barely hold their excitement. After all these years the actual, physical Promised Land was in full view. They'd arrived.

The tribes generally remained together within the camp at Acacia Grove around the Tabernacle but with the city of Heshbon at their disposal many ventured some distance to shepherd the large Amorite flocks they'd inherited. The lands of Moab adjoined the area around Heshbon and many from there also wandered about the land to survey and see first-hand the scale of destruction of their arch enemy – the Amorites.

The land of the people of Midian adjoined Moab and the two nations had peacefully coexisted for centuries. The Midianites were descendants of Abraham's second wife, Keturah, so spoke Hebrew. While they kept their own identities, they shared territory with Moab and freely intermarried. It was difficult to mention Moab without associating Midian.

When it came to the Amorites however, the situation was the opposite. War had been the status-quo forever, even though nobody, not even their rulers, could explain why anymore. The fact stood; the two sides simply loathed each other. The conquering army, Israel, instantly became their hero and saviour. Moab were descendants of Lot; the nephew of Abraham and they also spoke Hebrew. The passage of time had caused some dialect idiosyncrasies but Israelites understood them with relative ease.

The leaders of Moab and Midian, after witnessing Israel's total annihilation of the Amorites, became consumed with fear, sure that they would be next. They had an extremely cunning priest of Yahweh named Balaam. He was renown through their region as speaking the oracles of Yahweh, but also to pronounce his own oracle if that served better. In his eyes, his words and the words of Yahweh were one and the same. Balaam counselled king Balak and the people to act shrewdly with Israel, become their friend, mingle and intermarry with them and become family. The people heartily agreed and set to the task with urgency.

Encounters with the shepherds of Israel ramped up dramatically. No longer were these just chance meetings between fellow wanderers, now entire Midianite families invaded the liberated lands of the Amorite searching for any son of Israel. Seemingly great friendships were cemented and before long their new friends were invited by these shepherds, into the camp of Israel. The young men of Israel weren't slow to recognise the beauty of the seemingly endless number of Midianite daughters and many marriages were cemented.

Othniel stood one evening in the camp, watching a group of young Midianite women dancing around a small crackling fire. The women had arranged their garments in such a way so it left a wide section of their midriff exposed. The flickering light of the fire enhanced the curves of their bodies and the articulations of their hips held the young men as if in a trance. Othniel was enthralled and moved a little closer for a less obscured view.

Othniel watched, entrapped in the rhythm, when suddenly a large hand landed firmly on his shoulder and a stern voice said, "Come away from here, son." It wasn't a suggestion and Othniel knew very well the voice as he turned to see the sadness in his Uncle Caleb's face. "These women will turn you from Yahweh. There are many lovely women in Israel," Caleb concluded. Othniel walked with Caleb back to his compound and the subject was never discussed again.

There were very many young men within the camp but unlike Othniel very few had a father figure in their lives. After forty years most of those who were of military age at the time

Plague Erupts

of the spies had died off leaving a great dearth of age-hardened experience. As Caleb often reiterated to Othniel, "There are not many fathers among us now."

This point was further demonstrated as the days progressed, when a large number of men who had selected Midianite wives were enticed to go with them and meet their families. This meeting included elaborate celebrations and ceremonies honouring their god, Baal of Peor. Some became intrigued with Baal and took it upon themselves to learned its ways. The Midianite brides of course continued in their Baal ways and back in the Israelite camp they pushed its worship to any who would listen.

As Yahweh saw all this His mighty anger grew strong. His first commandment was pretty plain. 'You shall have no other gods before me.' Yahweh called Moses to the Holy Place. Some minutes later Moses emerged and summoned his young men to quickly gather the Generals of each of the tribes.

General Caleb of the tribe of Judah responded immediately and Othniel tagged along in case his assistance was needed. Twelve men stood around a very angry Moses as he reiterated the command of Yahweh. "Yahweh is very, very angry and a plague has already begun in the camp. Many are dead and many more are dying. He has decreed that to appease His anger all the instigators and offenders are to be rounded up and hung. Not until they're hanging in the sun before Yahweh, will His fierce anger abate. Each one of you Generals are to arm your men and kill all who have joined to Baal of Peor," Moses concluded.

As Moses was speaking the screams and wailing of those affected by the plague were clear for all to hear. Othniel could feel righteous indignation welling up within. How thankful he was now for those timely fatherly words of Caleb just a few weeks ago.

The group were about to break up and set to their task when a young man, with his young Midiante bride happily hanging off his arm, swaggered by giggling romantically. The pair disappeared into a nearby tent and lashed the door. Young Phinehas, the eldest son of Eleazar the High Priest of Israel, was standing beside Othniel, saw the blatant act of the young man and his Baal serving bride. He shouted with rage, grabbed a nearby spear and rushed the tent of the embracing couple and in one single action thrust them both through with his spear and he cried, "Judgement in the name of Yahweh. He is the only God and the God of Israel!"

Moses and the Generals who had followed Phinehas to the scene applauded the young man as he retreated from the tent where the young couple lay dead on the ground. Just at that moment the voice of Yahweh sounded from the Holy Place. "Phinehas the son of Eleazar, the son of Aaron the priest, has turned back My wrath from the children of Israel, because he was zealous with My zeal among them, so that I did not consume the children of Israel in My zeal. Therefore, I give to him My covenant of peace; and it shall be to him and his descendants after him a covenant of an everlasting priesthood, because he was zealous for his God, and made atonement for the children of Israel."

Eleazar the High Priest, beaming with pride, walked over and patted his son on the back and said, "Bless you son."

The Generals were disbursed to carry out their orders to hang all the instigators of the defection. Othniel, together with several other zealous young men of Judah, went with Caleb and quickly rounded up those that were still alive from the plague who had encouraged the Baal worship and foreign marriages. Later that day fifty-three men of Judah hung dead from hastily made gallows, plain for all to see Yahweh's thoughts of those who turn to worship other gods.

Othniel return home in a sombre mood and as he approached his compound his oldest sister Edna came running out to meet him. "Where have you been?" she screamed, "We've looked for you all over."

"Why, what is it?" Othniel replied.

"It's Mother," Edna answered. "She was down at a friend's tent this afternoon. Her son apparently had a Midian wife. I'm sure mother never knew," she sobbed.

"And..." Othniel begged.

"Suddenly the plague hit and everybody in the tent died. Mother is dead." Edna broke off into tears but Othniel had heard enough. He hung his head and walked into the compound where his mother's body lay, wrapped in a burial cloth ready for the grave.

It turned out that Othniel's family was not alone that evening in burying their dead. A total of twenty-four thousand people had died that afternoon from plague or hanging. Most houses had someone to mourn. Many small noisy groups gathered in the plains well outside the camp as light gave way to darkness. Othniel and his younger brother Seraiah dug a shallow grave and sadly lowered their mother into it. Their four sisters watched on weeping uncontrollably, their children in the care of their husbands back at the camp. Othniel thanked Yahweh for providing him and his family with such a wonderful mother. He then put his arm over his sixteen-year-old bothers shoulders and said, "Come on, let's go home. It's just us now but Yahweh is our strength and He will take care of us."

Next day Caleb suggested the two boys move into his compound and share their evening meals with him. Othniel quickly agreed and the move was finished in a matter of hours. The home and compound of Kenaz and his wife Charna ceased to exist. They had lived through the forty years of wilderness living but because of the curse brought about by the spies, they never set foot in the Promised Land.

Othniel stood alone looking at the empty space that moments ago was his family compound. The words of his father resounded strongly in Othniel's ears. 'You are my heir, son. You will take up my vineyard for me!' "Sorry father but it's going to be an olive grove," Othniel said.

"Who you talking to?" a female voice asked.

Othniel, totally lost in his own thoughts was jolted back to the moment by the familiar voice. Without looking up he said, "Nothing to worry about, Achsah." Turning towards her he continued, "I was just reminiscing about... What have you done to your hair?" he asked, as he gazed at her, as if for the very first time. He'd known Caleb's youngest daughter Achsah since he was a child, they played together, raced donkeys and she'd served him his meal countless times. Yet today a woman of great beauty stood before him but she spoke with Achsah's voice.

No longer was her long, often scraggly, hair hanging loose., Today it was neatly wound up into a ball and pinned together revealing a long slender neck. His eyes continued as he surveyed her maturing body. This girl, four years his junior had suddenly become a woman and a very beautiful one at that. "My mother decided I should dress like the woman I am within," Achsah answered. "Not sure I agree though, I'm still just me."

"I'm on your mother's side, I'm afraid," Othniel replied, his composure returning. "I have to say Achsah, you look absolutely stunning."

Now it was Achsah's turn to be stunned as the compliment hit home and she surveyed her old friend Othniel in this new light. Rugged, tall, good-looking and a hard worker. Keen to follow Yahweh and, what's more, father already liked him. Achsah's mind spun into overdrive, then desperate to demonstrate composure she casually asked. "I'm off to pick up some cloth from my mother's family. You want to join me?"

"You bet," Othniel replied, perhaps a little too eagerly.

Numbers 22:1-3, Numbers 25;1:18

20

Second Census

Othniel woke to the sound of a trumpet blast, a long continuous blast that seemed unable to stop. 'A continuous blast,' his foggy mind determined, that was for general assembly; what can this mean?' It was still dark out as he stumbled out of his bed sack and began to dress. His mind backtracked on the events of the night before; the celebration of his achieving military age – twenty years old.

The compound of General Caleb was one of the largest in all of Judah. Not because of family but because Caleb held court there. Much of Caleb's day was spent settling disputes, apportioning blame or witnessing transactions. Last evening however, its purpose was family. Caleb's sons had managed to secure a couple of young rams which they'd slaughtered ceremoniously and here they hung, sizzling, roasting over a large fire in the middle of the courtyard.

To one side sat Caleb, now eighty, with his eight sons whose ages spanned the generations. Mesha his firstborn was forty years old and his youngest Sheva only eight. Othniel, the guest of honour, sat opposite with his brother Seraiah and his four brothers-in-law.

On their left the women formed their own circle. At their head was Caleb's wife Mishael and although she was in her seventies, she didn't look a day older than thirty-five. Beside her sat Caleb's two concubines, Ephah and Maachch. Despite having three wives, between them they'd only produced Caleb one daughter, Achsah, who she sat next to her mother Maachch. Also included were Othniel's four married sisters Edna, Jael, Adina, Tamar and Caleb's sons' wives plus about a dozen young children.

It was true family life and Othniel, despite having lost both parents, knew he belonged. His heart was warm, his joy complete.

A shout went out and food was served, Yahweh was thanked and the feast began. In addition to the roasted lamb the women had scored a range of vegetables grown around the captured Amorite villages. The younger generation, who'd rarely eaten vegetables in the wilderness, treated the delicacies with stern suspicion. Those few who remembered Egypt however, fell on them with great fondness, savouring every mouthful. It was a feast fit for a king.

With sweet fruits devoured and qom consumed the music and dancing began. A bright and bouncy melody sprang from a variety of skilfully played stringed instrument which induced harmonious dancing. Groups of young women swirled in a circle waving banners and jingling tambourines. The young men formed their own circle around them skipping forwards then out again as if their circle breathed. Around their loop revolved as the encompassed women rotated in the opposite direction, the exuberant joy impossible to suppress. The pretence for the celebration was Othniel's becoming of military age but the real vibrancy sprang from the fact the after forty years of talk the Promised Land was now in sight.

The moon was high as the celebrations drew to a close and Othniel retreated to his tent content and seasoned with joy. Watching Achsah sway and swoon to the rhythm of the music had been the highlight of his evening. Her slender figure, her long dark hair and those bright bubbly eyes... Suddenly he was jolted back into the moment by a shout from near his tent. "Wake up Othniel, that's the trumpet for general assembly," Caleb announced.

A vast mass of bleary-eyed men watched as Moses took the stand ahead of them. Othniel stood with General Caleb who, because of his status, had been awarded a front row position. "Yahweh has told me to take a census," Moses began with little fanfare. "Every male from twenty years old and above is to report to the General of their tribe, report their age and ancestry. The General will record the details and report the numbers back to me. I want the census completed within the next five days," Moses concluded as he left the platform to resume his daily duties.

"Well, that was short and to the point," Caleb announced as he turned to find a Levite scribe.

Second Census

"You don't suppose it could have been done *after* sunrise," Othniel suggested, as his body begged for a quick return to slumber.

Within a couple of hours, a table had been set up near the entrance to Caleb's compound. Behind it sat General Caleb and one Levite scribe holding a quill at the ready on the head of a large scroll. The title read, 'The names of the army of Judah.' The first name on that list was Caleb, son of Jephunneh, age eighty years. Othniel had been commissioned to keep the lines of waiting men orderly to ensure the process flowed quickly.

Late that evening the lines had diminished for the day and Othniel saw his opportunity. "May I enrol now, General?" Caleb asked. "There's no one else in line today."

"Very well," Caleb replied as the young scribe began his questions.

"Name?"

"Othniel," was the echoed reply.

"Ancestry?" the Levite requested.

Othniel quickly trotted off his well-rehearsed family line, "Son of Kenaz, son of Jephunneh, son of Caleb, son of Hezron, son of Perez, son of Judah, son of Israel."

"Age?"

"Twenty years," Othniel blurted, proud to finally qualify.

"And who vouches for this man?" the scribe asked.

"I do," Caleb replied firmly.

"There," the scribe said as he finished up his writings and rolled up the day's scroll. "You're all done and so are we," he said with a smile.

The next day was a mirror of the one before as each of the men of Judah took their turn to register. Finally, near the end of the sixth day the last of the stragglers were recorded and a careful count of the numbers began. After some considerable time and much debate, a final tally was recorded. The army of the tribe of Judah stood at seventy-six thousand five hundred. Amazingly, among all the names recorded, only one person, Caleb, was above the age of fifty-nine.

The certified numbers were delivered to Moses who after the Sabbath set to work with Joshua to combine the totals from all the tribes. Late that day the Generals were summoned. Othniel, keen to be in the know, attended as an assistant to his General. Moses, business-like as usual, announced the total army of Israel from all tribes except the tribe of Levi was six-hundred and one thousand, seven hundred and thirty. "Also," he continued, "we have checked with the original census of forty years ago and not a man named in that list made it onto this new list except for Caleb son of Jephunneh and Joshua the son of Nun. This is just as Yahweh said. They have all died in the wilderness because of the evil report brought by those other ten spies.

"Oh, if you're interested", Moses continued, "we've also numbered the Levites from a month old and above. Their number is twenty-three thousand exactly. As with the other tribes, not a man among them is older than thirty-nine. Praise Yahweh, He is always completely faithful to His word."

Next day General Caleb order his assistant, Othniel, to round up one hundred young army recruits and meet him on the edge of the camp for training. Othniel and Elah knew what to expect this time but the innocence of the other young men was obvious and, it's fair to say, that over the course of the initial training days some injuries were sustained although, fortunately, few were of a serious nature. Caleb's brutal training methods worked brilliantly and within a couple of weeks a fierce breed of warrior matured.

With the skills of the first one hundred at a reasonable competency they in turn were each required to recruit and train one hundred other men in the same manner. And in turned once they were finely tuned, they too would select a hundred each for training. In just a few short weeks the entire seventy-five thousand five hundred men of the army of Judah had been subjugated to the unorthodox but highly successful training methods of General Caleb. Remarkably there had been no deaths, not because of the particular skills of the recruits but, perhaps only because of the grace of Yahweh.

The use of real-world live weapons training rapidly shaped the army of Judah for a large group of eager men to an amazing army fully versed in attack and defence. A lethal machine backed by the arm of Yahweh.

During the course of the training Caleb and his right-hand man Othniel, had been observing those who displayed particular skills or courage. These men were given separate training which included ways to encourage and motivate the troops. Those successful in this training were appointed captains over ten thousand troops, who then appointed others over a thousand, a hundred and others, over ten. With authority and reporting lines clearly established a command from a General could reach every man in the army of Judah within minutes. This truly was a lean mean fighting machine.

After several weeks of intensive training by all the twelve tribes the twin trumpets blew one morning and the entire Army was gathered near the entrance of the Tabernacle. Moses stood and addressed the crowd. Despite just having turned one hundred and twenty years old Moses had the looks and vigour of a forty year old.

"As most of you know," Moses began, "Aaron and I disobeyed Yahweh at Meribah, with that whole rock striking business. Aaron is already dead and Yahweh has told me I too must die soon before you cross the River Jordan. In my place Yahweh has chosen my faithful servant Joshua to lead His mighty Army and conquer the Promised Land, the land of Canaan. I've called you here today to witness his inauguration."

Moses called Joshua to join him together with Eleazar the High Priest. Moses then walked up to Joshua and placed both his hands firmly on Joshua's shoulders. "Yahweh has decreed," Moses began, "that you, Joshua son of Nun, the one who has the Spirit in him, will guide this great Army wherever they go. You will lead them into battle, so this nation of Yahweh will not be like sheep without a shepherd.

"I now lay my hands upon you to transfer some of my authority to you today before the whole community of Israel, so that they will obey you.

"When direction from Yahweh is needed, Joshua, you will stand before Eleazar the priest, who will use the Urim— one of the sacred lots cast before Yahweh – to determine His will. Thus you, Joshua, and the rest of the community of Israel will determine everything they should do."

With that said Moses lifted the hand of Joshua high in front of all the people and shouted, "Behold Israel, your new leader Joshua, appointed by Yahweh, who will lead you in conquering the Promised Land. Be strong and courageous my faithful servant."

With the ceremony complete and the people dismissed, Caleb, and of course Othniel, hung back to be the first to greet his fellow spy, old friend, and now Yahweh appointed leader. As Caleb finished hugging Joshua he said, "This is my faithful servant, my nephew Othniel, son of Kenaz."

"Oh yes Othniel, I knew your father well, he was acquainted with Moses."

"Pleased to meet you Sir," Othniel replied.

"I've been watching you training your troops," Joshua continued. "You're quite a fighter, I see." Othniel flushed with pride. "I can use a man like you," Joshua added.

"Not too quick, Commander," Caleb quipped in laughter.

"Whatever Yahweh wills," Commander Joshua replied with a knowing laugh.

Numbers 26 and 27.

21

War Begins

"Othniel, Elah, come now. I've got a mission for you," Caleb shouted as he strode into his compound. Othniel sprang to attention, all ears at the unusual statement. Cleaning his donkey stall could wait.

"I've just come from Moses," Caleb began as his two lieutenants hung on his words, eager to accept any mission, preferably dangerous, from their General. "He has asked that each tribal General assemble one thousand men, prepared and ready for war. He's ordered them to go out and take vengeance on the Midianites. You'll recall it was their deceitful women who caused our last plague." Othniel in particular nodded his agreement, as he recalled his mother's recent death.

"We're in," both young men confirmed in unison.

"Well, not so fast," Caleb cautioned. "I haven't decided who will go yet. I need you two to go through the camp of Judah and spread the word asking all those that are willing and able to assemble here at day break tomorrow morning."

Next morning close to ten thousand men armed and ready for war hovered outside Caleb's compound, each eager for war. Caleb marched out, every bit the General and without any to-do shouted, "Okay, so all you guys are fit and ready for war, are you? Thing is I only need one thousand men, not this huge crowd. We need men who are fit, who're able to run at the enemy and keep at it for hours."

A knowing grin crept across Caleb's face as he stood looking at his troops. "Down this path," he said pointing towards the edge of the vast camp, "is the camp edge. Every man who wants to go to war is to run from here and go twice around the entire camp. Not yet," he scolded, "on my orders. The first fifteen hundred men back will be chosen for training through which I'll eliminate a further five hundred. You are to carry your weapon and whatever else you're currently holding. Go," he shouted without further ado and immediately the majority of the men sprung to their feet and raced off with Othniel and Elah near the front of the pack. "What's with you guys?" Caleb asked.

"Sore leg, can't run fast," were the common excuses.

"Achsah, come," Caleb called. Eager to please her doting father, Caleb's only daughter, now a mature sixteen years old, quickly appeared. "Seems all my sons are otherwise occupied so I need your help. Walk with me," he ordered.

Caleb and Achsah stationed themselves at the edge of the camp to ensure two rounds were made and also to count in the first fifteen hundred. Caleb had no idea of the distance around the camp but figured that those who made it round twice would have a good fitness level. Given the distance from the centre to the edge was about two kilometres the actual distance was close to twenty-five kilometres for the two circuits.

The sun was well ablaze by the time the first runners appeared and Achsah shouted various forms of 'encouragement' from her vantage point as her father watched his men, eager to spot those with that extra edge. Down the pack a little but in a very respectable position came Othniel followed closely by Elah. "Move those scrawny legs. This isn't a Sabbath stroll," Achsah shouted as her friend Othniel raced by.

Exhausted but determined, Othniel pushed on, buoyed by the banter of his General's daughter. One day he thought, 'when she's aged some more, and I can afford to pay the proper dowry, I'll take her for my wife. Not only is she a thing of beauty, she's a hard worker, a good friend with a quick and fiery wit.'

The majority continued for the second circuit but the race was doing its job as a few thousand called it quits, limping by their General, back to camp after the first pass. Finally, with the sun now near mid-day the first of the runners came into view for the second time and Caleb and Achsah counted them off. Othniel received number one hundred and thirty-four and Elah one hundred and sixty-two.

During the next five days Caleb pushed his men to the point of daily exhaustion as they practiced warfare with running battles using real, lethal weapons – Caleb's favourite training method – and a very rapid learning curve ensued. Some injuries resulted but fortunately nothing too serious and those only eased the elimination process. Each day Caleb tapped a few men 'suggesting' they return to their homes and by the end of the fifth day he had a team of exactly one thousand. Each one, a lean, mean, fighting machine; all be it a very exhausted machine. Othniel and Elah stood proudly among the selected Judah soldiers.

Four days later Moses addressed the ten thousand strong army reminding them not to pity these Midianites. "Utterly annihilate them," were his exact words. Leading them was Phinehas, the son of the High Priest Eleazar.

Quickly the twelve groups, ten thousand strong, crossed the old border of the Amorites and spread into the territory of Midian and fell upon the unsuspecting, mostly un-walled, villages and cities destroying every male, young and old. Homes were looted, the women and infants rounded up, together with their livestock, then to ensure no possible return they burnt their homes to the ground; hence the origins of the term 'scorched earth'.

Othniel found that with a force of thousands and villages and cities of hundreds there was not a lot of fighting to be done and surprisingly the majority of the work was the ultimate destruction of looting and fire, followed by supervision of the women and animals. Cooperation by these recent widows was often not as forthcoming as required, however, but a few deadly examples seemed to bring the desired result, all-be-it a begrudging one.

Mesha, Caleb's oldest son, being hardened in war through the Amorite campaigns, was the captain of the Army of Judah. He had 'learned' from one of the captives that five kings of Midian had called a conference to seek guidance from their guru Balaam in a small non-descript village not ten kilometres away. Leaving the majority of the men to clean out the recent captures Mesha took the informer as a guide, together with five hundred men, and set out at dusk to jog across the plain. Rounding a small rocky range, the target lay right below them.

Night fires flickered as the sound of evening chatter rose from the unsuspecting encampment. Mesha gathered his men in silence, instructing them to quietly encircle the village. Once everyone was in place, he advised that then he would signal the advance with three short blasts on the shofar. "So listen up," he warned. The informer guide, having served his purpose of leading them to his leaders, received Mesha's appreciation; a quick thrust of a spear to his heart.

"We can't allow him to shout an advanced warning," Mesha explained.

Within minutes the small unsuspecting village was surrounded by five hundred men focused solely on destruction. Othniel crouched in the darkness behind a small building and scoped the path ahead of him. Not more than fifty paces away six camels stood at the ready, tethered to a pole. He moved a little nearer for a closer look, these were no ordinary camels, the gold clasps on their reins and saddles gave the clue. These surely belonged to the five Kings.

Othniel signalled to Elah who had taken a position beside him and together they hatched a plan. First, they would release the camels and send them packing, cutting off that means of escape. Next, they would attack, one to each side of the building immediately adjacent to the camels. "I reckon they're sitting in the courtyard at the front of that building. I can see the glow of a small fire there," Othniel whispered.

No sooner was their plan hatched then three short shofar blasts resounded across the subdued hamlet. Othniel and Elah had decided not to shout, as they raced towards the camels, believing instead that all the noise from opposite directions would distract their opponents. With the reins sliced through a quick solid slap on the hindquarters with the side of a sword released the startled camels who shot off into the darkness, their panic adding to the wild confusion as they went.

Othniel stood by the edge of their target building, spear and sword at the ready, and ventured a quick peep. Not more than two metres ahead a tall heavy-set man strode purposely, directly towards him. His goal; his faithful camel which he'd tied close by for this very eventuality. All Othniel's reflexes kicked in, a spear was readied as the escapee rounded the corner. Without warning or breath of alarm, Othniel's spear, driven by all his strength and the man's increasing momentum, pierced directly through the heart and a giant of a man crumbled, dead before he hit the ground.

War Begins

Elah had attacked from the other side, his surprise incursion quickly dispatched another of the Kings. The three remaining Kings, reacting to the invasion, focused all their attention solely onto Elah, conveniently, with their backs towards Othniel. Moments later death due to sword strike caused the remaining three Kings to fall to the ground.

Their prophet Balaam now stood cowering against the wall, pleading for his life, affirming that he spoke the oracles of Yahweh and that he could bring a blessing to the people of Israel. "Oh," Othniel replied, "the same way you enticed your young women to cause many in Israel to kneel to your useless wooden god, Baal?"

"Ah, yes, about that...." Balaam began as a sword penetrated his heart.

"In the name of the only living God, Yahweh," Othniel shouted as he extracted his weapon.

After a short period of coaxing, at the point of Mesha's razor-sharp sword, a young man confirmed the names of the slain men. They were Evi, Rekem, Zur, Hur and Reba, the five Kings of Midian, all sons of the recently deposed Sihon, king of the Amorites. The other wiry old man, he agreed, was their prophet Balaam. Othniel and Elah were briefly commended as the remainder of the killing came to completion and the looting began. Every building was searched, spoil was loaded on the captured donkeys and every building set ablaze. What hours before was a peaceful village closing off another day now sat a smouldering heap of ruin, strewn with dead and dying.

As the dawn broke the captive women were employed to herd and drive the captured sheep and cattle back to the army base camp. Mission accomplished; all the leaders of this once proud nation were dead.

Later that day Masha's warriors, together with their captives and spoil, returned to the main group. Over the next three days the final cities and towns were mopped up and Phinehas declared the mission at an end. As the men assembled to ready for their return to the camp of Israel a thorough count of the soldiers was made. Every tribe reported back to Phinehas, "Not a single man of theirs was missing." Ten thousand went out and ten thousand returned. Upon hearing the numbers Othniel couldn't help but marvel at the careful and strong hand of Yahweh. His General Caleb's part, however, could not be denied either. Yahweh had seen to it that every man was thoroughly trained, competent for his required role in the war.

Word of the victorious returning warriors quickly spread through the camp. Moses, Eleazar and all the tribal Generals strode out of the camp to greet the victors. With official pleasantries exchanged Moses turned his attention to the captives and immediately his anger bust.

"Why have you let all these women live?" he demanded. "These are the very ones who followed Balaam's advice and caused the people of Israel to rebel against Yahweh at Mount Peor. They are the very ones who caused the plague to strike Yahweh's people. Here's what you must do," Moses demanded. "Kill all the boys and every woman who has had intercourse with a man. The young girls who are virgins, only these you can keep alive for yourselves."

With his instructions understood Moses turned his attention back to the men. "Listen up," he said, "in accordance with Yahweh's laws, all of you who have killed anyone or touched a dead body must stay outside the camp for seven days. You must purify yourselves and your captives on the third and seventh days. Purify all your clothing, too, and everything made of leather, goat hair or wood."

Eleazar the priest stepped up and said, "In addition to what Moses has advised you, Yahweh has this legal requirement also: Anything made of gold, silver, bronze, iron, tin, or lead – that's all metals that do not burn – must be passed through fire in order to be made ceremonially pure. These metal objects must then be further purified with the water of purification. But everything that burns must be purified by the water alone."

"On the seventh day," Eleazar continued, "you must wash your clothes and be purified. After all that then you may return to the camp."

"Well, that wasn't quite the welcome I expected," Othniel complained to Elah. Elah's reply was interrupted by angry orders barked by Masha who also seemed unappreciative of the welcome.

"Get those women lined up now so we can do what we're told," he ordered.

A short time later two groups of women were formed and the much larger group of nearly one hundred thousand women and infant boys were marched off some distance from the camp and Moses's orders were carried out. All the returned men were ordered to take part in the mammoth slaughter but even so the killing took hours. Othniel's heart wasn't in his work but it was an order from Yahweh; a sentence of justice on these women who had caused the recent plague in Israel. It became even harder as he came face to face with a terrified young woman, about the same age as Achsah, holding her infant son. "In the name of Yahweh," he screamed as he wielded his sword in a most efficient manner.

Next day the cleansing began. All the remaining women were ordered to shave their heads, strip their clothes and wash in the nearby Jordan River. Clean clothes were bought out from the camp and the women dressed afresh. After seven days they would wash again then assimilate into the camp as slaves or wives but first would be allowed forty days to grieve the loss of their families.

The men likewise, in accordance with the Law washed their bodies, cleaned their clothes and attachments. All the metal objects were purified with fire as instructed. The final three days were spent counting the spoil. The scale of their two-week operation surprised everyone. Phinehas read out the totals before he handed it to Moses;

- "Six hundred and seventy-five thousand sheep,
- Seventy-two thousand cattle
- Sixty-one thousand donkeys
- Thirty-two thousand virgin women.

War Begins

"Moses has commanded," Phinehas continued, "that ten percent of that must go the Yahweh and be given to the Levites. Of the balance, half is shared among all the other tribes of Israel with the other half divided evenly among you guys." A hearty shout of approval arose from the rested warriors.

Next day Othniel received his share;

- One virgin
- Two Donkeys
- Three cattle
- Twenty-eight sheep.

Two donkeys will be very useful, Othniel reckoned, but a farmer, he was not. Perhaps one cattle he'll give to Caleb to celebrate the victory but the other two and the sheep would be sold. Unfortunately, the sudden glut of livestock had dampened prices dramatically in Israel but eventually one of his fellow fighters from the tribe of Gad made an offer. His family were big into sheep and planned to remain this side of the Jordan. Ten shekels wasn't much but at least that burden was gone.

As for the virgin she was only aged about seven years so way too young for a wife. A slave to fetch water and cut wood could be very useful though, Othniel decided.

"One final thing," Phinehas announced as they all washed again on the final day of cleansing. "Since Yahweh has spared the lives of every one of us, then every man is to bring an offering to Him. Please offer Him items of gold from your share of the plunder—armbands, bracelets, rings, earrings, and necklaces. This will purify our lives before Yahweh and make us right with Him."

Each man quickly stepped forward and made his offering, there was plenty to give. Othniel offered the gold clasps from the Kings camels' reigns and saddles. Back in the camp the gold was weighed and the total recorded; sixteen thousand seven hundred and fifty shekels of gold. "Praise Yahweh," Eleazar the Priest declared.

In addition to his donkey and slave, Othniel had done very well. Back in the camp he counted his personal spoil which weighed in at three hundred shekels of gold and fifty shekels of sliver. "I like the spoils of war," he announced.

"You aint seen nothing yet," Caleb reminded him. "You wait until we cross that Jordan in a few weeks. Then you'll see the real blessings of Yahweh."

Numbers 31. Deuteronomy 21:11-13.

22

Joshua Takes Over

———————

"So, I see you've got yourself a woman," a sarcastic voice announced.

"A slave," Othniel corrected. "And a seven-year-old at that," he added.

"Whatever," the voice replied as it walked away. Othniel turned and watched Achsah as she stomped away in a sulk. 'Whatever has got into that girl. Ever since I've been back, she's hardly talked to me and when she has it's been like that,' he complained to himself. 'Besides,' he reiterated 'there's no way I'd want a seven-year-old kid as a wife! Very useful to fetch water, clean and cook though,' he quickly added.

His thoughts were interrupted by a shout, "Othniel, come!" Caleb shouted. Othniel jumped up from his lazy musings and walked into Caleb's compound, who was sitting chatting to Joshua. "I've been hearing stories about you, young man," Joshua began sternly as he jumped to greet Othniel. Othniel squirmed internally and wanted to blurt, 'What stories?'

Instead, Caleb interrupted his concerns with a hearty laugh. "Just messing with you, son. Take a seat," he added.

A much relieved Othniel took a seat beside his General across from the Commander-elect of all the tribes of Israel. "Tell us about the fate of the five Kings of Midian?" Joshua asked. Othniel thought for a minute as he collected his thoughts.

He hadn't given the battle much consideration since that day as the recent slaughter of all those captured women and infants was still prominent in his mind. "I came across them purely by chance when we attacked their village with Mesha," Othniel began. He recounted how because of Caleb's great training he and Elah had been able to hatch a quick plan to first cut off their escape then surprise them. "It was all over in seconds," he concluded.

"Well five Kings killed by a young man in his first battle is no mean task," Joshua stated.

"Four actually, Elah killed one," Othniel corrected quickly. "Yes, he'll get his reward too but you're the man we're talking to now," Caleb replied. "We both wanted to honour you, Othniel. It was a very gallant thing you did. You probably saved years of hit and run attacks on our people," Joshua said. Othniel felt himself blush as the magnitude of what he'd done began to hit home.

"As a reward," Caleb continued, "I'm appointing you today to be my personal lieutenant, second to me over all the tribe of Judah."

Othniel's emotions swelled to bursting, "That would be my absolute honour, Sir," he replied in the calmest voice he could muster.

The trio sat and talked for a while longer and drank a little Qom after which Joshua rose to his feet and said his goodbyes. "I believe there's a call to assembly soon," Joshua advised. "Moses is continuing his reading of the Law. I'd better get prepared."

A very contented Othniel began a dreamy walk over to his nearby, expanded compound. As he rounded a tent Achsah suddenly appeared in front of him and much to his surprise she learned forward and gave him a quick peck on the cheek. "Oh, my, what was that for?" a pleasantly surprised Othniel asked.

"I was listening to your story about the five Kings and I think you're a hero," Achsah replied.

"So, I'm forgiven then?" Othniel asked.

"For now," Achsah answered, "but I'll be watching you like a hawk."

Othniel smile as he reflected on it later. Women are impossible, he surmised. A few hours ago, she was berating me, then moments later she's giving me a congratulatory kiss! Before he had time to ponder further a long blast of the twin trumpets sounded. "Another general assembly," he complained aloud.

Moses stood and read the Law of Yahweh to the entire congregation of Israel. There was little doubt in his strong voice about the need to obey. Othniel listen intently even though most of it he'd heard before while studying under the Levites. This time Moses added a new section which included all the blessing that would result from following Yahweh and curses for turning away from Him. Moses presented them as absolute certainties and right at that moment Othniel quietly resolved within himself that he was going to pursue the blessings of Yahweh – with all his might.

Every day for a whole week the call went out, the people assembled and the Law was read. The Sabbath however, bought a welcome break from standing in the hot sun. "So, what have you named your girlfriend?" Achsah asked as Othniel sat enjoying a late evening meal with Caleb, the Sabbath now ended.

"We're back to that, are we?" Othniel replied. Then without allowing a reply he quickly added. "I'm going to call her Charna, after my mother. She died because of those Midianite women so it's only fair her acts of service should be replaced by one."

The forty days of Charna's mourning as required by the Law were about half way done but she had asked for things to do to relieve the boredom. Othniel had checked and it occurs that if she wanted then she could serve. His tent was spotless, as was hers. Wood for the fire was stacked high and pitchers of water stood full. He hadn't tried her on cooking yet, but all in good time. She could speak Hebrew, which was a blessing, all-be-it with a very strong accent. One thing she was not, was a wife or a lover. Besides only being seven years old she was a Midianite and he had long since vowed that no Midianite was ever going to share his bed.

Next day was an early call to assembly and it was barely daylight when all the tribes stood before Moses in the refreshing cool of the morning. "Today," Moses started, "is the day that Yahweh has decreed that I must climb to the top of Mount Nebo. From there Yahweh has promised to show me the Promised Land and then I must die." A collective gasp, followed by a subdued mutter, broke out from the assembled tribes. Moses had been there for the entire lifetime of the majority of those present.

"We have already inaugurated Joshua and from today he'll be your leader," Moses continued. "In the same way I have led you all these years, so will Joshua be to you. Yahweh will speak to him and he to you. Eleazar the High Priest remains with you and Yahweh will lead you into the Promised Land. He will be with you and bless you if you continue to serve Him with all your heart."

"Joshua," Moses called, "please join me here?" Moses walked forward and placed both his hands on Joshua's shoulders and said, "be strong and courageous, for you are the one who will lead these people to possess all the land which Yahweh swore to your ancestors to give to them. Be strong and very courageous. Be careful to obey all the instructions that I have given you. Do not deviate from them, turning either to the right or to the left. If you do then you will be successful in everything you do."

Moses turned to the people and lifted up his hands and said, "That wonderful blessing Yahweh dictated to my brother Aaron, I speak over you now. Yahweh bless you and keep you; May Yahweh make His face shine on you and be gracious to you; May Yahweh turn His face toward you and give you true peace."

Without uttering a further word Moses turned, walked off the platform, across in front of the people towards the outskirts of the camp, heading directly to Mt. Nebo. The entire congregation stood watching him go. Mixed emotions stirred in every heart as their undisputed fearless leader for the past forty years walked proudly out of their lives.

Othniel stood beside Caleb, his disbelieving eyes trying to make sense of what was actually happening as a million doubts and questions swirled in his mind. Moses was the man who spoke face to face with Yahweh, could Joshua really do that?

Much of the crowd disbursed quickly as Moses disappeared from view. There were sheep and cattle to tend to, chores to be done. Othniel however, joined several others and made their way to the outskirts just in time to witness the figure of a vigorous one hundred and twenty-year-old man striding purposefully with the energy of a forty-year-old across the plains of Moab straight towards Nebo. Othniel watched with a heavy heart as the fading figure began the climb up the mountain onto Pisgah Peak. That was the last time anyone ever saw the man Moses again, dead or alive.

The very next morning, much to Othniel's surprise, the twin trumpet blasted early for a general call to assembly. Joshua stood on the platform and addressed the expectant hoard. "Moses, the man of Yahweh is dead," he stated with purpose and authority. "The customary period of mourning is thirty days. Today every person in Israel will begin this period of mourning. We will not move on, complete any manoeuvres or training until that period is over. You all know what to do," Joshua announced as he retreated from the platform. And just like that, the transition of leadership was complete. All of Israel obeyed Joshua and accepted him as their undisputed leader.

Deuteronomy 34, Numbers 6:23–26.

23

Jordan River

"Othniel," Caleb bellowed from his compound. "Come on. That was a single trumpet blast for all the Generals to assembly and since you're now my lieutenant, that means you too." Othniel jumped, eager to be doing anything. The boredom of the thirty days of mourning had got to everyone.

Joshua's words were clear. Every tribal General is to go through the camp and warm all those in their clan and give the following message. "Get your provisions ready. In three days, you will cross the Jordan River and take possession of the land that Yahweh, your God, is giving you." A mighty cheer went up from all those assembled as they quickly broke away eager to spread the word.

Caleb, Othniel and several others they'd recruited, quickly set to work and their enthusiasm was rapidly matched by all those who heard the news. It was fair to say that such was the uptake that by nightfall that first day the vast majority were packed and ready to go.

Jordan River

Prior to giving the order to prepare, Joshua had sent two young warriors across the Jordan to spy out the land and in particular the first city in their planned path, Jericho. Caleb, Othniel and several other Generals and their lieutenants sat eagerly soaking up their report. "The whole land is in dread and terror of our arrival. They've heard what we've done to the Kings on this side of the Jordan and their honest belief is that we can't be defeated" the men recounted. "As for Jericho," they continued, "its locked up better than a donkey in heat. We met a prostitute there, named Rahab, who took us into her house and protected us on the basis we do the same for her when we eventually attack the city. Hope it's all right but we accepted her deal?"

"I'll check with Yahweh," Joshua answered. "But since you've already confirmed this with her, I'm sure Yahweh will approve."

"Anyway," the Spies continued, "we did manage to get a bit of a look around Jericho. Once we get beyond the city walls then taking the city will be easy."

"Excellent," replied Joshua, "Yahweh has already been talking to me about those walls."

At first light on the third morning the Cloud lifted, the shofars blew and a very excited army moved out of Acacia Grove, where they'd camped for the past several months. That night they settled right on the banks of the River Jordan. Despite being in flood, just one hundred metres of slow moving water now separated the Tribes of Israel from the Promised Land.

Othniel walked down to the edge of the river as the day faded to night. The current wasn't strong but it looked deep and much wider close up. "How on earth are a million people and even more livestock going to get across there?" Othniel wondered aloud.

Caleb placed his hand firmly on Othniel's shoulder and said, "Son, throughout my life I've seen Yahweh do so many things. All the plagues in Egypt, the parting of the Red Sea and all His provision throughout forty years in the wilderness. He never failed us once, He came through every time. I'm absolutely certain this time will be no different."

Next morning Joshua's orders came thick and fast. This time the Levites spread the commands. "When you see the Priests carrying the Ark of the Covenant of Yahweh, move out from your positions and follow them. Because you have never travelled this way before, they will be your guide. Stay about a kilometre behind them, keeping a clear distance between you and the Ark. Make sure you don't come any closer." The instructions were clear and all those that understood the holiness of the Ark were very keen to obey.

Very early next morning the Cloud lifted and all the tribes broke camp in their designated order except this time the Ark of the Covenant went out first, followed at a safe distance by the Tribe of Judah. Othniel, marching beside his General, got a front row seat. Without hesitating the priests carrying the Ark marched straight in to the river but miraculously the very moment their feet touch the water at the edge of the river, the whole river dried up. Somewhere upstream the flow had stopped and the crossing point was now dry. Othniel gasped as he witnessed the very first miracle of his God, Yahweh. He'd seen His protection in battle but this was completely different. This was undeniably the raw power of his sovereign God. "I did tell you, Othniel," Caleb reminded.

The priests stationed themselves in the middle of the now dry riverbed upstream from the crossing point as the entry to the land began. Caleb marching at the head of Judah, the leading tribe, strode ahead and stood on the opposite bank and cried out loudly, "Hallelujah, Yahweh. Glory to your name because you are faithful. After forty years you have brought me back here just as you said."

With tears of joy in his eyes he turned to Othniel and said, "There are only two men in the whole of Israel who are old enough to understand all that Yahweh has done to get us here. Never forget that. If Yahweh says He will do something He will ALWAYS do it." Othniel agreed, he was beginning to understand. To hear about what He'd done was one thing, to experience His action first hand was entirely different.

Setting up camp that night somehow seemed different. The grass appeared greener, the trees more vibrant and the bird song more dense. Little of that was fact but to the Israelites, weary after forty years of waiting, everything seemed alive. Finally, they were in the Land.

Joshua had called the priests after the final person had crossed and as they retreated from the river, down came the water and the normal flow resumed.

Next morning the call for leaders to assemble came early. "All the time that we've been in the wilderness," Joshua began, "none of our boys have been circumcised. Yahweh had decreed that now we're in the Land every male must be done." Othniel grimaced as he digested the news. "Please have your males assemble now so the Levites can complete this as soon as possible. Nothing to worry about as they've all got new and sharp flint knives."

Over the next few days every male that was born since they'd left Egypt was rounded up and a very personal procedure was efficiently undertaken. Othniel was 'encouraged' by Caleb to set the trend for his tribe and to be one of the first. Stripped from the waist down, sitting on a hard rock while someone, another man, whom he'd never before met took to his most private part with a very sharp knife was something he could not watch. Surprisingly the procedure was quick, relatively painless and not as much blood as he'd expected.

The advice was to wrap the wound in a light cloth until the bleeding stopped. Wash it thoroughly every night and morning. For the next few days there was standing room only along the Jordan banks as the washing was strictly adhered to. All the men were very eager for full healing and restoration in the shortest time possible. Much to the surprise of most, instead of the anticipated several weeks of healing and recuperation, things healed rapidly with not a man experiencing any infection or ongoing problems. Within a week the camp was back to all men at full strength. Most, however, were very thankful for the respite of staying put until they were whole again.

Next was Passover and what a Passover it was. Joshua repeated the recent words of Yahweh that through the circumcision and now Passover in the Land, "He had rolled away the shame of your slavery in Egypt." While the men were busy nursing their pride, the women had quickly descended on the nearby fields and discovered several concealed grain storage huts, which were quickly emptied. The feast of Unleavened Bread, next day after Passover, was celebrated using produce from the Promised Land.

From that very day, the Manna that had fed all the Children of Israel the past forty plus years, stopped. The abundance of stored grain, wine, olives and vegetables was more than enough to feed all the people for a whole year.

Joshua stood before the armies of Israel, the Passover week now over. "Yahweh has laid out His plan to deal with the walls of Jericho." Joshua began. "We'll march from here and around the city once each day. The trumpeters will march ahead and I want each of you to utter not a word. Complete silence, not a word. Is that clear?" He asked. "We'll do that each day for six days but on the seventh day we'll go round seven times. When we've done all that, then I'll shout for every one of you to do the same. Then we'll see Yahweh act.

"One more thing," Joshua continued. "Since this is the first city to be taken, all the spoils of war from this city belong to Yahweh. Not one man is to take any personal spoil for themselves or their families. Is that clear?" No answer was forthcoming, his words left little doubt.

The trumpets blew, the men marched in order around the city and were back at camp a few hours later. The first day or two it was easy, however from about day four the grumblings started. "What's the point? This is achieving nothing.

"Let's attack now!" were the common 'suggestions'. The General however, allowed none of it.

"Joshua has ordered silence and you will all obey the words of Yahweh," they scolded.

Finally, the seventh day came and the mighty, silent Army of Israel, led by a team of very noisy trumpeters marched round the city seven times. The rope dangling from Rahab's house on the wall was very prominent for all to see each time they passed by. At the end of the seventh circuit the entire Army was spread evenly around the perimeter of the high walled city. The trumpet blowers had caught up with the tail of the last tribe.

"Shout," Joshua cried. Immediately an army of six hundred thousand roared at the top of their voice. The noise was deafening. No sooner had the shout started when suddenly the entire city wall slid straight downwards and crumbled to a heap. It was like the earth had opened below, it dropped straight down.

Every man raced straight ahead directly into the startled city and the slaughter began. Less than an hour later every living being, human or animal, was dead except for Rahab and her family whose section of wall never fell. She was quickly rescued by the very young men she'd previously protected.

Othniel led the way and thrust his sword at everything that moved. However, it very soon became apparent that when a force of six hundred thousand enters a city of perhaps twenty thousand the burden on each individual soldier is light. Those that fought were dead in minutes. Those that hid were mopped up quickly as the buildings were searched and destroyed. The rapid demise of the city surprised even the most hardened fighter.

With the spoil gathered the city was set alight. The smoke of the burning a clear signal to all other cities and villages in the area – Israel is here.

Joshua 1, 2, 3, 5 and 6.

24

Achan's Sin

Joshua stood before his Generals and their lieutenants in a council of war. "Now we've got rid of the fort city of Jericho the city of Ai is next. I propose we send some young men up there to take a look and let us know what might be required." The Commander's words were not a suggestion. "Othniel," Joshua continued, "will you put together a small team from as many tribes as possible to go up there and bring us back a full report?"

As the meeting ended the majority of the Generals' lieutenants lingered behind and hovered in Othniel's direction. Quick to pick up on the blatant clue, Othniel said, "So, any of you guys interested in a quick run up to Ai?" Every hand of those present shot up and Othniel had his team and within an hour they were on their way.

Several hours later Othniel and his team stood before Joshua and the war council. "We've taken a good look and we're all in agreement," Othniel began. "There's no point sending up the entire Army of Israel as the city is small with not many men of war. We recommend a force of only three thousand."

"Three thousand it is then," Joshua confirmed as he turned to his Generals. "Select two hundred and fifty from each of your tribes and Othniel can lead the attack first thing in the morning."

Othniel spread out his three thousand men as they approached the city. "Let's form into a curved line in front of the city so when they attack, we can close in and surround them," he ordered. He's barely finished his speech when suddenly the doors of the city burst open and several thousand men, hell-bent on revenge for Jericho rushed out yelling and waving their weapons menacingly. Othniel's confidence and assurance of Yahweh's support only seconds ago, vanished. A massive dread filled his heart, something wasn't right.

"Attack" Othniel screamed in his strongest voice but his words came out feeble and weak. Not a man moved despite the advancing hoard. The same dread and fear he felt had also encompassed them. Let's get out of here the man next to him suggested. While tempted, Othniel was determined his first leadership would be a success.

Before he had further time to react, the attackers had reached the first of his men nearest the city. Without hardly offering a fight they fell one by one. As he watched his earlier fear and dread increased, his whole body was shaking uncontrollably. "Sound the retreat," he ordered. Immediately the shofar blasted, all his men turned and ran, many discarding their weapons as they went.

Safely hidden now some distance from the city Othniel and his men regrouped. The attackers had abandoned their pursuit and returned to the city. "Did you guys all feel the dread?" Othniel asked.

To a man, every one answered, "Heck, yes." After a thorough count, he determined that thirty-six of his men had been killed. All in the space of a few minutes, he lamented.

As the embarrassed men stole back into camp Othniel's great pride of leading the attack of just a few hours ago was replaced by outright shame. He had failed all of Israel. As soon as the news reached the people the panic began, "We're all going to die."

"When the Land's inhabitants hear they'll be quick to attack."

"We're all going to die!"

Joshua and all the Generals lay prostrate before Yahweh, crying out to Him to help. "Why, why, why?" was all Othniel could utter. The crying was, however, abruptly ended when Yahweh answered Joshua, just as dusk began.

"Get up!" Yahweh answered. "Why are you lying on your face like this? Israel has sinned and broken my covenant! They have stolen some of the things that I commanded must be set apart for me. And they have not only stolen them but have lied about it and hidden the things among their own belongings. On

Achan's Sin

hearing these words Othniel suddenly brightened. That was the reason. It wasn't his battle skills after all.

Yahweh continued. "That is why the Israelites are running from their enemies in defeat. For now, Israel has been set apart for destruction. I will not remain with you any longer unless you destroy the things among you that were set apart for destruction."

"Get up!' Yahweh continued. "Command the people to purify themselves in preparation for tomorrow. For this is what Yahweh, the God of Israel, says: Hidden among you, O Israel, are things set apart for Yahweh. You will never defeat your enemies until you remove these things from among you."

"In the morning you must present yourselves by tribes, and I will point out the tribe to which the guilty man belongs. That tribe must come forward with its clans, and I, Yahweh, will point out the guilty clan. That clan will then come forward, and I will point out the guilty family. Finally, each member of the guilty family must come forward one by one. The one who has stolen what was set apart for destruction will himself be burned with fire, along with everything he has, for he has broken the covenant of Yahweh and has done a horrible thing in Israel."

Next morning the assembly trumpets sounded early and when all the tribes were together Joshua recounted the words of Yahweh and what was about to transpire. Othniel's heart sank a little as the tribe of Judah was selected. Caleb standing next to him said, "Did you take something from Jericho, son?"

"Of course not," Othniel replied indignantly.

"Then you have absolutely nothing to worry about. Yahweh is scrupulously fair in His judgements," Caleb answered.

Next each clan of Judah came forward, and the clan of Zerah was singled out. Then the families of Zerah came forward, and the family of Zimri, Othniel's grandfather, was singled out. Every member of Zimri's family was brought forward person by person, and Achan was singled out. Othniel was horrified. Achan was his mother's younger brother – his uncle. He'd been to his house so often when he was younger although he'd not spoken much over the last few years.

Joshua marched up to a trembling Achan and said, "My son, give glory to Yahweh, the God of Israel, tell the truth. Make your confession and tell me what you have done. Don't hide it from me."

Achan replied, "It is true! I have sinned against Yahweh, the God of Israel. Among the plunder in Jericho, I saw a beautiful robe from Babylon, two hundred silver coins, and a bar of gold weighing about ten ounces. I wanted them so much that I took them. They are hidden in the ground beneath my tent, with the silver buried deeper than the rest."

Joshua quickly dispatched some men to make a search. They found all the stolen goods hidden there, just as Achan had said, with the silver buried beneath the rest, and brought them to Joshua in front of all Israel. They laid them out on the ground in the presence of Yahweh.

The evidence was impossible to deny so Joshua and all Israel took Achan, the silver, the robe, the bar of gold, his sons,

Achan's Sin

daughters, cattle, donkeys, sheep, goats, tent, and everything he had, and they brought them to the valley of Achor.

Arriving at an appropriate spot Joshua turned to Achan and said, "You have brought trouble on us. Yahweh will now bring trouble on you." And he picked up a nearby stone and hurled it at him. Immediately all the Israelites followed suite and a great mountain of stones rained down on Achan and his family.

After burning their lifeless bodies, they piled a great heap of stones over then. So it was that then Yahweh was no longer angry with Israel.

Next morning Joshua stood addressing his war council. "This time," he said, "we'll all go up. Yahweh has told me not to be afraid, we will definitely be victorious this time. Othniel, I want you to lead thirty thousand men, twenty-five hundred appointed by each tribe. I want you to hide behind the city and when they come out to attack, we'll feign retreat which will draw them out of the city. I'll give you a signal to get up, ambush the city and set it on fire. As soon as we see the smoke we'll turn and annihilate those murderers. One other thing. Yahweh says we can all take plunder this time."

Later that afternoon the Army of Israel set out for the short walk up to Ai. Othniel and his chosen men set off in a different, much longer direction in order to come round behind the city unseen. Darkness was falling as Othniel and his men took their cover. Joshua, Caleb and all the remaining Army of Israel camped in the valley directly in front of the city that night.

At first light the massive gates of the city sprung open and the confident warriors of Ai raged out, charging the waiting army who immediately feigned defeat and began to withdraw. This only served to boost the confidence of the Ai men who surged out leaving the city wide open and completely unguarded.

Joshua, seeing his brilliant plan unfold exactly, signalled to Othniel and his men to make their attack. Eager to extract revenge, Othniel and his troops rushed the unprotected city and immediately began setting fires. Suddenly the Ai soldiers spotted the smoke and their hearts sank as they understood they'd been led into a trap. Immediately Joshua and his army turned and viciously attacked. Not willing to be deprived of a battle, Othniel and his men rushed out of the burning city to attack the rebels, sandwiching them between themselves and the main Israel Army.

The battle quickly became a slaughter and before long all the men of Ai lay dead. The attention was turned to the city which was diligently searched and all the women, boys and male infants were dispatched by sword. The virgins, the silver, the gold, the clothing, anything of any value, were taken as spoil.

Once the city was cleared of everything of value, all that remained was burned to the ground. What, at the start of the day, was a thriving city of some twelve thousand now stood a smouldering heap of rubble. A clear witness for all to see the destructive power of the Army of Israel led by their mighty God Yahweh. **Joshua 7 and 8.**

25

Gibeonites

Othniel sat in his tent going through his spoil from the destruction of Ai. It wasn't much, only a few gold coils and trinkets. What really excited him though was a beautiful gold necklace encrusted with several bright stones. He pulled it out for another look and polished the gold and stones until they gleamed brightly. He knew exactly what its destiny was to be.

The woman he'd retrieved it from was already dead, burnt in the initial fire that cemented the ambush. The stench of her burnt flesh was still firmly etched in his memory. Who was she he wondered, as he examined the handcraft, yet again? Obviously, someone of importance, the wife of a city chief, a mother of several prominent sons?

His morbid thoughts began to close in on him as he allowed his imagination to run wild. They ran on to a peaceful city with close-knit families celebrating birthdays, weddings and achievements. The children playing games, laughing while the men sat drinking Qom, recounting wise theories. Now because of his sword they all lay cold, entrapped in death. Their memories and lineage forever erased, their bodies burned and destroyed.

As Othniel sat darkness oppressing his soul he suddenly saw another vision of these very same families sitting around a fire honouring the wooden images they call their god Baal, calling out curses against the wonderful name of the only living God, Yahweh. His spirit began to stir within him as his righteous indignation raged. "How dare they speak against my Yahweh," he cried aloud, the darkness now shattered.

"Are you alright in there my Master," a female voice called.

"Go call Achsah from Caleb's compound," Othniel requested of the voice, his young slave Charna. Some minutes later Othniel sat in the common area of his small compound and a beautiful seventeen-year-old women sat opposite him.

Suddenly Othniel was overshadowed by an entirely different emotion; one of nervous embarrassment. He sat in silence struggling against the unusual sentiment. He'd known this young lady for years; they'd grown up together, competed against each other in donkey races and enjoyed so many happy moments. Yet now, the simple act of presenting her a small gift, made him tongue tied.

"Come on man, spit it out," Achsah joked as she laughed, while flirtatiously brushing back her long dark hair. "Or did you invite me over here just to gaze at my magnificent beauty?" Achsah, while a stunning beauty was also a very capable young woman, very determined and she knew how to get exactly what she wanted. She had long considered Othniel much more than a childhood friend.

Finally, Othniel broke out of his trance. "Achsah," he began, "you mean everything to me and I think you know that one day soon, when I have the right dowry, I intend to ask your father for you to be my wife." Achsah sat drinking in every word; finally he'd come to his senses.

"Your father is the General of the tribe of Judah, a very important mans" Othniel continued, pausing for effect. "The dowry for such a man's daughter is not just a few goats or some silver coins. Besides you're a thing great beauty thereby demanding a worthy price." Achsah blushed at the depth of honesty gushing from her friend. "I'm his lieutenant," Othniel continued, "and I fully intend to prove my worth to him to the full extent of my life. I have learned from him that if I continue to faithfully serve, Yahweh will honour that and in time, I will have more than enough for your priceless worth." Tears of joy filled Achsah's eyes as she soaked up Othniel's kind words. Her mother had told her that marriage rarely involved love, it was about respect, service and bearing his offspring. Achsah was determined to change that and her marriage was to be based on love. Right now, her chosen man was verbalising all the right stuff and it seemed to be coming from his heart.

Othniel wasn't finished. "Joshua has warned us to expect a long campaign starting very soon, as we spread out and take this Land." Othniel advised. "Your father told me he thought this could take about two years. What I'm saying is, we're going to be separated for a period while I serve in the Army of Israel.

You will be safe here in the camp at Gilgal. It's a nice spot and food is plentiful here. Now," he continued, adding excitement to his voice, "I want to give you something to remember me by while I'm gone. Consider it a down payment on your dowry."

Othniel retrieve the necklace he had concealed under a nearby mat. "Here, this is yours," he said as he handed the ornately carved necklace to his intended bride.

Achsah gasped as she took it in her hands. "Oh my, Othniel, this is so gorgeous. I shall wear it every day until you return with the balance for my father," she joked with loving joy.

"I got it from..." Othniel began.

"I have no desire to hear how you obtained it," Achsah interrupted.

The admiring complete, Othniel help fasten the clasp that held it together around her neck. "That's securely held together now," Othniel commented. "I don't think it's made to take on and off too often."

"Don't worry," a very contented Achsah replied, "it's going nowhere. Thank you so much," she said as she leaned forward and kissed him meaningfully on his cheek.

The two sat and talked totally content in each other's company. Romance apart, the two had much in common and truly enjoyed each other's company. The love fest however was abruptly ended as a long blast from a single trumpet sounded from the Tabernacle. "That's a call for the elders to meet. I'll have to accompany your father, the General," Othniel said as he got up to leave.

"We have visitors," Joshua announced as the Generals and their men assembled. Othniel noticed a group standing off to his left looking bedraggled and tired from a long journey. "These men tell me, through their translator, that they're from a far country," Joshua continued. "They had heard about the might of our God, Yahweh, of all He did in Egypt. Also, what He did to the two Amorite kings east of the Jordan River—King Sihon of Heshbon and King Og of Bashan.

"This man tells me the elders of his people instructed them to take supplies for the long journey. Go meet with the people of Israel and tell them, "We are your servants; please make a treaty with us? What say you?" Joshua asked of his Generals.

The Generals sat in silence as they surveyed the visitors. "How do we know their story is true? Perhaps they just live nearby and intend to trick us?" one of the Generals questioned. The interpreter jumped forward ready to answer a question he seemed to have anticipated. "The best way to answer you is to show you," the man said as he walked over to his camel and removed some items from a sack.

"See this bread," he said, "it was hot from the ovens when we left our homes. But now, as you can see, it is dry and mouldy. See these wineskins, they were new when we filled them, but look, now they are old and split open. And our clothing, our sandals they're worn out from our very long journey to reach you."

Several of the men got up and inspected the bread, wineskins and finally their clothing. The evidence seemed to confirm their story but something wasn't right. Joshua thought for a while then asked, "So where do you come from, where is your country?"

The spokesman answered quickly, "Your servants have come from a very distant country. We heard there, of all the might and power of your God, Yahweh and we've come to see for ourselves."

The mention of interest and acceptance of Yahweh struck a chord with the doubtful Generals and the atmosphere eased dramatically. Joshua and his twelve Generals came together in a huddle to confer. After much muttered discussion Joshua turned towards the visitors and said, "We have discussed the situation and your evidence bears witness to your words. Okay, we'll make a treaty with you and teach you the ways of Yahweh."

The spokesman turned with a broad smile to his fellow travellers and in a loud voice spoke to them in an unknown language for a time. As he concluded he raised his hands in the air to celebrate approval. Without a question or a word, the entire company of foreigners also raised their hands with relieved celebration. "We accept your offer," the spokesman said as he turned towards Joshua.

Joshua confirmed, that in the name of Yahweh, they may live among Israel where they would be safe and protected. All the Generals stood and confirmed their agreement. "Peace and protection are bestowed upon you and your families by all of Israel. We swear it this day in the mighty name of Yahweh."

A place was quickly found for the new comers to lodge near the outskirts of the camp and the integration was complete.

Othniel lay in his bed that night and sleep evaded him. His preference was to reflect on his delightful encounter that morning with Achsah but even that eluded him. His mind kept pondering on these visitors. Something wasn't right but he had no idea what. Besides, all the elders of Israel had made a treaty with them so who was he to question his elders.

Next morning, still unable to shake the doubt, Othniel caught up with Caleb as he went about his morning chores. "I have a question Sir, about our visitors yesterday," Othniel began.

"Sir?" Caleb answered. "What, am I no longer a friend, and uncle?"

Othniel flustered for a bit then said, "No, I mean that as my General not my father's brother," he explained. "Why didn't we inquire of Yahweh yesterday before we made peace with those foreigners?" Othniel asked.

Caleb thought for a minute then replied, "Joshua is the one who talks to Yahweh and he seemed to think it was okay. Besides it's not always essential to bother Yahweh with every detail. He did give us common sense for a reason. Sometimes things are just right," Caleb concluded.

Caleb's answer made sense but deep down Othniel still couldn't shake his uncertainty. A couple of days later he decided to wander down to see the newcomers. Not that he'd be able to speak with them as he had no idea of their language, unless he could find their interpreter again. As he approached the area a young boy was trying to manoeuvre a very stubborn donkey and Othniel stopped to help.

With an extra push the donkey finally got on with things and Othniel asked the boy if he knew where to find the new people. The ones that just arrived here recently? "Of course," the boy replied in clear accented Hebrew, "that's my people."

"So how did you learn Hebrew so fast?" Othniel asked quickly. The young boy's face dropped and he went white as a sheet, dropped the donkey lead and started to run. Othniel quickly chased and, mostly because of his much larger stride, he caught the young boy quickly. Holding him by the scruff of his neck he said, "You're coming with me son."

Some minutes later Othniel sat face to face with a very scared ten-year-old now well secured to a nearby post. "Okay, the full truth?" Othniel demanded. After a few stammering starts the boy, fearing for his life, finally revealed all. His people were from Gibeon a city less than a day's journey from Gilgal.

"We were so afraid of you people that we decided this was our only hope of staying alive after we heard what had happened to Jericho and Ai," the boy explained. "Am I going to die now?" the terrified boy asked.

Gibeonites

"Probably not, so long as you tell everyone the full truth from now on," Othniel answered.

Othniel had the boy repeat the truth to Caleb who in turn had him relay it to Joshua. The rest of his people were quickly rounded up and all the Generals assembled. Again, the boy explained the full truth and this time it was his clan that turned white and shook with fear.

The General retreated and much angry discussion ensued with the clear majority recalling in hindsight they too always had much unvoiced doubt, little of which was fact. Finally, they reached a conclusion and they returned to the trembling captives, certain their last hour had come.

Joshua addressed the men and said, "You have lied to us. We know now you live nearby. But because we made a treaty with you in the name of Yahweh, we're unable to kill you. However, you are cursed. None of you will ever be freed from being our slaves. From now on you are bonded to be servants of the Tabernacle, cutters of wood and carriers of water. You lied before Yahweh, therefore, you're now His slaves."

An audible sigh of relief sprang from the captives as they willingly accepted their new role, ecstatic their lives had been spared.

Caleb walked beside Othniel back to his compound. "You were right, Othniel," Caleb said. "There is never a time when Yahweh shouldn't be consulted. Never let us forget that." And Othniel firmly resolved to never forget the lesson. **Joshua 9.**

26

The Longest Day

"We're starting our campaign to conquer this entire land," Joshua explained to his Generals. "It will be army only from now on. All our women, children and those unable to fight will remain here in Gilgal. However, they will need protection. I require you to reorganise your tribe so that they're secure. Build perimeter fortifications and make this place a fortress. We'll station a guard of ten thousand men around the camp who'll be rotated with our main army on a monthly basis. Each tribe will be responsible for one month each year."

With the orders issued the men disbursed and set to work. Othniel looked around his compound and quickly decided without him there, it might as well be incorporated into Caleb's. His younger brother Seraiah now seventeen was too young for war and while he could look after himself, he still required supervision. Then there was his servant Charna. She could cook and clean for Seraiah but there was no way he could leave her under the care of a hormone rampant seventeen-year-old.

Achsah came to his rescue. Charna would be her servant while Othniel was away and she would make sure Seraiah was fed and his tent remained presentable.

With his compound eliminated Othniel focused his attention on building a protective, defendable perimeter. Fortunately, with the destruction of Jericho there was an abundance of stone and rubble nearby and, in a few days, presentable fortifications adorned the camp. The tribe of Asher drew the lot for the first month of home guard duty and their troops were selected and stationed. Joshua inspected the ramparts and commended his men for a job well done. The safety of their loved ones was now secure.

The very next day it began. Othniel busied himself making final preparations, loading his donkey with a tent, some weapons, some cooking utensils together with a few supplies. Suddenly the twin trumpets blew, seemingly with some urgency. It was a general call to assembly, but at this late hour; it was almost dusk.

"We have a messenger from our slave city, Gibeon. His people have asked for our very urgent help. It seems that five Canaanite kings have assembled a large combined army to wipe the city off the map." Othniel was tempted to cry out, 'So what, they're all Canaanites. Let them fight each other.' Instead, he bit his tongue and continued listening to his commander.

"We made a treaty with these people, therefore an attack on any of them is an attack on us. We must defend and do so immediately. Get ready. We'll be marching out at night fall and we'll keep going all night."

The six hundred thousand strong army rapidly dispersed eager to finally confront the enemy again. With his final preparations complete Othniel said farewell to his brother Seraiah, warning him again to stay well clear of his servant girl. Next Othniel turned to his Achsah, standing expectantly nearby. He had no idea what to say but decided a long close hug would say it all. As they pulled apart Achsah said laughing, "You stay away from those Canaanite girls. They'll put a knife in your back as quick as look at you."

"No fear of that," Othniel shouted in reply as he led his donkey towards the compound entrance. My focus will be on securing that dowry." Achsah didn't reply but the satisfied smile across her face said it all as she proudly watched her twenty-one-year-old man march off to war.

All night they marched, pushing hard through the moonlit sky around the side of the mountainous hills and finally the city of Gibeon came into view. In the distance beyond the town stood the flickering watch fires of the Canaanite army. Their battle lines were drawn up so as to lay siege to the city leaving their outer flank virtually undefended. Joshua praised the name of Yahweh as he drank in his scouts' report.

Joshua assembled his Generals and explain the plan. "Yahweh has told me not to be afraid of them. He has already given us victory over them. Not a single one of them will be able to stand up to us." Othniel, standing beside his General, particularly enjoyed the sound of those words.

"The majority of us will continue along this hillside until we're directly opposite them, at which point we'll rush down with a surprise attack. I'm sure they've got no idea we're anywhere near here." Joshua named off three Generals and said, "I want you to take all your men and scoot round the lower side of them to cut any possible means of escape.

"This battle doesn't end until every man is dead, particularly the kings; Adoni Zedek of Jerusalem, Hoham king of Hebron, Piram king of Jarmuth, Japhia king of Lachish, and Debir king of Eglon. Any questions?" None were forthcoming so Joshua dismissed them saying, "Let's get going. I want to hit them before the sun comes up."

A short time later just over half a million battle hardened warriors rushed the unsuspecting sprawling camp of the attacking kings. Panic does little to describe the result within the emery camp, the majority of whom were still asleep in their tents. The kings' men put up very little resistance as their sole focus was escape to retain their lives. The slaughter was quick and on a grand scale.

Because of the vastness of their camp the Army of Israel was unable to enclose them completely, which left a large escape route to the rear. Joshua quickly saw the problem as did many thousands of the kings' troops. He ordered Caleb to take at least six other tribes with him and follow their retreat, while Joshua and the rest mopped up any survivors left in the camp.

Othniel was dispatched to find six Generals and report Joshua's orders.

Thankfully dawn was well broken and spotting the Generals in the chaos was relatively simple. From his vantage point he dispatched two men to take a different path to reach each one. Before long a seventh General had sounded the retreat for his own men. Moments later at least three hundred thousand men sprang into action, at Caleb's command, to follow hard after and destroy everyone who had escaped – especially the five kings. "Go," he shouted.

Despite having marched all night none of the men felt exhausted. An inner energy drove them on, harder, quicker faster. Retreating soldiers fell, struck from behind by the much superior, fitter and healthier Army of Israel, fuelled by the Power of Yahweh.

Despite the hard pursuit all the kings and more than half of their army were outpacing their pursuers. Joshua had climbed a ridge to the West of Gibeon and from there he could see the retreating kings and troops in the distance. While there was little doubt victory had been won Joshua was bent on annihilation, how else were they to drive out the inhabitants of the land.

Despite having attacked at dawn the sun was now near mid-day. Joshua knew that when night fell the battle would be over as the attackers understood the lay of the land much better than his men. Joshua, remembering the words of Yahweh immediately prior to the attack, "Not a man shall stand before you," spoke to Yahweh calmly in the hearing of his men. "Let the sun stand still over Gibeon, and the moon over the valley of Aijalon." At that very moment the sun, restrained by an unseen obstacle, stopped in its tracks high above Gibeon and remained stationary for a whole day.

Meanwhile Othniel and his men ran hard after the retreaters but they had spread out wide upon the way ahead. The stragglers were easy pickings but distance between each man made the killing long work. Focusing hard on their given task Othniel hadn't noticed the darkening sky overhead, least not until the rain expectantly began and rain it did. Except this was no ordinary summer shower. The rain quickly morphed into a hail storm. Massive hail stones thundered to the ground immediately ahead and Caleb blew a shofar as he ordered his men to hold their positions.

The rain around them stopped as quickly as it began but not so on the way ahead. Massive stones the size of bricks thundered down, blitzing the retreating army. Men fell, never to rise again as the mighty force of the hail killed many more than Caleb's men could hope to reach. Caleb slapped his hand on Othniel's shoulder and began to laugh. "We might as well sit down and rest for a bit, Othniel," Caleb shouted between the laughter. "Yahweh has taken over and is fighting for us."

Othniel, seeing what his General had done, joined in the merriment. He and all the pursuing Army of Israel, glad of a little respite found a spot and relaxed. They took out some provisions and refreshed their souls as the hail did their work. "Dinner and a show," Othniel joked.

As the hail eased ahead of the men, having finished their refreshment break set off eager to complete Caleb's orders to mob up the wounded and escapees. Caleb stood up to survey the scene and their next tactic when a welcoming voice said, "Some storm, General."

Caleb turned to his Commander and said laughing, "Yes just purely by chance too."

"I'd like to chat Joshua," Caleb advised but I need to move my men down and get the killing done before darkness falls. We only have a few hours."

"Ah, about that," Joshua said. "Yahweh has helped out with that also. You can't see it from here because of all the cloud but back over Gilgal the sun has stood still. I asked Yahweh to do that until we have the job done."

"Excellent, excellent," Caleb answered. "Run with me, Commander."

Othniel kept a clear distance ahead to guard the way for his General and Commander from a surprise attack by a hiding enemy. As he finished off a reluctant assailant a messenger approached. "I have a message for the Commander," he said. "Do you know where he is?"

"Come with me," Othniel replied.

"Commander, I've just come from the Makkedah where I saw all five kings enter a cave to hide out from the storm and our sword," the man reported.

The Longest Day

"Great news. Good work," Joshua replied. "Take twenty-five men with you and get back there as soon as you can. Roll several large rocks over the cave mouth and all of you stay and guard the place ensuring nobody goes in or gets out. We'll continue with the pursuit and deal with them later," Joshua ordered. The young runner beaming with pride quickly counted off the required number of nearby soldiers and raced off to complete his important task.

"Now let's push on hard, men," Joshua bellowed. "Do not allow any of them to enter their cities or towns."

For hours the vast Army of Israel scattered across the area striking down every man they saw. Thousands already lay dead from the hail and now thousands more lay dead from the sword. Every man did his utmost to prevent any escape but a few swift runners did manage to retreat into their fortified cities. As the killing came to a close the sun again began to move from the place it'd been fixed to for one whole day.

The retreat was called and all the Army of Israel assembled and made camp in the fields around the city of Makkedah. Despite none of the men having slept or even rested much for the past two whole days none were faint or excessively exhausted. It was fair to add, however, that there were few complaints when the retreat was sounded and the command to make camp given.

Joshua gave the order and the kings were extracted from the cave and paraded in front of the Army. Five kings, Adoni Zedek of Jerusalem, Hoham king of Hebron, Piram king of

Jarmuth, Japhia king of Lachish, and Debir king of Eglon, all once mighty warriors stood with heads drooped in shame as Joshua passed judgement.

"These men dared to rise a hand against our mighty God, Yahweh." Joshua declared. "Men of Israel, be strong and courageous, for Yahweh is going to do this to all of your enemies." As he spoke, he strode up to each man and dispatched them with a sword thrust to their heart. "Hang them on those trees," Joshua ordered. "Let their dead bodies be a clear sign to each one of you. Nothing can hold back the hand of Yahweh."

As the men carried out Joshua's hanging orders, he called his Generals together. "Men I'm hungry as I expect are most of these men. Any ideas on where we can find a good feed in these parts?"

One of the Generals replied quickly with a smile, "Sir, there's probably an abundance of food stored in that city right beside us here. We could go and relieve them of it?"

"Great idea," Joshua replied, "Ready your men. We've got about three more hours of daylight."

A short time later the defences of Makkedah were breached and six hundred thousand hungry men poured into the city. Moments later all the inhabitants, men, women children and infants lay dead, defenceless against such overwhelming force.

As the sun finally descended Joshua ordered the hanging kings to be removed and entombed in the cave that once protected them. The Army of Israel ate well that evening, retreating to their beds early to rejuvenate their weary bodies, a successful and very long day's work complete.

Joshua 10:1-28

27

Jabin of Hazor

Following the battle from the longest day Joshua and his men rested at Makkedah for two days then observed the Sabbath. Next morning Othniel was startled awake by the blast of the single trumpet. He quickly dressed, ready to join his General at the council of Elders.

Joshua looked agitated as he stepped up to address his men. His focus and style were in marked contrast to Moses. Joshua was about business, getting the job done. Moses was about the detail, doing it right.

"I've just received word that while we were busy with our destructions last week," Joshua stated, "one of the most powerful kings to our North has put together a formidable force." Joshua leaned over and picked up a small scroll. "According to this report," he continued as he began reading the scroll, "this man Jabin, King of the city of Hazor formed a coalition of about twenty Kings from the mountains in the North to the plains in the South and the Mountains of Dor in the West. In addition are Eastern people, the Amorites and Hivites and those from the land of Mizpah. They've all assembled at the waters of Merom, where I'll guess they'll organise themselves for a few days."

Joshua paused and looked up, "For your information, Merom is a lake about sixteen kilometres (ten miles) to the north of the Sea of Galilee. It's a formation along the River Jordan, "he explained. "According to this report his army is as the sand of the sea and he has many chariots and horses. Any questions?" he asked laughing.

"Thing is, we've never faced chariots before and we need to stop this guy before he gets organised. I suspect his camp at Merom is just for establishment and he'll move South once he's ready." Joshua advised.

"I suggest we march up there immediately and make a pre-emptive attack on him before he knows we're there," offered one of the Generals.

"Actually, that's pretty smart," Caleb agreed.

After much discussion it was decided that after they'd consulted Yahweh, they'd march long days to reach there in only three days. The order was given to prepare the troops. About an hour later six hundred thousand men set out on the rapid run North.

Two days later, after a few hours rest and sleep, the trumpet sounded for general assembly. Joshua stood before his men and announced. "I have heard from Yahweh and He has told me, 'Not to fear or to be afraid because of these people'.

Tomorrow, about this time, early dawn, He will deliver them into our hands. We are to burn their chariots and hamstring all their horses."

A mighty cheer went up from the men and they marched off to the chant, "Great is the name of Yahweh."

It was just getting light next day as Joshua and his army reached the brow of a hill to the West of the lake and he ordered his men to rest. Joshua sent some scouts out who soon reported that the enemy camp was indeed sprawled out in a plain just on the other side of the hill. With the breaking dawn some men were already stirring, beginning their day while others still slept in their tents. All the chariots were neatly lined up along one side with their horses grazing happily some distance away.

Joshua developed a rough plan and began dispatching orders to his Generals. One was commanded to take his tribe and set fire to the chariots. Another he ordered to attack the horses and render them useless, then set them free. "The rest of us," Joshua ordered, "will rush them from here. As soon as I give the command shout the name of Yahweh loudly and rush the enemy."

Moments later six hundred thousand men race down the small incline into the sleepy camp, the roar of Yahweh's name was deafening. The effect on the camp was catastrophic as thousands of terrified sleepy men piled out of their tents, some still searching for their weapon of choice. In the half light of dawn, they saw everything that moved as an attacker and, conveniently, more were killed that day by friendly fire then those killed by Israel.

Joshua commanding his tribe of Ephraim circled round the sprawling camp and quickly found the command post just as all the kings were desperately applying their armour ready to fight. Because their focus was towards the noise of the Westerly attack the Kings ignored their Eastern flank until Joshua, and his thirty thousand men, burst into their dressing rooms. No mercy was shown even though very generous terms were loudly shouted by the desperate defenders. Within minutes every King and their Generals lay dead.

Devoid of any orders or signals, chaos ensued within Jabin camp. Men slashed at everything that moved, fires raged and the injured, startled horses rampaged through the camp. Israel's job was relegated to mopping up and destroying the timid or injured. Before night fell not a man of Jobab's remained alive. Their unused chariots now a smouldering heap of twisted iron, with not a horse to be seen.

Joshua blew his shofar; the battle was over. His troops had fought gallantly and causalities were light but the destruction total. "We'll plunder this mess in the morning but first we'll eat and sleep," Joshua ordered. A content and weary army slept well that night.

Next morning Joshua ordered five thousand men to guard the camp remains and burn the dead while the rest of the army pushed on to take the nearby cities. Jabin's city Hazor was a few hours march away. That would be the first target. Joshua and his army reached the city about the middle of the day. Despite being so close, not a word of the demise of Jabin's mighty army had reach the city, so complete was Joshua's victory. As they approached, the highly fortified city lay wide open, oblivious to its imminent destruction. The Army of Israel simply marched, or perhaps we should say, charged in, through the main unguarded gates.

All the able-bodied men of war from Hazor had been conscripted into Jabin's army. The remaining inhabitants put up little resistance. The battle became a slaughter and by nights end it lay quiet, overwhelmed by death, not one soul remained.

Next day the looting began and anything and everything of value was removed. Hazor had been a large prosperous city, sitting on a major East to South trade junction. Gold, silver and precious stones were found in abundance. Camels and donkeys were laden with food and clothing, and a massive train was dispatched to Gilgal.

With the looting complete Joshua gave the order to set the place on fire. Because of the abundance of trees in the region the majority of buildings were of timber construction and it burned impressively. Within five days of Joshua's arrival a once thriving bustling powerful city lay deserted and in complete ruin, never to be inhabited again.

Joshua sat with his Generals as they pieced together exactly who were all the Kings of Jabin's confederation. As best as they could determine by the spoil they appeared to be from the North; from the Valley of Lebanon, to the South from Megiddo and Carmel and numerous other surrounding cities. "With the leaders and top warriors from these cities already dead, now is the perfect time to attack and destroy their inhabitants." Joshua advised. "I propose we spread across the land to the North then across to the East and make our way South until we arrive back at Makkedah."

Next day the triumphant Army of Israel marched out and over the next year city after city fell to the invading hoards. Not one city offered terms of peace, each and every one came out to fight and each and every one suffered the same outcome – total destruction of every living soul, exactly in accordance with the word of Yahweh.

Except for the city of Hazor, which Joshua made an example of, none of the structures within these cities were destroyed. Once devoid of inhabitants the cities were cleaned of all their spoil and left ready to be indwelt by the Tribes of Israel. The spoil was loaded onto the captured donkeys, oxen and carts and sent back to the dramatically expanding camp at Gilgal.

Week after week the routine was the same. Find the next nearest city, work out a plan, destroy the people, remove the spoil and move on. Not every battle was easy and nor was every one without causality among Joshua's men, but every battle did end in absolute victory.

Othniel, while a very apt and able fighter, didn't always see the thick of battle. As Caleb's chief lieutenant and right-hand man his role was command and control; relaying orders, encouraging his men and reporting progress. The times, the ones he enjoyed the most, was when he was charged to lead a special assignment. Usually involving the taking out of a strategic enemy commander while the bulk of the troops fought an opposite flank.

Whatever his fighting role he always got to 'assist' with the looting. As time progressed, he accumulated a respectable pile of silver and gold, his personal fortune. He focused on things of general purpose, things that were not specific to a region. He knew he hadn't yet found his own inheritance although he'd seen some beauties. Clothing was in abundant supply but apart from a few changes that didn't really interest him. He did however accumulate a respectable pile of female attire which he sent back to his beloved Achsah awaiting him in Gilgal.

Eventually the massive killing machine, the Army of Israel, began to run out of cities and towns within the North of the country and they returned again to the ruined city of Makkedah they'd set out from in a rush nearly one year previous.

Joshua 11.

Jabin of Hazor

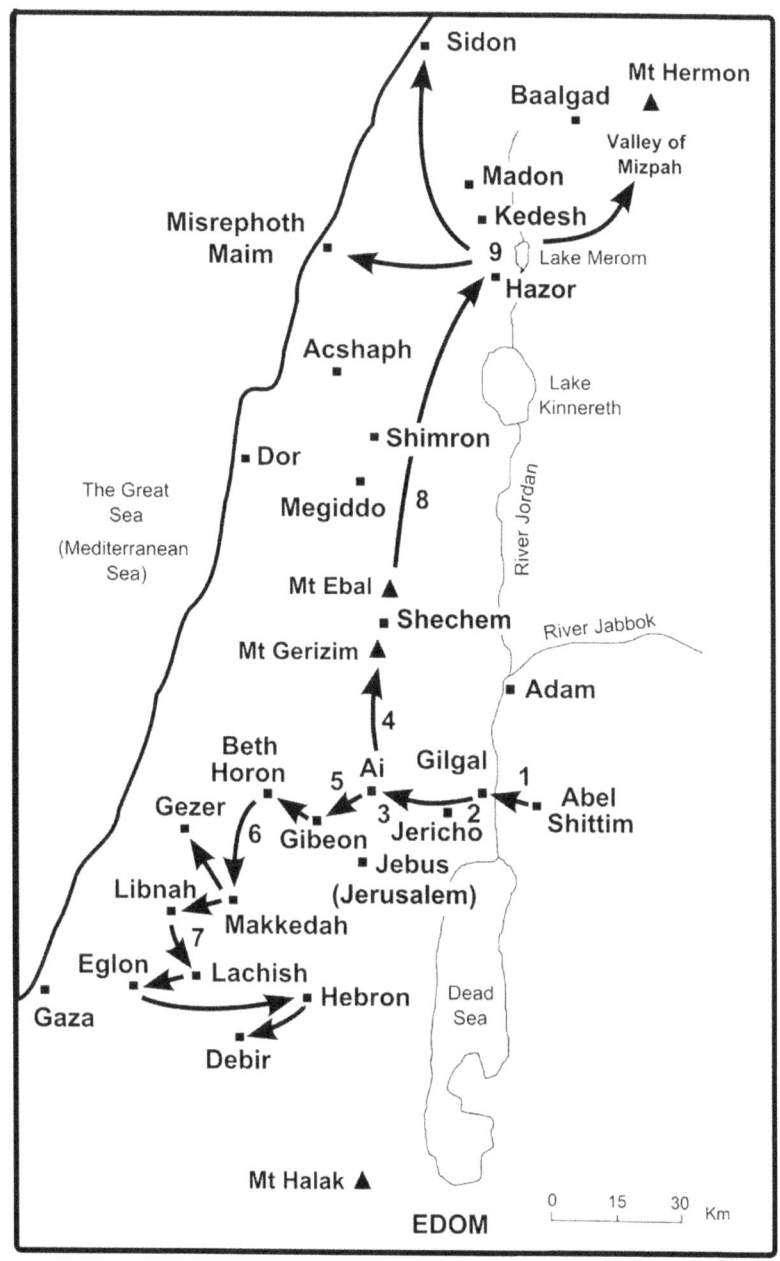

28

Caleb's Demand

After a few weeks rest and relaxation at Makkedah, Joshua addressed his troops now eager for the next move. "Yahweh has blessed our way thus far and has told me to continue for more of the same," he announced. "Today we're setting out to march against Libnah and we'll do the same to it as we did to Hazor. We leave as soon as the sun is warm."

A small contingent had been left at each of the emptied cities to guard from occupation by escapees or wild animals. Usually, these men were the recovering injured, the older, less agile men or the weary. The rest of the army meanwhile marched off to Libnah.

Unlike Makkedah which had walls made of timber, Libnah had high walls of stone and was seemingly impenetrable. As the Army set up camp a safe distance away Joshua and his General walked the perimeter. "I'll ask the advice of Yahweh," Joshua suggested after observing no obvious flaws.

Next morning Joshua, seemingly brimming with ideas ordered men to begin several different tasks. He stationed archers back from the city, along a particular sector, with strict orders to shoot anyone or anything that appears over the top of the wall. Next, he summoned the troops to work in shifts of ten thousand men to work for half a watch each and dig along a section of wall. "Yahweh, revealed there is a weakness in this wall here below this soft ground," Joshua advised his Generals.

For several days the men worked in shifts each day creating a massive hole under the wall exposing its meagre foundations in that area. Above, several anxious on-lookers made their observation but were immediately fired on by the archers. A few deaths however, seemed to cure their curiosity. On day five Joshua decided the right length was exposed and ordered the men to begin breaking out the rocks from the wall, beginning at the base. Joshua ordered the Generals to arm their men and prepare for war.

Just at the start of the second watch a mighty shout went out from the workers as they scattered in every direction, followed closely by the sound of cascading rock as a large the section of wall crumbled to the ground. "Advance and attack, in the mighty name of Yahweh," Joshua shouted as the rock noise subsided.

Thousands of men poured into the well populated city and again the killing was swift. The defences within the city were quickly thrown aside and little further resistance matured. The King was captured and hung on a nearby tree as a witness to all.

Later that day with every resident, young or old, dead, the Army of Israel ate well. Every house was searched and everything of value uplifted. Next day a small garrison was left to defend and ferry resources back to Gilgal. Another foothold in the Land had matured.

From there they marched to Lachish where, only the next day, the city gate was breached and once again the Army did what it had become very expert at. Not a soul from Lachish remained alive by nightfall.

After a few days rest Joshua held a war conference with his Generals. "Gezer was next," Joshua announced.

"I know you have a plan, Commander," Caleb interrupted, "but it's going to take us decades to destroy this people if we continue at this rate. It seems to me to be a bit of an overkill to use a force of half a million to overrun cities of only twenty thousand."

"I see your point," Joshua answered as several other Generals also nodded their agreement. Despite being seasoned warriors with fearsome battle experience, the ten other Generals were at least forty years younger than Joshua and Caleb. None had been registered in the first census back in the early wilderness days. For this reason, while they all had opinions, some of which were strong, they rarely spoke up out of respect for their much older colleagues. This time however, their support for Caleb's suggestion was plainly obvious.

"I suggest we break into divisions and branch off in different directions, widening the swathe we take as we sweep across these mountain regions," Caleb offered. The acceptance of the plan by the younger Generals was undeniable. Joshua's plan for Gezer was in tatters but he too had to agree with Caleb's idea.

"Alright I'll ask Yahweh's opinion," Joshua confirmed.

"One further thing, Commander," Caleb continued. I want to head to the city of Hebron. You'll recall Joshua, when we passed through there forty something years ago, we saw the descendants of Anak there. Those massive giants of men who made Israel trembled in fear just through hearing their name. They are the reason we spent forty years in that dry, forsaken wilderness.

"I want that mountain. In the name of Yahweh, we will destroy the sons of Anak," Caleb slammed his spear into the ground as he finished, emphasising his point. Othniel standing near his General couldn't help be stirred in his spirit too. He was in for interesting times.

"Don't see why not," Joshua answered, "I'll add that to my list to hear from Yahweh on".

Next morning Yahweh was clear on His confirmations, Joshua confirmed; Caleb had his wish. "One thing," Joshua said. "You and the Tribe of Simeon are to go together. You are to fight together to clear your territories."

"No problem with me," Caleb confirmed as did Mishma, the General of Simeon.

Joshua discussed the partnership and directions of all the other tribes, blessed the Generals and set them to their tasks.

"Each of you is to send a messenger to me with a report of your progress each seven days," Joshua ordered as the group broke up.

Caleb's troops marched off towards the city of Zephath. His tribal methods were just as efficient as the combined army and Zephath soon lay with a dearth of residents. Towards the coast they pushed towards the territories of Gaza and Ashkelon, who suffered a similar fate. City after city, king after king, fell to the skilful sword of the joint tribes of Judah and Simeon.

After more than a year of fighting, taking cities and occupying lands finally Caleb's chosen city of Kirjath Arba lay directly ahead. "Now where are those feeble giants?" Caleb asked aloud.

General Caleb sat with General Mishma, his lieutenant Othniel and several other of their advisors, together on a grassy knoll overlooking the city of Arba. Their purpose was to spy out the land and strategize attack scenarios. It was a beautiful day, a warm gentle breeze, cooled by the surrounding hills, added to the lure. Caleb was in a relaxed mood.

"Not much has changed since I was here forty-six years ago," Caleb said thoughtfully. "I loved the area then and nothing has changed. See that city," Caleb continued as he pointed at Arba. "That's one of the oldest cities in the world. I'm told it was built by the mighty giant Anak, seven years before Zoan in Egypt. Kirjath means city," Caleb explained. "The City of Arba. I think I'll rename it after it's ours."

Oblivious to their presence the residents of Arba went about their daily chores. Olives, sheep and goats seemed to be the popular occupations but there were also several small fields of sprouting grain and vegetables. Off to their right a young boy sat alone tending a small flock of goats. "Othniel, why don't you try to disguise yourself as a traveller, go down and capture that lad. I bet he could tell us a lot about who lives in that city."

As short while later Othniel returned to his base camp with a terrified twelve-year-old boy bound, gagged and strapped across his donkey. "Look what I found sleeping on the job," Othniel laughed as he released the boy. Caleb, Mishma and Othniel sat with the boy, offered him water and some sweet treats recently arrived from Gilgal.

"We're your friends," Caleb assured him. "If you tell us all about your village, we'll let you live. If you don't then were going to cut your fingers off, one by one."

The boy starred at Caleb with abandoned eyes, his life as he knew it was over, whatever he did. Caleb grabbed the boy's hand and said, "Okay, your choice. Shall we start with this one," he asked as he reached for his dagger.

"No, no," the boy cried, his tears flowing freely, "I'll tell you everything."

Next morning with an attack plan cemented, Kirjath Arba's end was neigh. They'd learned that three giant men, descendants of Anak lived there. The boy had described the men as being three metres high and as strong as twenty camels and that they ate three sheep every day between them. Caleb knew these giants were the boys only hope so why not grossly exaggerate them. Reality would soon be proven.

The three giants ruled with an iron fist and everything was theirs first and they like to drink wine. "They'd drink it at every meal if they could find enough," the boy explained. Recent pillaging of nearby cities had produced an abundance of wine and there'd been several occasions when Caleb had restricted his men's consumption. Suddenly Caleb knew the answer. One of his men, he'd newly learned, had a great love of snakes and he'd recently found several local vipers which inhabited these parts.

Several new wine skins were filled and placed in a pit with the man's captured snakes. The wine skins were essentially just that, the leather skin of a sheep or goat cut out and stitched together to form a teardrop shape. A long stick was used to move the wineskins aggressively and on queue the snakes struck, latching hold of the skins as they neatly inserted their deadly poison. Since the skins were new the puncture marks from their fangs quickly sealed without a mark. Eventually determining the skins weren't actual foe or prey the snakes tired and gave up the strike. Caleb however was convinced that each skin should now contained enough poison to kill a hundred elephants, he declared the job done. A runner was dispatched, under the cover of darkness to deliver the skins together with an array of fresh fruit at the main gate of the city of Arba.

Early next morning Caleb watched from his vantage point as the gates were opened. The waiting gift was quickly snatched up and rushed inside. Caleb had little doubt that the chieftains would demand their fair share first.

Two mornings later, well before daylight, the Army of Judah and Simeon surrounded the city and set fire to the wooden city gate. Attempts were made from inside to douse the fire but the damage had been done. Caleb's men charged the gates with tree logs, smashing them to kindling and burst inside.

One hundred thousand men of Israel did what they had done for months now; slaughtering everything that moved. The leaderless defenders fled before their attackers, but to no avail, death awaited all. Caleb, seeing the lack of giants knew quickly his plan had worked. He and his handpicked team, under the guidance of the captured boy, headed straight for the houses of the sons on Anak. Once inside little resistance was encountered. The giants were alive but the toxic wine, while not deadly had done its job well. They thrust and swung but their strength was gone and they were quickly captured and strongly bound.

Later that morning as the killing ended Caleb and his troops stood in front of the three restrained and very lethargic hulks. "I have a message for each of you in the name of my God, Yahweh," Caleb shouted. "Because of you my people spent forty years wandering in desert places. I said it then, and I declare it again now," he continued, "the power of my great God Yahweh has given us absolute victory over you today."

"In the name of Yahweh," he cried as he thrust his spear through their bodies and they crumpled to the ground. Not satisfied he grabbed his sword and removed their heads. "Now they're dead, dead – twice dead – through the power of Yahweh. Throw their bodies into that ravine," he ordered.

In the days that followed the city was cleared; and the captured boy? Well yes, his life was spared. He was given some supplies and told to run throughout the remaining Canaanite cities and towns telling them everyone he met what had been done to Kirjath Arba. Be sure to tell them that the much-feared descendants of Anak, Sheshai, Ahiman, and Talmai are all dead through the mighty power of Yahweh.

Next day a messenger came from Gilgal telling Caleb he had yet another grandson; they'd called his name Hebron. "From this day forward this city is named Hebron," Caleb declared.

**Joshua 10:29-36, Joshua 14:6-15, Joshua 15:13-14
Judges 1:17, Numbers 13:22.**

29

The Challenge

Caleb had marched his men to the West, onward towards the Great Sea looking for the next conquest. After the destruction of Hebron Caleb sensed a satisfaction deep within himself that he hadn't felt for the past forty-five years. Those giant sons of Anak, that had made the heart of Israel faint, were all dead. He had secured his inheritance; he had arrived.

Most of the towns they'd encountered since Hebron were small and essentially their mission had been a mopping up exercise, securing the area from any random revenge. This morning Caleb sat on an embankment overlooking the descending hilltops as they gave way to the plains and the sea. Below lay a green fertile valley just above which stood a small fortified city. It was early morning and its residents could just be seen as they went about their usual morning activities in the warm morning sun.

"Is that our next target General?" one of his men asked.

"Actually," answered Caleb with a broad developing smile, "I thought we might do something different with this one. I'm eighty-five years old but as you guys all know, I've got more stamina than most of you young guys. I've got my inheritance so I'm going to sit this one out," he continued, then paused for effect.

Just at that moment Othniel who'd been otherwise occupied, joined his General who was now pointing out the strengths and weaknesses of the observed fortified city. "That city is called Kirjath Sepher, the city where Sepher, a son of Anak, or his descendants live. Whoever kills that giant owns that city," the General explained. "I've demonstrated how we deal with giants through the power of Yahweh," Caleb continued. "Now it's your turn. I want to see if any of you men have learned anything from me. So here's the deal," Caleb announced as he rose to his feet to address his men. There's a prize for whoever leads the attack on that city and takes it. Whoever does that is rewarded with my only daughter Achsah as his wife." A cheer went up from several young men, the beauty of his daughter was very well known and highly discussed in Judah. Caleb looked at a stunned Othniel for a moment and slowly walked back to his tent as several dozen young men broke off into excited huddles.

Othniel was in shock. He had taken for granted that he would return from this prolonged war with a nice nest egg, pay the dowry and take his bride. The taking of Kirjath Sepher certainly was a worthy dowry but the competition was not. His spirit stirred as visions of his beloved Achsah shot through his mind. His emotional fest was rudely interrupted by a slap on the back from his best friend, Caleb's young son Elah. "Why are you just sitting there, man?" Elah asked. "I've just heard the news. That's what you've always wanted, isn't it? Let's get moving."

Othniel and Elah walked back to camp, talking excitedly as they went. "The General says that whoever kills the giant has the city," Othniel reiterated. "We don't need a vast army to do that, we just need a cunning plan," Othniel continued.

"And some men to help mop up the locals afterwards," Elah added.

"Ok let's round up one hundred trustworthy men and hit the road. We can discuss tactics on the way," Othniel stated. "Oh, yes, let's make sure they're all married men, I don't want any internal competition," Othniel added.

In less than an hour one hundred gallant warriors stood before Othniel and Elah. "We're leaving now and march while its still daylight," Othniel ordered. "We'll leave inconspicuously, the General's the only one that needs to know." Moments later Othniel reported to Caleb that he was on his way to collect his prize.

"May the power and strength of Yahweh go with you," Caleb blessed.

In order to avoid detection Othniel led his men out to the side of the camp to the North but once out of sight they circled back and began to jog. Othniel had earlier spotted a well-used track heading West which seemed to lead straight to the city.

He calculated the distance to be about eighteen kilometres (eleven miles) so they should make it in about three hours, well before sundown.

Rounding a small hill as the sun began to descend, Othniel bought his men to a holt. The city lay just ahead, in clear view. Over to their immediate right side were two women tending their olive trees. Silently Othniel and a couple of his men snuck around behind them while Elah causally approached as a traveller. Before he had time to engage them Othniel grabbed and quickly gagged them.

Back under the cover of nearby trees Othniel and his men 'pressed' the terrified young women for information about the city and it's king. Before long he learned that on the far side of the city wall there was a secret night gate, that the king's house was central, near the main city gates.

As evening approached the city drew to a close for the day as Othniel and his men watched from their seclusion. They could have rushed the city which would have gained them access but then how would they defeat a giant of a man twice their size. Surprise was the preferred option and the cover of darkness was the best time to deliver it. The men ate some food and rested up until darkness was complete.

Othniel took three chosen men and set off with one of the captured women. Elah followed close behind with the other and some men. Around to the extreme West of the city his unwilling guide pointed to a small rocky pile. "Remove those and you'll find a gap in the wall where that stream exits," she said. The men quickly set to work and sure enough a space sufficient for a man to crawl through was revealed. One by one Othniel, his men and his guides entered the sleeping town.

The partial moonlight gave just enough light for him to see as Elah with the other guide made their way over to the main city gate. His orders were to silently eliminate any guards and open the gates for their remaining troops to enter and await Othniel's orders to attack. With just the one sleeping doorman rapidly dispatched the gates were quietly opened and Elah was guided back to the king's residence.

Othniel arrived first and quickly set to work. He'd carried a nice length of twisted rope with him which he tied between two buildings at shin height just above the ground, about twenty paces from the entrance. With Elah and another holding the two captives secure in direct view and about fifty paces from the entrance. Othniel and two others ran into the dark recesses near the giant's doorway. Othniel gave the signal and the girls gags were removed. With the encouragement of the tip on Elah's dagger both the women began screaming wildly for help. Not only was that to be a call to arms for the king, it was also the signal for the rest of Othniel's men to attack the city through the now wide-open city gates.

Othniel's heart was pounding as he watched his plan begin to mature. He had one shot at this and if it went wrong, even if his life was spared, Achsah was lost. That could not be an option. He was rudely snapped out of any self-doubt as the door to the giant's home burst open and a mighty roar went out. "What's all this noise, I'm trying to sleep," he bellowed.

Seeing an opportunity to save their lives the two women screamed vigorously for their leader's salvation.

The three metre (ten foot) tall mammoth stood and surveyed the scene for what seemed to Elah to be an eternity. He then uttered a contemptuous unconcerned grunt, reached around and grabbed his spear from inside and began to amble towards the screaming. Othniel and his men held their ground behind him silently watching, daring not even to breath. Focused solely on the noise, the giant paid no attention to the path as he gained pace in the darkness.

Suddenly one of his legs caught on Othniel's low strung rope and over he went, hitting the ground with a mighty thud. Before the stunned giant had time to react Othniel leapt forward and thrust him through with his spear, then quickly severed his head. "Dead, dead," he shouted repeating Caleb's words in Hebron. Relief flooded his body as he watched this giant of a man in his dying moments. "Great is the name of Yahweh," he yelled excitedly.

Elah released the two captive women who ran screaming into the darkness only to encounter the rest of Othniel's army coming the other way. Their final end was silent and swift. Once the giant was dead, very little resistance was encountered as the rest of the city was eliminated. All the men, women, children and infants were slain and carried outside the city to be burned.

As daylight broke the killing drew to a close and the massive pile of bodies was covered in branches from the nearby trees and set alight. "That should send a signal back to Caleb," an ecstatic Othniel announced. His mission had been incredibly successful his bride was paid for – in full.

He'd barely finished talking when another of Caleb's men appeared together with about two hundred men of his own. Othniel knew him, Jeroham was his name. Although he was older, he too had decided Achsah was a prize to fight for and had left his camp at break of dawn to attack Kirjath Sepher. Disappointment was insufficient to describe Jeroham's emotion. His dreams and hopes lay as dead as the pile of burning bodies blazing ahead of him. After quickly inquiring who had led the attack, he turned on his heels and announced to his men. "Othniel, son of Kenaz has stolen my prize. We're returning to camp."

For the next few days Othniel and his men looted the city. To their amazement the industry of the city had been one of record keeping. Thousands of clay tablets were found being records of travels, produce and commerce throughout much of Canaan. At the height of Pharaoh's reign, he had controlled most of the cities in the area. He'd set up a king in each major city to lessen the likelihood of a coordinated revolt. Each of these Kings were required to report their revenue and movements to Pharaoh via the tablets inscribed in Kirjath Sepher and from them he would determine his tribute. The system had become so entrenched that now nearly fifty years after Pharaoh's demise the records were still produced although it seems that little of the collected revenue had actually been passed on during those intervening years. Their giant king not only enforced the tribute but protected the city from revolt.

After learning the full extent and reasons for the tablets Othniel stood and praised his God, Yahweh. "This very city," Othniel declared, "collected the money that help pay the wages of Israel's slave masters in Egypt. Now Yahweh has seen it destroyed." It was also very apparent that scribing was a very prosperous occupation, gold and silver were abundant.

Laden with a very healthy bank account, and a well-paid army, Othniel and his men returned to Caleb's camp to a hero's welcome. Word of his gallant attack was well disseminated and Caleb welcomed his new, and only, son-in-law with a hearty greeting and much newly acquired wine. Safely back in Gilgal, Achsah, the subject of the celebrations had no knowledge of its reason.

The once industrious city of Kirjath Sepher stood deserted, every building perfectly preserved but devoid of residents. "Turns out," Othniel advised Caleb, "that Sepher did represent the name of its king. It means books of records in their language. Matters not though as I'm going to name it Debir from this day forward."

Joshua 15:16-17

30

Gilgal

The campaign of destruction through Canaan had taken nearly five years but now finally the majority had been conquered and the killing came to an end. The order went out from Joshua for all the armies of Israel to return to Gilgal and reunite with their loved ones and families.

Caleb assembled all his troops at Hebron and thanked his fellow General, Mishma, head of the tribe of Simeon. News of a return to family bought a lift to the men. Hebron sat at about nine hundred metres (three thousand feet) above the sea among the mountains South from Jerusalem. The shortest route back to Gilgal was via the Dead Sea which was three hundred metres (one thousand feet) below sea level. As Judah and Simeon descended, the frequent topic was thankfulness for the fact they were not journeying in reverse. Going down was much easier than climbing up.

The men's eagerness grew as the three-day journey came to an end. Along the shore of the Dead Sea, then follow the Jordan

River turning inland to Gilgal as the ruins of Jericho came into view.

Othniel walked up the path of the familiar camp that had been his home for the past twenty-five years. The location had frequently changed, the layout remained exactly the same. His compound, used only by his younger brother during the past five years, soon appeared. He was home but something was missing - Achsah. She was now his wife, paid for in full. 'I wonder if she knows?' he pondered.

His thoughts were short lived and his question answered as his ears filled with the excited scream of a beautiful young woman running in his direction. Achsah rushed up to Othniel, flung her arms around his neck and her legs around his waist and clung to him like a rock limpet. Fortunately, his quick reflexes, honed through years of war, helped him brace as he replicated his excited wife's embrace. Achsah kissed his neck and hung on. Othniel was taken aback. This was delightful but not the welcome he'd envisaged however this was her boisterous unexpected nature, which he also loved. Eventually Othniel, fearing an imminent and embarrassing toppling said, "Okay, you can release the bear-hug now, I need to take a breath."

Othniel took a step back as Achsah jumped to the ground and he looked at his bride as if for the very first time. Well certainly the first time in five years. No longer was she a maturing young girl, she was a mature and exceptionally beautiful twenty-year-old young woman. Her face was more symmetric, her eyes brighter and deeper, face so soft and silky and her hair was long, black, gracing the ensemble perfectly. She was tall, confident, with a trim, well developed body. Every bit of that race to Kirjath Sepher was absolutely worth it.

Achsah was finally the first to speak. "So, I hear, my Papa sold me as a prize?" she said laughing.

"Well not exactly a prize," Othniel answered. "He provided me a method to pay your dowry," Othniel affirmed gallantly.

"Yea, right," Achsah teased, "I heard you ran all through the day to make sure you got there first. Anyway, tell me," Achsah continued, "who was your competition?"

"Several actually," Othniel replied honestly, "Your old friend Jeroham came closest. He missed out by a day."

"Yuck, he's horrible," Achsah exclaimed. "Dealing with that Sepher giant would have been nothing compared to your dealing with me if that idiot had won," Achsah declared. "Anyway, I'm supposed to tell you to get wash up and come across for dinner. We've got a special meal prepared," Achsah said.

"We all stopped off and had a good scrub in the Jordan earlier today, on your father's orders," Othniel replied.

"Well, you'll still need a change of clothes," Achsah answered. "See if you can get your handsomeness to match my stunning beauty." Othniel watched as his bride left his compound and returned to hers. 'She might have matured,' he reasoned, 'but she'd lost none of her incredible personality.'

That night was a celebration fit for a king. Caleb, all of his sons, his grandsons, his sons' wives and daughters sat around with Othniel and Achsah to praise Yahweh for an inheritance secured and a safe return. The meat, the vegetables, breads and dips together with an abundance of wine, all the product of an abundant land, was consumed with a very thankful heart.

Next day Achsah walked with Othniel arm and arm to a large shady tree near the outskirts of the camp. "Tell me all about Kirjath Sepher?" Achsah asked as they made themselves comfortable on the grass.

"It is the most beautiful place on the face of the whole earth," Othniel began extravagantly. "From the hill above the city you can see the Great Sea. We went close to it on our warpath to the South. They say it continues on all the way to the end of the West," Othniel continued, keen to impress his wife of his recently obtained worldly wisdom of geographical knowledge.

"All the homes in the city are made from stone. No longer will you have to live in an enclosure made of animal skins. Also, there's an abundance of stone on the hills so that as the number of sons increase, we can add more rooms to our house," Othniel added with a loving smile.

"Or daughters," Achsah added quickly.

"Sons are heirs," Othniel replied firmly. "We'll see," Achsah answered with equal firmness. "It takes two to dance," she added.

31

Eastern Tribes

Achsah, her mother, her aunts and sisters-in-law busied themselves with a myriad of tasks to prepare for the wedding. Caleb, the head, the elder and General of the tribe of Judah, his only daughter was to marry the hero warrior of the tribe. Nothing could be left to chance.

Othniel had tried to be useful but the consensus, which became substantially firmer as time progressed, was 'weddings were women's business.' Instead, he hung out with his General.

Now the war had ended the urgency had been placed on allocating the lands. Gilgal was too confined with the Army reunited and the order was given to move out for one last time before the people disbursed to their inheritances, inland some ten kilometres (seven miles) to the small city of Shiloh.

Situated on a hill, Shiloh could easily be protected but importantly, it had an abundance of grassy hills and valleys surrounding it that could easily accommodate the tribes of Israel well into the future.

"We'll set up the Tabernacle here," Joshua decreed. He then instructed Eleazar the High Priest to make the Tabernacle secure as this will be the place it is to remain. "This will be the place where the feasts of Yahweh are to be held each year," Joshua instructed.

Eleazar busied himself developing plans to build a more permanent structure over time, while still maintaining the array of daily offerings. Joshua meanwhile had sent out a team to go through the land to survey it, dividing it up into parts so it could be allocated to the tribes. Judah, at Caleb's insistence, had been given a large territory in the South, the hills that flowed out South from Jerusalem. The Hebron area was specifically Caleb's. Since Judah's lands were more than enough a big chunk of it had been surveyed off for another tribe, potentially Simeon.

The tribes of Ephraim and part of the tribe of Manasseh had fought hard and carved out a big block for themselves along the Jordan River. Half of Manasseh took the Western side while the other half remained in the East. Two other tribes, Gad and Reuben, because of their extensive livestock accumulations, had also decided to remain to the East of the Jordan on the fertile plains that once belonged to Sihon of the Amorites.

These two and a half tribes, however, were required by Moses to go over the Jordan with the rest of Israel to fight with them until the land was conquered. This they had faithfully done and now, after nearly five years away, they asked to return permanently to their families. Joshua called them together, blessed them and they set off with their share of the spoil. Very few sad faces were evident as those gallant fighters set off to return to their homes and loved ones, assured of a warm hero's welcome.

With those tribes gone the focus shifted to the division of the land among the seven tribes yet to receive their land, which was to be decided by lot. The description of the land had been recorded in a scroll and the heading of each description was given a number. These numbers were written onto small stones and placed in a clay jar. The General from each of the seven tribes was asked to assemble and one by one they came forward then blindfolded. That General ceremonially reached into the jar and withdrew a stone. The number on the stone was their territory.

Othniel sat and watched the entertainment, content in the knowledge his inheritance was already allocated. As each number was drawn the usual shouts of excitement sounded as did the occasional negative, from a disappointed tribe. By and large however, the process was smooth and by nightfall all the land had been allotted.

Next came the allocation of cities for the Tribe of Levi. Because they were appointed to the service of the Tabernacle, they didn't receive a heritance of lands, but rather were given cities. They were to receive the tithe – ten percent of all the produce – of all the other tribes. Joshua decreed that the names of groups of cities within each tribe, be placed in a jar and the heads of families with Levi were asked to draw a name. Both Hebron and Debir were included.

Much to Othniel's and Caleb's dismay both Hebron and Debir were drawn and given to the sons of Aaron, the High Priest of all Israel. There was little Othniel could do to object but he couldn't help a small pip of pride in that at least it had gone to those of noble blood. It was however, made very clear to the Levites that they were only receiving the city and its surrounding common grounds; only land sufficient for subsistence gardening for fresh vegetables. All the fields surrounding Hebron, the farmlands and villages belonged to Caleb. This was so for all the Levite villages since they received their produce from the people's tithe, not from farming. Othniel regained his composure as he realised that while his Debir city was gone he still owned all the surrounding farmland and of course, a beautiful wife.

Othniel broke the news to Achsah but she was too distracted with wedding preparations even to care. "We'll have plenty of land to farm," she answered. "You always told me how vast and expansive our estate was," she added somewhat sarcastically.

A few mornings later the single trumpet sounded and Othniel joined his General with a very agitated Joshua. "I've just received a report," Joshua began, "that the two and a half tribes that fought beside us for these past years, that we said goodbye to only days ago, have turned aside from Yahweh already." A collective gasp of disbelief rose from the assembled group. Joshua paced, searching for words, his anger and frustration raging.

"Please explain, Commander," Caleb asked cautiously.

Eastern Tribes

"They've built an impressive alter on the frontier of the Land of Israel, by the Jordan River." Joshua answered. "I made it clear to them that the Tabernacle in Shiloh is where they come to worship Yahweh, yet now less than a week later they've built their own. For what; to save them a day's walk!"

The general consensus was that such actions required annihilation – immediately. Such blatant disregard of the Laws of Yahweh had to be dealt with quickly and severely. "All Israel must be assembled and we'll wipe them out," one General demanded. After much debate Caleb finally spoke.

"Let's not rush things," he suggested. "We can wait a few days while we send Phinehas the son of Eleazar the Priest, together with a representative from each tribe. They can meet with the Elders of Reuben, Gad and the Manasseh half tribe and ask them directly what their intentions are."

Caleb's suggestion hit a chord with the assembled men. Deep down none of them really wanted to go to war with these men whom they fought beside for the past five years. However, if Yahweh had been disobeyed then every man was clear on the required action.

Next morning Phinehas and ten other tribal representatives set off for the half day march to the Jordan River. Othniel proudly stood for the tribe of Judah. He was quite glad of the distraction as he was well done with the panicked excitement of wedding planning.

Later that day they arrived at the Jordan and sure enough there was a very impressive but disused alter. Onward they went, across the Jordan River and finally they announced themselves to the assembled two and a half tribes. A somewhat surprised group of their elders quickly assembled and Phinehas got down to business immediately.

"The whole community of Yahweh demands to know why you are betraying the God of Israel." Eleazar began bluntly. "How could you turn away from Yahweh and build an altar for yourselves in rebellion against Him? Was our sin at Peor not enough? To this day we are not fully cleansed of it, even after the plague that struck the entire community of Yahweh. And yet, today, you are turning away from following Yahweh. If you rebel against Yahweh today, He will be angry with all of us tomorrow." On and on Eleazar went, his anger obvious to all.

Finally, he ended and demanded a reply. One of the Elders of Gad stepped forward and began. "Yahweh, the Mighty One, is God! Yahweh, the Mighty One, is God! He knows the truth, and may Israel know it, too! We have not built the altar in treacherous rebellion against Yahweh. If we have done so, do not spare our lives this day. If we have built an altar for ourselves to turn away from Yahweh or to offer burnt offerings or grain offerings or peace offerings, may Yahweh Himself punish us.

"The truth is, we have built this altar because we fear that in the future your descendants will say to ours, 'What right do you have to worship Yahweh, the God of Israel? Yahweh has placed the Jordan River as a barrier between our people and you people of Reuben and Gad. You have no claim to Yahweh, because YOUR descendants may prevent OUR descendants from worshiping Yahweh.

"Therefore, we decided to build the altar, not for burnt offerings or sacrifices, but as a memorial. It will remind our descendants and your descendants that we, too, have the right to worship Yahweh at His sanctuary with our burnt offerings, sacrifices, and peace offerings. Then your descendants will not be able to say to ours, 'You have no claim to Yahweh.'"

As the visitors listened, the explanation relaxed their mood dramatically. Their reasoning made perfect sense. The men conferred separately for a short time then, after returning, a much calmer Phinehas said, "Today we know Yahweh is among us because you have not committed this treachery against Yahweh as we thought. Instead, you have rescued Israel from being destroyed by the hand of Yahweh."

Next morning a very relaxed group led by Phinehas set off for Shiloh. Back home all talk of war was quickly abandoned and wedding plans again took centre stage.

Joshua 18:1, Joshua Chapters 14-20, Joshua Chapter 22.

32

Wedding

The serenity within Othniel's compound stood in stark contrast to the whirlwind within Caleb's. Today was Achsah's day and every woman in Judah, it appeared, was determined this would be the wedding of the century. Caleb tried to help but clearly his wedding expertise extended only to setting out tables or moving tents. Tiring of the bustle he wandered across to Othniel's quarters to offer assistance.

Entering the neighbouring compound Caleb found it deserted; well almost deserted. Charna, Othniel's slave had been ordered to tidy house and prepare for the arrival of a woman. She rattled around in the sparse compound, adding a feminine touch and removing the last vestiges of bachelorhood. "He's bathing down at the river, Master," Charna stated in reply to Caleb's casual appearance.

Othniel had finished bathing and was relaxing in the sun on a grassy slope as Caleb approached. "What do you mean just lying there," Caleb fake scolded. "You're getting married

Wedding

in a few hours and you're not even in your wedding clothes?" The two laughed as Caleb flopped onto the ground beside his future son-in-law.

"You know," Caleb reflected, "I'm eighty-five years old, and have been married for over forty of those to my three wives. I've got eight sons but only the one daughter. Six of my sons are married and their days came and went with little fuss. But when my daughter is married the whole tribe of Judah seems to be involved. What is it about women and weddings?"

Even though Caleb's question was rhetorical Othniel considered an answer should be presented. "That's because your daughter is the most beautiful in all of Israel," Othniel answered proudly and honestly. Much to Othniel's surprise Caleb threw his head back and laughed heartily.

"You're so full of young man's drivel," Caleb announced.

"You think you're marrying for love and indeed that is a good reason." Caleb continued as his laughter subsided. "Romantic love, I mean. You only see the good in her, her beauty, her youth, her shapely form. But those attributes will fade, she's going to get older and believe me she's going to do and say things you'll take offense to. What of your romantic love then, my boy?"

Othniel considered Cable's question. He understood the need for a deeper bond other than physical attraction but he believed he was already good friends with Achsah. Caleb watched his pondering for a time then added. "You and Achsah are already good friends, I've seen you grow up together and it's obvious you have a mutual enjoyment. What created that bond? That's my question."

Othniel saw his point, "I suppose it was because we did so much together. We did things together; even if it sometimes was only chores and jobs we didn't want to do," Othniel answered.

"My point exactly," Caleb said emphatically. "Keep doing that and you'll have a long and very happy marriage. As for trying to understand the inner workings of her mind – forget it. That's an impossible conundrum."

A few hours later a sprightly dressed twenty-five-year-old stood on a grassy knoll with his younger brother Seraiah, his friend Elah and several other young men, awaiting his bride. But not just any knoll, this one had been decked out fit for royalty. Large wooden poles marked the perimeter with ropes strung between then. Over the ropes were draped colourful cloths that fluttered in the warm, gentle afternoon breeze. Tables, laid out with every type of edible treat, were arrayed around the edges. A large chuppah, or canopy, had been erected in the centre, its bright red cloth covering, supported by a post at each corner, accentuated its importance.

Wedding

Traditional Chuppah.

To the Western edge stood a prominent, but cosy tent, also ornately decorated. Othniel's heart flooded with mixed emotions as his eye caught the tent. The thought of being intimate with his young wife, yes very appealing. However, why did it have to be so public?

Othniel's thoughts were interrupted as a shout went out, the bride is near. Othniel and his friends quickly retreated out of sight leaving the beautifully prepared wedding place deserted.

Achsah continued her assent held aloft in a sturdy aperion by four strong men resting its poles on their shoulders. Another marched ahead blowing a shofar, announcing for all that the bride had made herself ready and was on her way to meet her betrothed.

A Traditional Aperion.

Behind the bride her bridesmaids were dancing, swirling and clanging tambourines. Behind them, a long procession of family and invited guests. Achsah was carried in and lowered beside the chuppah. Immediately her six bridesmaids, all dressed in long colourful gowns, rushed to her aid, helping her alight. Gasps of wonder flowed from the guests as Achsah, adorned in a long flowing white gown, was escorted under the canopy. She was covered from head to toe with just a hint of sandal concealing her toes.

Suddenly several young men began playing lyres and Achsah and her bridesmaids began a hypnotic dance as if entranced by the music. They swayed and swirled as if under

Wedding

the spell of an unseen arm. They leaned forward, eyes straining, their hands shielding the suns glare from their eyes. All the while they sang, "My bridegroom, where is my Groom." Suddenly a squeal of delight broke from Achsah lips, "There he is. Behold my bridegroom!"

Othniel, enjoying the theatre, marched out from his hiding place and strode over purposely and stood beside his bride. The music stopped, the bridesmaids retreated and the couple stood alone under the chuppah. Othniel turned toward his bride and took her hand in his. She was covered from top to toe and at that very moment a thought raced into his mind. He shouldn't, but he had to know, as he finally muttered, "That is you under there, Achsah?" Othniel begged.

"Of course, my lovely," a calming familiar voice replied as she also gave his hand a reassuring squeeze.

A young Levite, who'd been hired for the occasion, stepped forward to give the blessing. As he began, he called Caleb to come and stand beside him. "Othniel, it has been reported that you betrothed this young woman, Caleb's daughter, because of a promise made to you," the Levite stated. "Caleb," the Levite continued, "Did you make a promise that whoever conquered the city of Kirjath Sepher, now renamed Debir, would receive your daughter as his wife?"

"Yes, that is correct," Caleb answered.

"And this man Othniel took the city to your complete satisfaction? the Levite continued.

"Absolutely," Caleb confirmed.

"On that basis," the Levite continued, "I declare this man has paid in full the price for your daughter." He broke and administered them a small portion of bread followed by a sharing of the cup of blessing, after which Othniel, as instructed, stomped on and shattered the small goblet. With the formalities complete the Levite announced, "They are now man and wife. I will now bless their union before Yahweh. 'What Yahweh has joined together, let no man separate. May Yahweh bless you and keep you; may Yahweh make His face to shine upon you and be gracious to you; may Yahweh lift up His countenance upon you and give you perfect peace'."

A mighty cheer went up from the invited guests and Elah, Othniel's friend and best man, stepped forward and ushered the couple away to the bridal tent. Without a word Elah lifted the opening and the couple disappeared inside. With the tent resealed Elah returned to the guests. "Let the festivities begin," Caleb shouted. The lyres sounded, the dancers swirled and the invited guests splurged on the food and wine.

Meanwhile within the confines of the bridal tent Othniel was first to speak, "Here, let me rip that thing off your face? I want to see and believe it really is you." Moments later the dim light of the tent accentuated the natural beauty of her facial profile. "Okay, I can relax now, that definitely is you," Othniel teased.

"What's with all the talk," Achsah demanded. "Just shut up and kiss me, won't you?"

Wedding

Sometime later a much-relaxed couple lay content in the warmth of a loving relationship, each one absorbed in their own thoughts. Finally, Achsah broke the silence, "You better throw this out for all to see," she ordered as she slid the bridal sheet out and handed it to her husband. Othniel opened the tent door a slither and threw the sheet across the side of the tent, the virgin status of his bride was clear to all. A mighty cheer went up from the outside guests with the proof displayed. "Now my father can truly celebrate," Achsah said. "His only daughter did maintain her virginity. I'm sure he doubted me at times but I never even came close."

As evening drew near, the festivities reached fever pitch. Achsah had changed from her long white gown and now adorned a long slender multi-coloured dress.

Othniel surveyed his wife as they prepared to leave their tent. "Very pleased to see this outfit is devoid a veil," he joked.

"It can easily be arranged," Achsah teased. "It has what they call a tease, I can pull it down over my eyes while I dance; see," and she pull up the small veil hanging down her back and partially obscured her face.

"That I can live with," Othniel replied.

The couple walked around greeting their guests, each keen to press the flesh of the newest couple in Judah. "I think the entire tribe must be here tonight," Othniel complained. Eventually the greetings ended and the party began. Food was in abundance as was the wine. Despite the liberal proportions few were drunk. Caleb, ever the General kept a close watch on his friends. Unbeknown to most his cautions were well placed and extremely effective.

Traditional Dancing Attire.

Wedding

Othniel and Achsah danced, ate and drank. Their hearts, while knit, were merry and this was a time of celebration. As the night progressed Othniel stood, content with the world, as he looked across the valley from his knoll. The moon was high, the air was warm, all was well. Suddenly a large hand gripped his shoulder. "Welcome to the family, son. You've earned the right to call me

Father," Caleb said. Othniel turned and hugged the man. It had been seven years since his own father had died and he missed him terribly. While he couldn't be replaced, Caleb was an outstanding substitute. The celebrations went on for two whole days.

As the festivities abounded Othniel found himself suddenly confronted by Jeroham his old contender for Achsah's hand. With him were six very sturdy Levites and their mood was serious. "You have broken the Law of Moses," Jeroham shouted. "We've come to arrest you!"

"Arrest," Caleb said stepping forward to intervene. "What's all this about?"

"Was or was not Kenaz your brother?" Jeroham demanded.

"Yes, of course that is true," Caleb replied.

Sensing a kill shot Jeroham beamed and said, "And Othniel here is Kenaz's son?"

"For goodness' sake man, what's your point?" Caleb demanded. "Anybody can get that from the census records."

"I did," Jeroham continued undeterred. "According to the Law of Moses nobody can marry a close relative. Othniel has married his close relative so has broken the Law and should be put to death." Jeroham stood back certain he'd delivered a death blow and Othniel's demise was imminent.

Caleb burst out laughing. "You stupid boy," Caleb scolded. "Firstly, I don't believe Moses's Law applies to first cousins. Second, if you had bothered to check the records properly you will see that, while Kenaz was my brother, he wasn't my blood brother. My father adopted Kenaz when he came to us in the first year in the wilderness. My father Jephunneh was a Kenite, as was Kenaz."

Jeroham and his henchmen had ensured their shouting would attract a strong crowd, which it certainly did. Now they looked like idiots, wishing for invisibility. "Ha," Jeroham exclaimed as he turned to leave. "You can be sure I'll check every word of your story," he shouted. Caleb didn't respond but laughed heartily as he watched the deflated egos make a hasty retreat. Very soon the whole crowd saw the funny side and the laughter grew to a roar.

As things quietened, Caleb turned to Othniel and said, "Somehow I don't think we'll be seeing him again in a hurry."

33

Inheritance

"I'm going to miss this place," Achsah announced as they stowed the last of their belongings onto their faithful donkeys. "This has been the only home I've ever known. It's been located in all sorts of places but the layout and tents have always remained the same." Othniel walked over to his wife, put his arm over her shoulder and held her close. He too had mixed emotions about leaving his boyhood home but they were setting off to take up their inheritance.

"We've sure had a lot of memories here," Othniel said consolingly. "But we're starting a new chapter in our book; the Othniel and Achsah chapter."

Achsah was quiet for a moment as she digested his words them burst out laughing. "You're so full of it, Mr. Othniel. Where did you learn that flowery line from?" Othniel didn't answer, his words weren't original but he thought he'd delivered them so well.

"Come on donkey, let's go," Othniel said picking up the lead animal's rope.

Caleb had organised all his offspring to travel together and it was an impressive train of thirty-five souls, plus twenty-two slaves, fifty donkeys, several hundred sheep and twenty-five oxen that set out from Shiloh. What once had been a large sprawling camp around the Shiloh Tabernacle was quickly being reduced to a remnant of scattered tents as trains of people ventured off to the unknown via all points of the compass.

Caleb, ever the general, led his clan slowly along the peaks and troughs of the hills that rose from the Jordan River towards the centre of the land. They followed a well-used trade route along the hills which supported a myriad of small towns, each one devoid of its original inhabitants. Some were claimed by weary settlers but even those were still sparsely populated. These towns did however make the journey easier. Their unused vegetable gardens, fruit trees and vines provided ample food and snacks. Their unused homes excellent overnight accommodation. Each morning they were careful to leave each lodging clean and tidy ready for whomever it now belonged.

It took seven days but finally Hebron came into view and with darkness invading, the clan quickly set up home in the almost empty city that Caleb knew so well. Later that evening Caleb drew together all the men to devise an allotment plan.

Squatting around a small fire to provide some light Caleb took the lead. "My sons, we can rest in this city for a few days but we cannot set up our permanent home here because this is a Levite city. You can see already that some have arrived," Caleb advised. "I do, however, own all the surrounding lands which contain a number of smaller cities. I suggest that, beginning tomorrow, all of you come with me while the women rest here and we'll scout those cities. They're all empty. I know we destroyed all their inhabitants."

Next morning Othniel said goodbye to his beautiful young wife and set off with his father-in-law and his sons to survey their allotments. "The best lands are to the South," Caleb advised as they left the gates of Hebron. As the sun reached mid-day, they'd covered about ten kilometres when Caleb brought the group to a holt atop a small hill. Below was a plethora of small hills, green valleys and six small villages. Each one secure but empty of residents and positioned perfectly to allow easy access to the adjoining fields.

"Right, this is it," Caleb advised. "All the lands you see before you, Joshua has awarded to me. There are six towns here and we are ten families; assuming my two youngest sons, Naam and Sheva, eventually find themselves wives!" The married sons quickly expanded on the light-hearted banter until Caleb pivoted the focus back to his plan. "We each have to select a town to share with others. These are cities of Judah and my guess is many will want to live here. Some already have," Caleb said as someone pointed out some villagers going about their daily routine.

"I suggest we take our time," Caleb continued, "this is our inheritance and it will be our home for generations, so choose well. Once we've got our cities sorted then I'll allocate each of you a field. Let's go."

During the next days the men spent at least two days in each of the towns, exploring the homes, the water and security of the village walls. Hebron was a large fortified city with stone walls and considered a stronghold; a place of refuge to run to if under attack. The fortifications of these city walls were generally made of wood and their purpose, while providing some security, was primarily for keeping animals either in or out. While not common in the area, bears and lions were part of the landscape and always on the scrounge for an easy meal.

Anab sat at the southern end of the cluster at the top of a hill. From it you could see all the other five villages and out towards the Negev desert further South. Othniel loved it immediately. Towards the West the land sloped away and was covered in a large olive plantation. The slopes in all other directions were smothered in grape vines, the harvest maturing. "I can see my Achsah settling in this place," Othniel said to Caleb as they sat drinking in the sight of rows of vines as far as the eye can see and olive trees waving in the light summer breeze.

"You're right there's something about this city," Caleb answered. "It means, 'The place of grapes,'" Caleb stated. "I wonder why they called it that?" he added with a chuckle.

The two men wandered among the vines then down through the olives. "You could make a nice living off this, Othniel," Caleb advised.

Inheritance

"You mean I could have this field?" Othniel asked excitedly.

"Potentially," Caleb answered. "We have to see what the other boys have decided on."

After two weeks of exploration, every corner of the enclave had been thoroughly explored. Caleb called his sons together and began dividing his inheritance. "Mesha, my firstborn and son of my wife Mishael, you can have the city of Eshan and the fields below it. I will take the city of Anab. When I eventually pass on, you'll inherit my land also and since it borders with Eshan then it will be easy to combine."

"Now to my sons from my wife Maachch. Sheber and Tirhanah you can have the city of Dunmah and its surrounding fields. That leaves Shaaph and Sheva to share the city of Goshen and its surrounds. That okay with you boys?" Caleb asked. The smiles on their faces answered Caleb fully.

"For the sons of my wife Ephah. Iru and Elah, you can share the city of Dannab with its fields. They're excellent for sheep grazing and you guys are great with sheep. Naam you can have the city of Arab." A shout went up from the three sons as their chosen towns were allocated to them.

"I'm also mindful of my brother Kenaz who didn't make it to this good land," Caleb continued. "But his son Seraiah did and he's travelled here with us so to you Seraiah I give a share with my son Naam of the city of Arab. It has a ton of lovely grape vines. I know it was always your father's dream to make the finest vintage known to man. Therefore, you can have as your own, a large vineyard there and live out your father's dream."

Caleb concluded his allocations and stood up suggesting the confab was over. "Ahem," Othniel coughed indigently. Caleb turned towards the cough in mock puzzlement while the other sons remained squatting enjoying the squirming of their sister's new husband. Caleb burst out laughing, unable to continue the charade. "Oh, of course, Othniel. I completely forgot," he teased. "You can share the city of Anab with me and I'll give you the whole field of olives on its West."

A much-relieved Othniel jumped to his feet and pumped his fist in the air and exclaimed, "Yessss."

With the division of the lands complete all the men sprang to their feet and congratulated each other. Seraiah was particularly excited and exclaimed so wildly to his brother Othniel, "Father talked so much about grapes and that was the only thing that interested me," he blurted.

"He sure did," Othniel agreed, "but it's always been olives for me."

Next morning the eleven excited men arrived back at Hebron to collect their wives, possessions and livestock. Achsah was keen to get there, excited to finally be able to set up house with her new husband. At first light next day Othniel, Achsah, their four donkeys, Charna their slave and fifty sheep set off for the city of Anab. "How'd you score the sheep?" Othniel asked.

"Let's just say I won a little wager with my brother Elah," Achsah answered. Othniel laughed. His wife was fiercely competitive and, in his opinion, Elah was very lucky not to have lost all his sheep, whatever the wager had been.

Inheritance

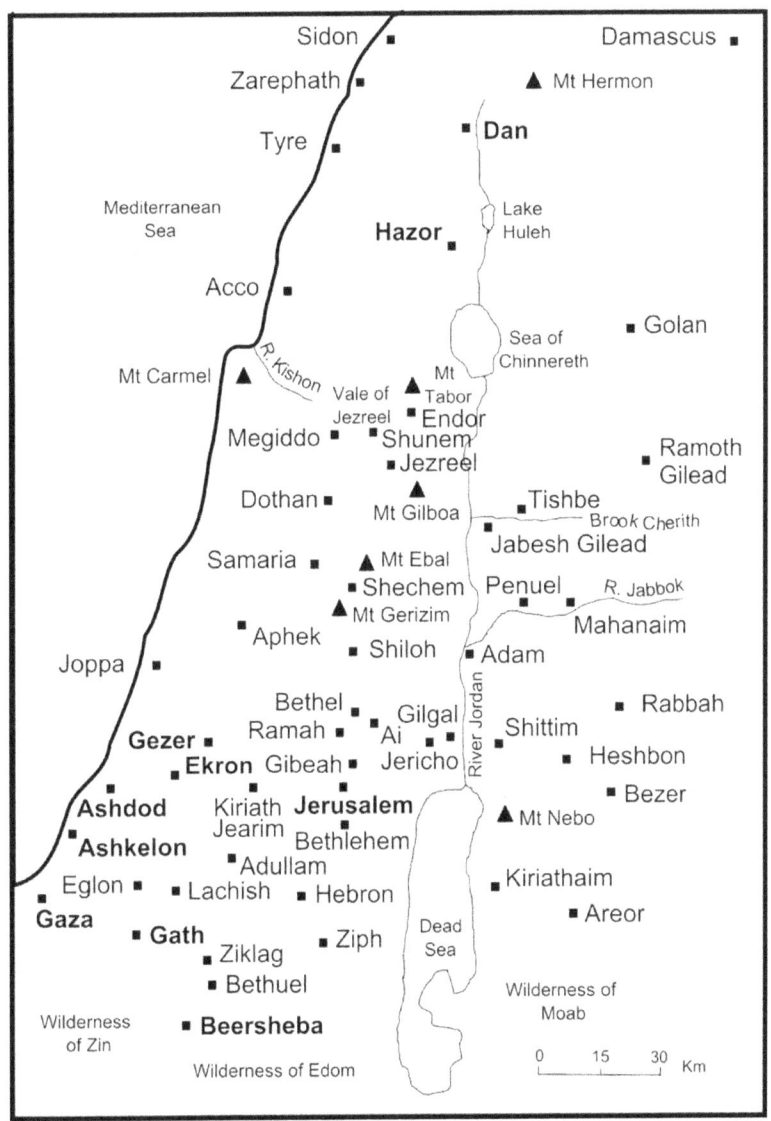

Map of Israel after settlement.

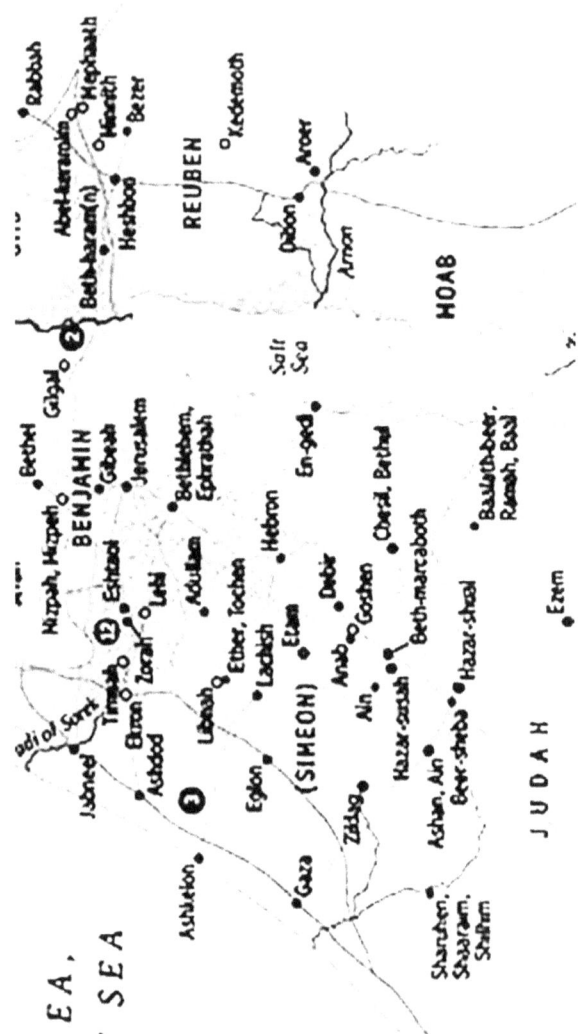

The Cities of Judah.

34

Springs of Water

It was well past noon when the young couple arrived at Anab. Achsah left the sheep with their slave Charna as she accompanied her husband into the town. "Which house would you like, my dear?" Othniel asked. Achsah didn't reply as a harsh reality began to hit home. Unlike Hebron which already had several hundred Levites in residence, this city of Anab was completely deserted. A few cats, dogs and a number of domesticated hens but not one single living soul. "What happened to all the people?" Achsah asked with genuine sadness.

Othniel didn't answer immediately. He knew his wife understood the fate of the locals but somehow admitting he'd been responsible for slaughtering them was hard to admit aloud. "Ah, they died," Othniel finally answered.

"Yes, but why did you have to kill everyone?" Achsah continued. "Surely some could have been kept for slaves and others banished," she suggested.

This wasn't the house hunting experience he'd envisaged but his wife's questions were valid. "The simple answer is that Yahweh told us to," Othniel explained. "These people in this land had moved so far from Him and worshiped all sorts of bits of wood and images, anything but Him. They practiced all kinds of evil things like sacrificing their kids to made up gods and different sexual rituals and practices which He hates. He didn't want any of them teaching those things to His chosen people Israel so that's why He demanded we destroy every living soul. No record of their sinful practices remained. Well not in this city, at least." Othniel concluded.

"So," Achsah asked, "how many young women, like me did you kill?" Othniel was often haunted by the many visions of terrified women and children, moments before they were silenced by his sword and the last thing he wanted to do was to re-live any of those, especially right at this moment.

He grabbed his wife and looked into her sparkling brown eyes and said, "None. I never found another woman like you in the whole of the land."

Achsah flushed at the loving compliment and simply replied, "Yea, right!"

"I like this house," Achsah announced as she marched inside. It was a stone house, solidly built. The floors were dirt but well hardened through years of use. The timber roof, a simple long gable, held up large clay tiles layered in a staggered array down from the centre. As she entered there was a cooking fireplace, a food storage and prep area with a small bed place for a servant. This entry kitchen opened out onto a large living space. On the other end of the living area were two smaller rooms, done out as bedrooms.

To say it was tidy was an understatement as it had obviously been deserted in a hurry and someone had ruffled through every corner looking for valuables. But everything was there including all the bowls for eating and cooking. The things for the fire plus water pitchers, one almost full. The bedding consisted of a layer of lamb skins stitched together and placed on a raised area in the corner. A change of clothes lay in a corner together with a small baby crib. "Absolutely perfect," Achsah stated. "You have excelled yourself, Mr. Othniel."

With the day drawing to a close Achsah helped Charna secure her sheep in the large enclosure near the city gate. The pair then set to discovering how to organise and cook on such a fancy fireplace. The only type both had ever used were makeshift fires that were easily moved. Eventually, after Othniel had welcomed the arrival of Caleb and shut the city gates, he sat on the floor of his living space and ate a delicious meal of hot bread, stewed lamb with vegetables accompanied by, in his opinion, the most beautiful woman in the whole earth.

Next morning the couple were up early and after greeting Caleb and his wives, Achsah released her sheep to a nearby pasture and set Charna to watch. "Let's go and explore," she demanded. Othniel, keen to show off his massive olive plantation, strode off purposefully, his practical wife at his side.

Much to Othniel's delight at the bottom of the olive trees they found a large stone building, purpose built for olive processing. A well-used wooden press with at least a dozen large clay pitchers. Most were empty but two were not. Outside, in a lean-to arrangement, were several skins full of wine, a basket of pomegranates, another of oranges and several large sacks of grain. "I thought my guys cleaned out this village," Othniel exclaimed. "They were supposed to send all this stuff back to Shiloh."

"Well I'm very glad they didn't," Achsah said.

"Come on let's look for a nice place to water my sheep," Achsah said. Up and down they hunted but no water source could be found, except for a small spring near the city which was only used for cooking and cleaning. "How am I going to grow my vegetables, where's the place for water?" she begged. "I'm going back to get us a donkey each."

"This is the end of our property," Othniel announced as the pair came to the end of the olive grove.

"I still don't see any water. Who owns all this land from here on?" Achsah asked.

"That belongs to your father," Othniel clarified.

"I don't care, I'm looking for water," Achsah stated as she rode off. Unsure what to do, Othniel followed. He already knew well that once his beloved got an idea in her head there was little he could do but follow along.

Springs of Water

Down at the bottom of their hill they rounded a bend and found a well-used path. "This must lead to somewhere," Achsah said and pushed her donkey on down the path. Around a further bend the track abruptly veered left around a rocky outcrop and ran into a stream. On the other side was a large flat pasture lush with a plentiful supply of green grass. "I told you there'd be water her somewhere," Achsah cried. "Let's find the source."

A couple of hours later Achsah and Othniel sat on a rock with their feet soaking in the clear bubbling waters of a spring, the main source of the stream they'd crossed. "This is a truly beautiful place," Achsah stated. Othniel had to agree, it was spectacular.

"There's just one teensy problem," Othniel replied. "This land and this water all belongs to someone else!"

"Details, details," Achsah laughed as she jumped up to mount her donkey. "Give you a race to the bottom."

The pair rode along following the stream when after rounding a bend it rapidly became very still and quite deep. "Oh my, this never stops giving," Achsah exclaimed as she jumped off her donkey to examine the small lake. Othniel was just as stunned as his wife, this was an unexpected find in such a deserted area. "You know," Achsah shouted excitedly, "look at the water bubbling over there, this is another spring. What do you know an upper and a lower spring? Water in abundance."

The day was hot, the pond inviting, so while their donkeys munched their fill on the fresh green grass the couple stripped off and washed and bathed in the cool waters.

With the afternoon about to give way to the cool of evening the pair set off on their trusty steeds for the confines of Anab. Round the path up the hill to their village Achsah shouted excitedly, "Hey look, here comes Papa."

Achsah raced off driving her donkey on, eager to greet her father. As she approached she slid gracefully off the side of her donkey and using every ounce of her womanly charm ran up to her father grabbed his hand and dropped to her knees. She kneeled silently gazing into his eyes with hypnotic charm, a well-practiced skill honed through years of living as an only daughter among eight male siblings.

Whatever Caleb's previous mood, it was now considerably softer. Othniel sat on his donkey nearby drinking in the masterly act playing out before him. He'd seen it many times growing up and knew well its outcome, at times to his peril. "What is it, my lovely Achsah?" Caleb finally asked.

"Papa, Papa, you've been so generous and kind. You've provided us a lovely house and a magnificent working olive grove," Achsah answered, pausing for effect.

Still transfixed by his daughter's charm Caleb said, "And?"

"There's no water for my sheep, Papa," Achsah answered. "Please will you bless me the upper and lower springs? We've just come from there and they're perfect for my sheep."

"Well, of course, my Achsah," Caleb answered, the spell of his only daughter complete. "I declare it now and will repeat it at our next family meeting. Achsah leapt to her feet and flung her arms around her father and kissed him on his cheek.

"Oh, thank you so much, Papa. You're such a kind man."

As a slightly bewildered Caleb continued on his way a confident Achsah jumped back on her donkey and began riding towards the house. "And that, Mr Othniel is how it's done. We've just doubled our inheritance and I have water for my sheep and it cost us zilch," Achsah stated calmly.

Othniel didn't answer. He couldn't answer. He'd seen his wife get stuff from her father before but the cold calculation of the act hit home this time. If he ever had a daughter, he decided, he would never succumb so easily.

Joshua 15:18-19, Judges 1:15.

35

New Life

Every day new travellers from Judah arrived at Anab. Everyone was looking for an inheritance, a place to settle and call home. The tribe of Judah covered a large territory with many cities but unlike Caleb most families had not been allocated lands. There was plenty to go round but the general rule was first in, first served.

Caleb and his sons had possessed the cities in the southern Judean hills and managed all the surrounding farmlands. But two families did not a city make. Most of Caleb's towns had fifty to one hundred homes, enough to easily accommodate three hundred people. Anab had a total of sixty-three homes. Caleb lived in the principal house at the head of the town. Grand and luxurious and very appropriate for the retired General of the tribe of Judah. He lived in comfort with his three wives and five slaves. Othniel lived nearby in a less modest abode but, none-the-less, one fitting for a war hero.

Caleb ran out the welcome mat and every visitor was greeted with friendly charm. However, in addition to a nice home most visitors were also interested in land; something to make a living off or to grow the fruit and vegetables needed to support their growing families. Since Caleb owned all the land around his villages attracting residents became much harder than attracting visitors.

Caleb, Mesha and Othniel met to discuss the problem. "I've got land, oxen and sheep in abundance," Caleb outlined, stating the obvious. "Thing is, nobody wants to work the land for wages. Everybody wants to own land, produce their own crops, wool or meat."

"You could sell some land," Mesha advised.

"Why would anyone buy land when they can walk over to the next village and get some for free?" Caleb answered. "Real estate is in abundance and thanks to our five years of war it's all for free." Point made, the trio discussed several options then discarded them.

After much talk and several cups of qom Othniel spoke up. "There's another problem we need to address," he said. "My olive crop is maturing and there's no way I can pick and press all those olives by myself. Perhaps we should form a co-operative and work together with each other to bring in our harvests?"

"Trouble with that is that all our harvests are due about the same time. It'll take weeks to reap all our crops by which time some will spoil," Mesha replied.

"Slaves are the answer to that problem," Caleb answered bluntly, terminating the labour discussion.

Eventually it was agreed that Caleb would begin a feudal system. He would own the land and it would pass on under inheritance but others would be allowed to farm it provided they paid Caleb a fee – fifty percent of all the land produced. "After the payment of Yahweh's tithe," Caleb confirmed.

At first the visitors weren't overwhelmed with Caleb's proposal and most moved on within a day or two. However, quality farmland became less plentiful as the land of Judah became settled again. Therefore Caleb's offer slowly gained acceptance and before long Anab was bustling with families. The majority were subsistence farmers utilising Caleb's lands. There were also many other trades; potters, leather workers, stone masons, black smiths and even a tailor.

Othniel's harvest came and went but despite being able to hire a few workers the majority of his crop spoiled. Achsah helped out as she could but she was busy with her own sheep plus running the house. And as for sixteen-year-old Charna, their one and only slave she worked from dawn to dusk and slept on Sabbaths.

"This is not the good life," Achsah scolded after a particularly difficult sheep day.

"Caleb tells me slaves are the answer," Othniel replied. "But I don't know where to find slaves anymore after we killed off all the locals. Besides Yahweh had forbidden us from keeping any of them alive."

"I don't care where you get them from but I need at least five and you could do with twenty, plus Charna needs some help to run the house," Achsah replied making her point with her usual clarity.

"I'll talk to Caleb in the morning," Othniel answered.

"It's Passover in a few weeks. Therefore, we're required to go up to Shiloh. Joshua will be there too, so we'll bring it up with him," Caleb advised. "We all need slaves, Sheber and Elah were complaining to me too, just yesterday."

Two weeks later all the men for Anab and its surrounding villages set off to celebrate the Feast of Passover at Shiloh, in accordance with the Law. Four days later Caleb's clan had their lamb slaughtered at the Tabernacle and enjoyed a large meal of roast meat and unleavened bread.

Next day was a Sabbath, the day of unleavened bread, but the following five were a time to mix and mingle before the final Sabbath day and disbursement. Being head of Judah, Caleb was cornered frequently to pass judgement on every matter, held off for the occasion, but finally on the fifth day both Caleb and Joshua found the time to connect.

"Because of my extensive land holdings my sons and I aren't able to keep up," Caleb complained. "Produce is wasting and Yahweh's tithe is diminished. All the sons of Israel are busy cultivating their own lands so there's no hired labour available. Slaves are the only solution as I see it and my boys have worked out that between us, we need at least one hundred and twenty of them." Joshua nodded thoughtfully as he listened to his old friend unload.

"Question is where, do we go to get them," Caleb continued. We could raid some remaining Canaanite cities to the West but Yahweh has forbidden we keep them alive in case they introduce us to their foreign gods. So, my friend, what do we do?" There's plenty of Midianite cities but what does Yahweh say about hitting them again?"

Joshua thought for a long time, chewing a dozen scenarios over in his mind when suddenly he jumped like he'd been hit with a bolt of lightning. "Gibeon," he shouted excitedly. "Why of course, I'd be delighted to hit back at those con-artists. Eleazar has used a bunch of them to fetch and carry for the Tabernacle here but there's hundreds of them. Their cities are Gibeon, Chephirah, Beeroth and Kirjath Jearim."

"Take as many as you like," Joshua added, "just don't kill any because we have a covenant with them." As Joshua got up to go, he grabbed his friend and gave him a manly bear-hug. "Thank you, Caleb, you've made my day. I'm still embarrassed about being fooled by those guys and it makes me feel so good to get one back at them."

Two days later Caleb and his sons marched into the cities of Chephirah, Beeroth and Kirjath Jearim and rounded up two hundred young men and women. Some were as young as ten with the oldest in their early twenties. Naturally the city elders didn't take too kindly to the forcible confiscation of their offspring and reacted with some displeasure.

New Life

Caleb desperately wanted to unleash his sword and deal with the problem in his accustomed manner. However, he restrained himself and demanded the elders assemble immediately. "You will please recall your old trickery when you lied to us about your status?" Caleb said as he addressed the angry elders. "You told us then that you'd travelled from a far country so we made an agreement with you to keep you alive. A few days later when the truth came out, we still honoured our word. We assured you then that we will not harm you but made it clear you would become our slaves. Some of you serve at the Tabernacle but now these folks will be coming with us to work on our land in Southern Judea. Have I made myself clear?"

There was no answer to Caleb's rhetorical question nor was there any further disagreement. There was however one request that the selected number be allowed to remain with their families one more night to say their goodbyes. Caleb agreed on the condition that if all the same two hundred didn't show up again next morning, then he'd go ahead and take an additional two hundred.

Just to be sure Caleb and his boys made a fire, heated the tip of a few old swords and used the hot tips to brand a triangle shape on the right arms of every slave.

Five days later Caleb, his seven sons together with Othniel and his brother Seraiah, arrived back at their homes with an abundance of free labour. The slaves were divvied up according to needs with Othniel receiving thirty-five. Twenty men and fifteen women. Achsah was delighted at her husband's acquisitions and immediately commissioned five of the women to run the house. Charna was promoted to overseer of household with a staff of five.

Othniel took fifteen men and five women to work in the olive grove and Achsah used the remaining five men and five women to keep her sheep.

Human nature being as it is not all the new slaves jumped to their chores with ardent enthusiasm but the ever-resourceful Achsah had the answer. If a slave didn't work, neither did they eat. Their portion sizes were strictly relative to their productivity levels. Within a month all the dissenters had succumbed to reason and the whole operation flourished like a well-oiled machine.

With her sheep shorn and an abundance of wool, Achsah acquired a spinning wheel and loom and began weaving woollen garments. A few of which were many times smaller than what was required for her, or her husband.

36

Family

"Life seems to be suiting you here my Achsah," Othniel commented as he sat admiring his beautiful young wife. They had been in Anab now for six months and winter was upon them. The winters weren't generally cold but the occasional days were, with snow falling three of four times most winters. The main feature was rain. Not frequent nor continuous but when it did rain it poured. Othniel had built a large lean-to roof along one side of his house, where he now sat while his wife toiled nearby.

Achsah was busy hovering over her loom weaving a new garment when Othniel's odd comment suddenly hit home. "Now why would you randomly say that, my husband?" she asked.

Rushing in where angels fear to tread Othniel blurted fearlessly, "Oh it's just that you look like you're putting on weight."

Achsah reacted in a manner that all women have maintained perfectly through to the present day. "So you're saying I'm fat?" Achsah replied, with well expressed hurt. Next moment she burst into tears and disappeared into the house.

"What did I say," a truly perplexed Othniel called after her.

Othniel was about to run after his weeping wife, determined to get to the bottom of her unprovoked distress, when her servant maid Charna suddenly appeared. "You stay there, Master," she suggested. "It's her baby that makes her easily upset," Charna continued knowingly, "I know how to calm her."

Charna's words hit Othniel like a camel train. Baby! "What, when, how, what," he muttered as he sank back into his chair. Then as quickly as he sat, he leapt to his feet and rushed off, not into his own house but straight to Caleb's. "General. I'm going to have a son," he shouted wildly as he burst in. Caleb was nowhere to be found but Achsah's mother was.

"Men, they're always the last to know," Maachch commented, mostly to herself. "Is she okay?" she asked.

"I don't know," Othniel replied, "she went running into the house crying when I saw her last."

"You fool, what did you say to her?" Maachch inquired, then without waiting for a reply she rushed out to be with her daughter.

"I only told her she looked fat," Othniel shouted after her.

Just at that moment Caleb appeared, "I see you're attempting the conundrum," he said laughing.

"Not intentionally," Othniel replied. "All I said was she was maturing in size," Othniel explained.

"Othniel, my man, let me explain something," Caleb stated. "There has never been a woman since the creation of Eve that has ever been fat regardless of how large they became. Every woman compares herself with another and takes great comfort in her belief she is slimmer and more attractive than her comparisons. That's her survival strategy. If she's more attractive, in her eyes, than another then a man is more likely to protect her and keep her as his wife. Telling a woman that she's fat, to her, is the same thing as telling her you're about to look for someone else. Someone more beautiful and more attractive."

"Your Achsah is a very beautiful young woman who frankly sets the standard for most others," Caleb continued. "To tell her she's past it, well, let's just say; don't go there again." Othniel stood for some time chewing on Caleb's words. This was all new information to him. On no level did he dream ever that his wife was no longer stunningly beautiful. Surely, she knew that.

Then discarding the subject completely, he blurted with excitement, "I'm going to have a son."

"Why the heck are you standing around chattering to me, you idiot," Caleb said with his usual charm. "Go to her, man."

Sometime later, with fences mended, a wiser and more sensitive Othniel sat chatting excitedly with his wife. Beauty and figure shape, strongly avoided. He learned his child, not necessarily a son, would be born about the time of the harvest. For days following Othniel walked with a spring in his step and a whistle in his heart. He was the most blessed man on all the earth.

As the weeks passed Achsah found supervising the care of her flock more difficult so she recruited a young woman, a daughter of a neighbour, to supervise her slaves in the care of her growing flock. The slaves 'recruited' from the cities of Gibeon were settling in with most resigned to the fact they'd never see their families again. Some had tried to escape but a public whipping witnessed by all the others put an abrupt end to their attempts. Work was getting done and the wheels were turning smoothly.

Othniel was walking through his olive grove and decided to check on something in his pressing factory. Walking down the path he thought he heard a woman scream. He paused to listen again and this time it was distinct. The hair on the back of his neck bristled with horror. The scream was one of terror of a woman in extreme peril, a sound that he'd heard many times during his fighting days. Dread flooded his body as he rushed towards the source, was he under attack?

As he neared his pressing shed, he heard a thud then the screaming abruptly stopped. He burst into the building to find Achsah's young recruit lying unconscious on the floor having just been raped by one of her slaves. "You filthy dog," Othniel roared as he rushed at the partially dressed young man and administered a massive blow to his stomach and several others to his head. He grabbed the now stunned man and shoved him head first into a large empty pitcher and tied his feet securely, hung the other end over a roof rafter and pulled it secure. Confident there was no means of immediate extraction he turned back to the young women who was beginning to awake from her attackers blow to the head.

Othniel carried the distraught woman and placed her carefully on a wooden seat in the centre of Anab. He quickly retrieved a shofar and blew a short blast on it repeatedly – a signal of urgent assembly. Within minutes almost the whole village had assembled and Othniel angrily explained the unprovoked attack on this innocent young daughter of the Tribe of Judah by this young heathen slave. Two sturdy men were dispatched to retrieve the attacker from his pitcher prison to stand immediate trial.

Hearing the shofar, residents of Caleb's other nearby cities also arrived. It was quickly agreed that all the slaves would be assembled to watch the trial and sentence. One hour later Caleb, the elder of the tribe, addressed the crowd. "This matter has to be judged in accordance with the Laws of Yahweh given to us through Moses," Caleb began. "The penalty for rape is death but the death penalty can only be carried out on the mouth of two or three witnesses."

"Then there's the woman," Caleb continued, "if she didn't call out then it means she consented which makes it fornication and she too is guilty of death." An audible gasp went up from several women in the crowd at Caleb's statement.

"We'll I can attest to the fact I did her scream very loudly," Othniel added.

"Okay we can accept that then. The woman did call out, therefore she is innocent. Now the man, are there witnesses?" Caleb asked.

"Again, I can confirm that this man was seen raping this woman as I approached," Othniel confirmed.

Caleb turned to the traumatised young woman and asked, "Was this the man that did these things to you?" Still unable to speak the woman nodded her confirmation. "Therefore," Caleb began authoritatively, "it is confirmed by two witnesses that this slave did rape this woman. Therefore I pass the sentence of death to be carried out immediately by stoning." This time the audible gasp arose from the one hundred and ninety-nine other slaves assembled to witness the judgement.

The rapist was led outside the village a short way then released of his constraints as the several hundred attestants select their stones of choice. Once freed the terrified man took one look at the angry crowd and began to run. He covered about three metres (ten feet) before hundreds of stones smashed against his flesh and he fell to the ground. Within a minute his lifeless body was covered by a great pile of rocks.

Walking back to the city Achsah caught up with her husband. "This man's death will serve as a deterrent to the other slaves," Achsah said. "But there are more than one hundred young men among them all. Can you guarantee me that none of them will ever repeat the crime someday in the future? It might be me next time?" That thought horrified Othniel who quickly found Caleb and relayed his wife's concern.

Next day a council was convened of all six of Caleb's cities and Caleb outlined the concern. There was some dismissal of the problem but the general consensus quickly became clear. This could never happen again. As to prevention, that too had a fast and clear solution – castration. "We'll do to them the same as we do to our animals we don't want mating," was the cry.

Nobody in the village had any experience in creating human eunuchs but that didn't deter suggestions on methodology. Everyone had a favourite from cutting to crushing. A couple of men favoured themselves as physicians regardless of their lack of any real training. Most methods were old wives' fables passed down through the generations. Eventually two men were awarded the task of using whatever means to transform one hundred male slaves into eunuchs.

The first slave was rounded up, ordered to undress and lie face down on a large rock with his legs well spread. With his private parts clearly exposed one man held a large rock directly on top of the stony bits while the other physician smashed a second larger rock onto it pulverising all fleshy items below. The hapless slave screamed in agony, leapt up, danced around holding his mutilated pride, bellowing in excruciating pain. A few seconds later he fell to the ground, passed out. The owner of the slave, Mesha, rush forward to retrieve his motionless workhorse. "You flaming idiots, you've killed him." Mesha roared. Just then the man groaned and took a gasp of air much to the relief of the two attending 'surgeons.'

Mesha 'suggested' they refrain from any further eunuch making until they understood the results of their first endeavours. His suggestion was quickly agreed to by the other slave owners not keen to see their labour force placed out of action indefinitely.

Hours later the man's parts had swollen to the size of a decent watermelon and two weeks later he was still unable to walk, let alone work. A conference of slave owners ensured, following further strong encouragement from their wives to get the job done. It was Caleb who finally ended the discussion. "I was almost forty years old when we left Egypt where we lived as slaves ourselves." Caleb began. "Just as we didn't like being mistreated there, neither can we treat our slaves here with contempt. Yahweh would not be pleased."

"I remember hearing of how the Egyptians dealt with those they wished to castrate. They tied the part up very tightly with a small strip of linen. I heard that even though it was painful it was bearable. The string caused the bean sack to wither up and drop off in a few weeks." Caleb's simple idea gained immediate acceptance and the two physicians were ordered to gather the required strips of linen thread and get to work.

Next day Caleb oversaw the implementation of his plan. The first slave was ordered to lie down naked while the same two doctors quickly tied a string. Mission accomplished, they stood back proudly as Caleb went in for a final inspection. "Not around the whole lot, you blithering idiots," Caleb roared. "How's the poor chap supposed to urinate? Just tie it around the part with the stones in it." Quickly the two doctors made the suggested adjustments and much to their surprise the slave was able to dress himself and walk away unaided.

Next day they checked in on the patient who, while in considerable discomfort was able to carry out light work duties. Caleb gave the green light for a mass program and within a few days all the male slaves in their six cities had begun the irreversible process of becoming eunuchs. The procedure took about a month to mature with all men recovering quickly, except for the first patient who even after six months still had not fully recovered.

As for Achsah; Just after the completion of the olive harvest, much to the delight of her husband she gave birth to a healthy baby boy. "I will call him Hathath," Othniel declared.

1 Chronicles 4:13

37

Time with Caleb

Othniel held his young son with great pride. He wished his own parents were still alive to see his magnificent offspring but this wasn't a time for sad thoughts, his child was to be enjoyed. He showed him off to Caleb, under Achsah's watchful eye. "You'll have to get him circumcised," Caleb advised. "The Law is very clear; it must be done on the eighth day." Othniel's eyes began to water at the thought as he remembered his adult circumcision as they entered the land only seven years earlier.

"I was hoping you could do it for me?" Othniel asked. Achsah gasped, her father was a lovely man but gentleness was not a strength. The thought of her dear little boy being cut about by such a character was a non-starter.

"Actually, Hebron is only a half days' walk from here and that city is full of Levites," Caleb answered. "They're the experts in such things, so I suggest you wander over there." A very relieved Achsah heartily agreed.

Time with Caleb

On his seventh day Hathath's parents placed him carefully on a donkey and set off for Hebron. It was the first time the couple had been back to the city since they camped out there when scouting out their land. They were shocked to find how full and bustling the city now was. Every one, a Levite, all relatives of the family of Aaron the Priest.

Their arrival caused quite a stir, not because of the hero warrior Othniel, nor his young progeny but his beautiful wife. Unbeknown to either parent the beautiful only daughter of General Caleb had become a legend throughout the land. Seeing her in the flesh seemed to only enhance the narrative.

Travelling with the beauty queen of Israel turned finding accommodation into a task of selecting the best offer. Slept and well fed the following day was serious business. One of the senior Levites was summoned to operate on the beauty queen's firstborn son. Using a very sharp flint knife the surplus foreskin was quickly removed and the wound wrapped tightly to stem the bleeding. Within half an hour the whole process was complete, much to Achsah's relief. Othniel handed the priest the required five silver coins for his son's redemption. "You must go up to Shiloh and present him to the Lord after your days of cleansing, Achsah."

Later that afternoon the family returned to Anab. Achsah continued with her forty days of purification and Othniel to the pressing of his olive harvest.

Finally, her days were up and she selected a couple of healthy male lambs, ordered her slaves to catch her at least four pigeons and provide cages for the journey. After a few days all was set and Othniel, Achsah and baby Hathath set off for Shiloh. Achsah brought along Charna and three other servant girls to drive the lambs and help with chores.

The five-day journey was uneventful except for the celebrity welcome Achsah received at each nights' accommodation stop. Othniel was the war hero but his wife, while a trophy of war, was renown throughout Israel as a beauty queen. Exactly how and when that occurred, he had no idea but he had no desire to smother the legend. It aligned totally with his own first hand understanding and as he witnessed, it certainly brought its benefits.

Arriving in Shiloh the couple made their first port of call, the Tabernacle. "This place has changed a bit," Othniel stated as they approached the large wooden gates. No longer were the walls of skins held up by stakes and strings, this was a permanent structure. They were in the Land now therefore having a removable fence around the Tabernacle was no longer necessary. This one was made to last. A large stone fence had been erected around the perimeter and while the animal sacrifice area with the bronze alter were still out in the open, a new stone area was being prepared at the West end to eventually contain the Holy Place and the Holy of Holies. In the meantime, the original skin covered structure stood to one side housing the menorah, the table of show bread and the golden altar. On the other side of the veil was the Holy of Holies containing the Ark of the Covenant and the Mercy Seat.

Othniel and Achsah stood before the officiating priest as he accepted Achsah's lamb and pigeon to cleanse her childbirth impurities in accordance with the Law. The lamb was quickly slaughtered and burned as an offering, as was her pigeon. With his wife cleansed Othniel stepped forward and presented his son. "This is my firstborn son," Othniel announced proudly. "We want to dedicate him to Yahweh and pay the offering." Achsah produced the cage containing the last two pigeons. The priest efficiently removed their heads and sprinkled a little of their blood on Othniel, Achsah and their young son, then offered the birds to Yahweh by placing them on the blazing altar. He took Hathath and held him aloft and, just like his father twenty-seven years earlier, the priest cried out to Yahweh.

"Yahweh, in accordance with his parents' desire, we dedicate young Hathath to you. May his days be many and may they all be blessed." He handed him back to Othniel who, just like his own father all those years ago, made no effort to conceal his joy.

With the official ceremonies complete Othniel and his family relaxed in Shiloh for a few days then made their way back to Anab. Again, they enjoyed their celebrity status securing prime accommodation at every night's stop.

Back in Anab daily life resumed, well at least for Othniel. Achsah's life however no longer focused much on her woollen fabric manufacture, instead it was consumed with raising a lively son and directing the household servants. Before long she became pregnant and gave birth to a second son, much to her husband's delight. This one they named Meonothai. Again, a cleansing time, a trip to Shiloh. Several months later she became pregnant again and this time birthed a daughter whom she named Rachael.

Much to Othniel's surprise he quickly became besotted with his only daughter. As Rachael matured, she portrayed all her mother's natural beauty and compelling charm. Othniel recognised the manifest reproduction of her mother's exceptional ability to weld her feminine wiles on any man to get her own way, but he didn't care. This was his daughter and he was determined to enjoy her.

As his family grew Othniel decided to take the time and enjoy life. He remembered his father, cut short at a relatively young age, with so much living left undone. Everyone hopes for a long fulfilling life but years weren't guaranteed so Othniel became determined to waste none of them. He was living in the Promised Land given to him by Yahweh. He had been blessed with large land holdings and many servants, he had huge reserves of silver and gold, the spoils of war. Now he had a wonderful wife and family, his wants were at an end.

Othniel had modified his house somewhat. He added some more rooms for his expanding family plus he removed its roof replacing it with a flat structure which permitted him to also build upwards, when the time was right. In the meantime, he'd built a parapet and used the large elevated platform to sit and relax. From it he could see down across the valley towards the city of Goshen and to his South, a great view of his massive olive plantation. He found observing and directing operations of his slaves somewhat effective and definitely more relaxing from his roof top than standing among the trees.

Caleb also had modified his grand home to add a large courtyard to one side for entertainment and holding court. Being the head of the Tribe of Judah meant much of his time was consumed in making judgements for his fellow clansmen. Most were simple disputes relating to land and boundaries which, once expounded properly, often resolved themselves. That said, Caleb too enjoyed a relaxing life and while he spent time with all his sons, Othniel, being his neighbour, was easiest to sit with in the cool of the evening and enjoy some wine.

Tonight was such a time, as Othniel expounded on all his blessings; his family, his servants, his land and his wealth. Caleb listened and reflected too on his own blessings then said, "I was a slave in Egypt for many years then Yahweh led us through the wilderness for forty years. He protected us miraculously through the five years of war as we conquered this land and now, He has given me rest in the land. Othniel, I believe this is the most dangerous time for us," Caleb concluded.

Othniel puzzled at his father-in-law's strange statement then with a chuckle answered, "Okay, I give in, why then is this blessed time of peace so dangerous for us?"

"Do you recall the words of Moses in his final address in the plains of Moab by the Jordan River across from Jericho?" Caleb asked.

Othniel, remembered the very long discourse over many days then asked, "Yes, of course but what specifically?"

"Let me recite what struck me most," Caleb answered.

"When you settle in this good land that Yahweh is giving you, if you fully obey Yahweh your God and carefully keep all His commands that I am giving you today, Yahweh your God will set you high above all the nations of the world. Then you will experience all these blessings if you obey Yahweh your God:

- Your towns and your fields will be blessed.
- Your children and your crops will be blessed.
- The offspring of your herds and flocks will be blessed.
- Your fruit baskets and breadboards will be blessed.
- Wherever you go and whatever you do, you will be blessed.

"He mentioned a whole lot more blessings then finished up by saying; 'If you listen to these commands of Yahweh your God and if you carefully obey them, Yahweh will make you the head and not the tail, and you will always be on top and never at the bottom. You must not turn away from any of the commands nor follow after other gods and worship them.

"I think you'll agree, Othniel," Caleb added, "That is where we're at today. We are walking in His way following in His commands and He certainly is blessing us." Othniel had to agree, he'd never actually viewed it as Yahweh's direct hand. He had felt it was more just the abundance of such a good land that Yahweh had blessed them with.

After a thoughtful pause Caleb continued. "The frightening thing is He also told us exactly what will happen if we don't follow His commandments. As I recall it, this is what he said about that;

"But if you refuse to listen to Yahweh your God and do not obey all the commands and decrees, all these curses will come and overwhelm you:

- Your towns and your fields will be cursed.
- Your fruit baskets and breadboards will be cursed.
- Your children and your crops will be cursed.
- The offspring of your herds and flocks will be cursed.
- Wherever you go and whatever you do, you will be cursed.

"As I recall it, His list of curses went on forever," Caleb added. "This is what worries me, Othniel. Joshua is a standard for the people of Israel and to a much lesser extent I'm a standard for the Tribe of Judah. Both of us have experienced first-hand all that Yahweh has done. We know and remember what it was like under slavery in Egypt. We remember what it was like to spend forty years in the wilderness. We saw His faithfulness at every point as we were faithful to Him."

"You and me, Joshua, we're are the only two people alive in Israel who have seen all these things and there is no way we would ever want to go back to the curses we experienced in Egypt. Following Yahweh is our sole desire. Many like you, Othniel, have experienced the wilderness and fought to gain your inheritance. It means something to you.

"What happens when Joshua and I die off, because we will eventually? All the older generation that experienced the wilderness and fighting for the land will die off. Your children will never have experienced that, they will only know the blessings. Will they continue to follow Yahweh with all their might? That's what worries me."

Othniel sat in silence for quite some time as Caleb's words sank in. He'd never thought ahead quite like that and Caleb had a very valid point. What was going to drive this next generation to follow Yahweh diligently. Would they become absorbed with all the blessings and treat Yahweh casually. The word was very clear on would happen should they turn away. "Well thanks so much for destroying my pleasant evening, General," Othniel answered with mock gloom.

Caleb laughed heartily then said, "It's up to you, Othniel. You're young, grow up as a living example of what it means to follow Yahweh with all your heart." Caleb paused for a bit, then said, "Please will you swear to me now before Yahweh, who hears everything, that you will follow Yahweh with all your heart, mind and strength and serve no other god all the days of your life?"

Just like as if someone had pushed him, Othniel dropped to his knees, looked up to the heavens and swore loudly by the mighty name of Yahweh to follow Him with all his strength for all his days.

Tears filled Caleb's eyes as he saw his young progeny's commitment. "Thank you, Yahweh, for giving me a son," Caleb spoke aloud.

Deuteronomy 28:1-6, 13-19

38

Passover

A few weeks after Othniel's declaration before Yahweh it was Passover time. The requirement was just for the men to present themselves each year for the Passover but there was nothing forbidding the presence of women, so Othniel decreed that this year the whole family would make the five-day journey. They would take their time and see the cities along the way then perhaps afterwards he would take his family to the river Jordan. This would be a teaching journey, a time for his family to see and hear the things that Yahweh has done.

Othniel had recently invested in a few camels. He remembered well his father's faithful camel and understood how much more they could carry and that they didn't possess that stubborn streak donkeys were renown for. Achsah wasn't convinced. Donkeys had served her well and she would be riding a donkey to Shiloh, thank you very much!

The winter had passed and spring was present as the family set off in train for Shiloh soon after the sun has risen. In tow were Othniel riding his camel, his two young sons now old enough to manage their own donkey, just. Next, was Achsah on her donkey which young Rachael also shared. The servant slaves bought up the rear with several more donkeys and a couple of camels all hauling supplies for the journey. Finally, were a couple of servants driving five young rams, one of which would be selected as the Passover lamb.

Later that day the family rolled into the large city of Hebron. Immediately a crowd gathered and a multitude of offers of accommodation were shouted to the famous neighbours. The Levites in Hebron, being the sons of Aaron, were required to attend the Tabernacle for a month on a rotating basis throughout the year. With Passover approaching additional priests had been called in, which left several vacant homes in the city as many priests had travelled with their wives and families for the extended tour of duty.

Othniel and Achsah were quickly allocated a large furnished home for a very comfortable night's stay. Simply providing a place to rest wasn't enough so a large hastily arranged celebration dinner was laid on with the beautiful Achsah the star attraction. Food was plentiful and the wine in abundance, dancing and festivities continued well into the night.

Othniel had never been so thankful for servants as he was when awoken early the next morning. Being excluded from the merriment of the previous night they had consumed their meagre rations and retired to bed early. When a sleep deprived master and mistress crawled from their beds all the children were up, dressed and fed and the animals loaded, ready to leave. Othniel staggered from his bed to his camel where he was offered bread and copious water and proudly led his family out of a very quiet Hebron in the breaking dawn.

Next night was a stop at the much smaller city of Gedor. Othniel had travelled the route many times on his way to and from Shiloh and usually followed the same trail each time. Gedor was familiar and an old army friend now lived there who always made him welcome. The home comforts were sparse in comparison to Hebron but the friendship was genuine. Othniel didn't care, he was very appreciative of a quiet place to retire to early that night. Next morning Othniel gifted his friend one of their male lambs and then set off for the city of Nob.

The path between Gedor and Nob followed along the ridges of the Judean mountains and just before the descent down into the city of Nob Othniel stopped and called his sons over to see the view from their vantage point. Directly across from them lay the stronghold city of Jebus (later renamed Jerusalem). "See that city?" Othniel asked his sons. "One day Israel is going to conquer it. We tried but those towering stone walls make it almost impenetrable. We did destroy their king in an early battle but could not take the city. One day...." he sighed and paused thinking.

"See that mountain just to the South there," Othniel continued as he pointed out a hilltop to his sons. "That's a very important place called Mt. Mariah. That was the mountain where Yahweh told our father Abraham to offer his only son as a burnt offering. You remember, I've told you that story many times and that at the last minute Yahweh told him to stop and provided a ram instead." The boys nodded their agreement as they recalled the scary account. Seeing the actual location cemented the reality of their father's teaching.

With the sightseeing over the family continued on to Nob, arriving not long before dusk. Again, a friend was their host in exchange for a lamb next morning. The following evening the family arrived at Ar, their final stop before Shiloh.

Othniel went looking for his friend only to hear he'd already travelled to Shiloh for the pending Passover. Another feature of Ar was that, unlike all the other cities they stayed in, which belonged to Judah, this was inhabited by those from the Tribe of Benjamin. And it quickly became apparent that hero status of Othniel's war efforts counted for little in the town as did Achsah's celebrity status – nobody other than Othniel's old friend had ever heard of the family before. While it would be unfair to say nobody welcomed them it was, however, true that offers of accommodation were silent.

The weary family sat, as is the custom, in the open square in the city centre waiting to be noticed by a potential host as darkness began to descend. This time it was the ever-resourceful Achsah who came to the rescue. Finding a private place to refashion her attire and spruce her appearance Achsah returned no longer a weary traveller but as a beautiful, delicate woman in desperate need of rescue from the unknown dangers of spending a night in the open city square. The impact was immediate and within minutes several hosting offers matured. A smug Achsah turned to her husband as the family was led to their lodging and said, "And that, my darling, is how it's done!"

It was mid-afternoon the next day when the family arrived at the surrounds of Shiloh. Already hundreds of families had arrived and set up camp on the hills and fields around the Tabernacle city. Othniel quickly found a spot beside some others from the tribe of Judah he was acquainted with and the family set up their small tent city to settle in for the fourteen-day stay.

"Come with me boys," Othniel called to his sons. "It's the tenth day of Nisan today and we have to take our lamb for inspection by the priest." Both boys eager for some action jumped at their father's call as Othniel selected the strongest of the three remaining lambs.

Arriving at the Tabernacle they soon discovered their five-minute task may take some time. There were several thousand Levites on duty this day but there were also several hundred thousand ram lambs to inspect. Othniel and his boys were well down the line. Eventually their turn came as the priest beckoned to present their lamb. Despite having performed the task a dozen times already that day, the priest's inspection was as thorough as if this was his first one ever. Every part of the lamb was measured and searched for any imperfections. "Every lamb offered to Yahweh must be spotless," the priest reiterated. "But it seems you've selected well. Take good care of it and bring it back in four days."

For the next four days the lamb had the run of their makeshift camp. The finest bed of straw was prepared, it ate and drank at will in plentiful amounts and was generally spoilt.

In every way it was treated as a bona fide family member even though it was to be a substitute.

On the fourteenth day Othniel led the happy lamb with his boys back to the Tabernacle. Again, it was rush hour except this time the outcome for the lambs wasn't so bright. The final process took less than a minute. The lamb was expertly place on its side on a low table, its head hung over one end. Othniel held the hapless animal's legs as a priest sliced its throat while another held a bowl to catch the pouring blood. Empty of its life-force Othniel picked it up and carried it back to his camp while the priest carried the blood to the blazing bronze altar and after sprinkling a little at the altar, he tossed the rest onto the fire.

Two very sober boys watched their father skin and gut the animal that been their playmate for the past four days. Later, as the offal burned on their camp fire, the lamb slowly roasted above. "Now boys," Othniel began, "do you understand this?" Without waiting for a reply, he continued. "When our fathers left Egypt, Yahweh commanded each family to take a lamb, kill it and paint the blood on their doorposts. The Angel of Death passed through the land of Egypt at midnight of the fourteenth day of Nisan and in every house that didn't have the blood on their post every firstborn person in that house died. The blood of this lamb, therefore, is a substitute for the blood of our firstborn. Yahweh commands we do this every year to remember that substitution." Hathath paled and gulped as the reality of the event hit home. Being a firstborn had its advantages but this was not one of them.

Passover

The teaching done, the lamb was cooked and the celebration meal began. It went on for hours as they ate roast lamb to their fill together with bitter herbs, unleavened bread and several goblets of wine. All the while Othniel recounted to his family the account of their people coming out of Egypt and their exploits in the wilderness over forty years. As darkness fell any remaining lamb was thrown on the fire and burnt. "Yahweh was very clear," Othniel stated, "none is to be left until the next day."

Next day was a Sabbath day, the day of unleavened bread. A solemn day of rest. "This is the actual day the Israelites triumphantly marched out of Egypt," Othniel taught. "Yahweh commanded we celebrate it as a day of rest."

With the holy Sabbath over the next six days were for relaxation, family and mingling with friends or business. Each day, except for the intervening regular Sabbath, Othniel and Achsah went their separate ways to seek out old friends and make new ones. Deals for the sale of olive oil were concluded as were sales of recently weaved woollen cloth. A very profitable time for the couple. Othniel even scored a great deal, he believed, for several oxen complete with a lovely new cart to be delivered within the month.

The final day of Passover concluded with yet another Sabbath day after which several hundred thousand happy Israelites disbursed to every corner of the Land.

Eager to complete his boys' education Othniel took his family back home past the remains of Jericho, along the Jordan river, around the Salt Sea, back up the valley to Hebron and then on to Anab.

39

Drawing Near

A few weeks after Passover Othniel, as promised, received delivery of his oxen and sparkling new cart. The incredible thing is he found so many essential uses for his cart that he wondered how he ever managed without it.

Later that year with the olive harvest complete and the pressing done it was time to deliver the tithe in accordance with the Law of Yahweh. Othniel gathered up a tenth of the olive oil, and a tenth of all his produce. Achsah rounded up a tenth of her lambs, their wool and her weaved cloth and Othniel drove across to Hebron, with the aid of several servants, to deliver all the offering.

To say Othniel was received in Hebron as a hero would be underwhelming. Anyone giving out free stuff is welcome but when it comes by the cartload it can cause quite a stir. The women gushed over Achsah's cloth which was instantly apportioned. The sheep were put to pasture and instructions were given as to where to place the large clay pitchers of olive oil.

As Othniel supervised the unloading he stuck his head inside a nearby well-kept small building. Too small for a house and not tall enough for storage he was curious. He lifted open a large door along one side to find a room bright and airy with a large mat covering almost the entire floor. Along the end wall were several large parchment scrolls with ornately crafted finials each end. Othniel walked over to take a closer look. He'd seen scrolls in the Tabernacle but they contained the Holy Torah. What pray tell were these?

Othniel stepped over to take a closer look and as he reached out a hand to feel the parchment a strong voice said loudly, "I wouldn't do that if I were you." A very startled Othniel jumped in the direction of the voice to discover an older man sitting quietly on a large bench. Strange he'd never noticed him before.

"What are these scrolls?" Othniel asked.

"They are a copy of the Torah, the Law of Yahweh. My brother asked me to make a copy and keep them safe here at Hebron," the man replied.

"Your brother?" Othniel questioned.

"Yes, my brother Eleazar, the High Priest," the man answered.

"Then that would make you, who?" Othniel queried.

"The brother of the High Priest," the man replied with a sly grin. After a short pause he added, "Ithamar. My name is Ithamar." "And you are?" Ithamar asked.

"Oh, yes, sorry," Othniel answered. "My name is Othniel, son of Kenaz of the Tribe of Judah," Othniel replied. "I live nearby in the city of Anab. I've just delivered my tithe which my servants are unloading next...."

"I know you. You're married to the most beautiful Achsah," Ithamar interrupted. Did nobody know him in his own right any more, Othniel pondered feeling slightly frustrated.

"Yes, that's me," Othniel replied with a sigh.

"Do you live here?" Othniel asked changing the subject.

"Of course," Ithamar replied. "I still do my regular service at the Tabernacle every few months but mostly I just sit here and guard these."

"So you're also a scribe?" Othniel asked.

"Yes, when my older brother was awarded the position of High Priest my father Aaron arranged for me to become a scribe and safeguard the Torah." Ithamar explained.

"Can you please teach me the Law of Yahweh," Othniel begged. "Yes, of course," Ithamar replied, "I'd be delighted to have a student."

"I was taught it years ago, in the wilderness," Othniel explained, "but there was a lot I didn't understand."

"Come back next week, after the Sabbath, we'll start then," Ithamar answered.

It was barely light on the first day of the next week as Othniel saddled up his camel and rode off towards Hebron. Less than an hour later the animal had effortlessly covered the ten-kilometre distance and Othniel arrived at Ithamar's tiny scroll shrine just as he was opening its' doors for the day.

With the greetings exchanged Ithamar carefully removed one of the scrolls, excited to have an eager student. "It's so nice to teach this to someone who is keen to learn," Ithamar commented as he began unrolling the scroll. "Most of my students attend because they are required to learn in order to understand their priesthood. Why is it you're so eager?" Ithamar asked.

Othniel hadn't thought about that question, he just wanted to learn. "Actually, I don't know the answer to that," Othniel replied honestly. "I just have this deep curiosity to learn more about Yahweh. He says He'll bless me if I follow Him with all my heart, which is exactly my desire. But I want to know why He's even interested in me? Why does He love me at all, what have I done to deserve that?"

"Wow, very deep questions there Mr. Othniel," Ithamar replied with a chuckle.

"I have a question before we start," Othniel said, "Why are these scrolls so precious to you? Why do you spend all your days in here?"

"Well, not all my days in here," Ithamar answered, "I go up to Shiloh twice a year for a month, to serve as a priest in the Tabernacle. Regarding the scrolls; apart from the fact they took me five years to copy everything and the fact that this is the only copy of the original in existence, do you mean?" Ithamar added with a strong tinge of sarcasm. "Besides that," Ithamar continued, "is that these scrolls represent the words of Yahweh. Moses may have written them but Yahweh told him what to write. The words record who Yahweh is, what He does for us, how we approach Him and how we can get to know Him personally like our Father Abraham did."

Now it was Othniel's time to say "Wow." He'd always regarded the scrolls as an account or record of Yahweh but seemingly we can get to know Him personally through them? That was new to him and he felt his zeal begin to swell. Right at that moment Othniel resolved to draw near to his God, Yahweh, and really get to know Him.

"We'll begin with the creation account," Ithamar began.

"Creation account?" Othniel asked, surprised. "I thought the Torah was only about the Law of Yahweh. Least that was the only part that the Levites read when I attended classes at the Tabernacle in the wilderness."

"That is a big part of it," Ithamar explained but Moses recorded a lot of history as well. That all helps us understand how we all got to where we are today and why."

For three days each week for the next six months Othniel got up early and rode to Hebron to sit and listen to Ithamar read the scrolls. Most days it was just him and Ithamar but at times other young Levites would sit in. Their attendance, however, was casual and they lacked the passion which consumed Othniel. Ithamar was an excellent reader but he also was a teacher. After reading a section he would stop and explain the sense and meaning, ensuring Othniel understood the context and purpose.

As the days progressed Othniel learned that each of us had been created by Yahweh, in His image and likeness. That the first man Adam had sinned through disobedience and because of that all men are born alienated from Yahweh. That without the shedding of blood there was no remission of sin. But that through a blood sacrifice it was possible for us to draw near to Yahweh. That Abraham had done just that and also because he obeyed Yahweh, and He had accounted righteousness to him. That Abraham talked with Yahweh and that Yahweh actually called Abraham His friend. That Yahweh chose Abraham, because of his faithfulness and promised him and his descendants would become a mighty nation and inherit all the land He'd promised.

Each day Othniel's passion for Yahweh grew as he heard all the promises that Yahweh had made throughout the Torah and that every one had come to pass, not a single word of Yahweh had failed. Othniel also understood clearly that in order to remain in the continuing blessing and promises of Yahweh then he had to continue to follow Him. He couldn't expect Yahweh to bless him if he disregarded Him.

Othniel enjoyed that his patriarch Abraham had talked with Yahweh so he began to set aside a time each day when he'd go apart by himself and just chat aloud quietly to Yahweh. Never did he ever receive an audible reply but somehow after he'd voice his concerns or questions, he usually found the answer would randomly occur to him or the situation would seamlessly resolve itself.

Thanks to the fatherly guidance Othniel, after having lived for more than thirty years, finally began to appreciate the reality and relevance of Yahweh, the God of Israel – his God.

Leviticus 27:30–34

40

Grandchildren

Today was a big day in Othniel's house. The servants had been busy for days preparing food and arranging supplies but now the oxen carts had been loaded, Othniel and Achsah's new clothes had been carefully packed. With Othniel on a camel and Achsah on her donkey the family set off for Hebron. Today Othniel's only daughter was to be married.

Othniel, now forty-seven, reflected on how the years had flown. By his count they'd been living in Anab now for twenty-two years. His olive grove had been extended to cover his entire valley and both his sons helped manage the expanding team of slaves and hired servants. Achsah's few sheep had grown to several thousand as the trusted pasture lands, fed by her ever resilient upper and lower springs, continued to flourish. Caleb now one hundred and seven still enjoyed life as his body aged.

Some time ago Othniel's daughter Rachael began accompanying him on his seemingly frequent trip to Hebron.

Grandchildren

His pretence was to deliver some ongoing part of his tithe but in reality, he simply enjoyed hanging out with a now very old Ithamar. Rachael's reasons were quite the opposite; there were an abundance of young men in Hebron. It seemed ten sons was the unofficial goal of every Levite father.

As Rachael matured her likeness to her mother was uncanny. Like her mother, having older brothers only served to sharpen her competitive streak. Donkey races were her favourite leveller and she often bragged she'd never been beaten in a proper race for years. As for her looks she certainly was her mother's daughter. Tall, with a slim figure, her long black hair enhanced her symmetrical face and sparkly brown eyes. Her personality was bubbly and seldom had Othniel heard her utter a cross word.

Shimei was the fortunate objective of Rachael's affection and much to the dismay of several hundred other young Hebrew men she had became smitten with him about a year prior. His father, one of the serving priesthood, was a man of meagre means and many sons so Othniel quickly agreed a token gesture would serve as a dowry. In the end the payment was a camel saddle. Shimei's had no camel nor any need for a saddle which had been gifted to him as a tithe from an enthusiastic saddle maker some years earlier. Othniel in contrast was delighted, another saddle was just the ticket for his growing caravan of camels. Rachael on the other hand was slightly peeved. The lowly dowry by no means reflected her true worth. Her beloved Shimei had indeed scored a bargain.

In contrast to her parent's wedding, with its focus on celebration, the ceremonial part of Rachael's wedding was of greatest importance. She was carried to the ceremony, just like her mother before her, in a traditional aperion and she was married under a chuppah but that was where the similarities ended. Since the majority of the guests were Levites, they wore the long gowns that had now become synonymous with belonging to the priesthood. Also, because not all Levites could become serving priests a popular occupation was musician. Harps, stringed instruments and cymbals were in abundance as were the players matching harmonies.

Shortly after Rachael had been carried to the chuppah and the bridegroom enticed from his feigned hiding place, a young ram and two young pigeons were slaughtered and offered as a sacrifice to Yahweh. Some of the lamb's life blood was placed carefully on the tip of the right thumb and right ear of both the bride and groom. Othniel didn't remember hearing that requirement in the Torah but these were Levites and Yahweh's priests.

Immediately the lamb was slain a vast chorus of perhaps one hundred musicians broke out in beautiful harmonic melody singing recently composed psalms to Yahweh. Several choruses later an elderly man stepped forward and took the couple's hands. Achsah nudged her husband and whispered, "Isn't that Eleazar, the High Priest?"

"Yes," Othniel replied, "apparently he's a close relative."

Grandchildren

The crowd hushed rapidly as the identity of the officiant sank in. Eleazar efficiently ambled through the brief marital vows then turned to Rachael and said, "Rachael, daughter of Othniel of the Tribe of Judah, you are today marrying Shimei a Levite of the tribe of Levi. By this you are becoming a Levite, a tribe dedicated to the service of Yahweh. Do you solemnly declare before Yahweh that you accept that all the offspring you bear will be Levites and brought up and instructed fully in the ways of Yahweh?" Racheal's agreement was superfluous but she acknowledged it anyway.

Eleazar lifted his hands, raised his voice impressively and stated, "I declare, before Yahweh and all present, that this man and his bride are now man and wife. What Yahweh has joined together, let no man separate. May Yahweh bless you and keep you; may Yahweh make His face to shine upon you and be gracious to you; may Yahweh lift up His countenance upon you and give you perfect peace."

As Eleazar retreated the praise team broke out in yet another extended psalm as Shimei and Racheal were led away to the bridal tent. The singing continued for as long as it took for the young couple to consummate their marriage in the confines of their bridal tent and wave the evidential virginity sheet for all to see. With the certainty the woman entering the Tribe of Levi was indeed a virgin all thoughts and praise of Yahweh were quickly abandoned and the festivities began in earnest.

Ten months later Othniel held his first grandchild, a son. Despite this child officially being deemed a Levite he was in

Othniel's opinion still of his bloodline, his flesh and blood – his grandchild to enjoy.

The next year both Hathath and Meonothai married. Hathath married a young lady from the village of Goshen and Meonothai one from the city of Arab. Keen to be about their father's business they both built new homes in the expanding city of Anab. Hathath, being the firstborn, was set to inherit the larger portion of his father's grand estate so he took over the day-to-day management of the olive grove under the careful and constant watch of his astute parent.

Meonothai, being close to his mother, took over her large flock. The breeding, shearing and weaving of cloth a constant occupation for several hundred slaves and a few hired hands.

Ten years after Rachael's Levitical marriage, and at the grand old age of fifty-seven, Othniel's children had produced a total of seventeen grandchildren. Seven for Rachael, and five each for Hathath and Meonothai. Othniel praised Yahweh as he took on the commitment of training another generation to grow up knowing the ways of Yahweh. Each day he thanked Yahweh for His constant and abundant blessings in the Land.

41

Joshua's Summons

Turning sixty-one was not a milestone birthday but it was a useful an excuse for a family celebration. The confines of the city of Anab placed too many restrictions so a secluded grassy enclave near the lower spring pool was the spot chosen for today's occasion – Othniel's birthday. The servants had been preparing for days and the result was a feast fit for a king; the bounty of an abundant land screaming for consumption.

Othniel sat with his two sons, his son-in-law, his brother Seraiah and his three sons plus an aging Caleb. The women gathered in their own group while the seventeen grandchildren, now aged from four to thirteen, played games and splashed in the spring lake. The day was peaceful and warm and all was right with the world. Having eaten his fill and consumed a good measure of wine, Othniel lay back to rest and quietly thank Yahweh for His many and abundant blessings.

Caleb had turned one hundred and twenty several months ago and almost the entire tribe of Judah turned out for that party. It had lasted five days. Despite his age Caleb kept in reasonable health and still held court two days each week. Two of his wives had died but Achsah's mother, Maachch remained despite being close to eighty. Caleb had enjoyed Yahweh's blessing all his days and found it very easy to enjoy life. The rough, brusque nature of his younger days had morphed into a kindly old great-grandfather. He claimed to have lost count of how many he had and indeed they were many.

As the contented men lay relaxing a young man rode up on a donkey and shouted, "I'm looking for General Caleb, someone in the city of Anab told me I would find him here?" Caleb sat up suddenly very alert, that was a title he hadn't been called officially in a very long time.

"I'm General Caleb," he responded.

"I have a message from Commander Joshua for you Sir," the young man said. "He's assembling all Israel to meet before him at Shechem in ten days. He wants you to send messengers throughout all Judah instructing them to be there – no one is exempt." Having delivered his message, the young man retreated to his donkey and was gone.

"Shechem, that's another day's journey past Shiloh," Caleb stated turning over the command in his mind. "Why not Shiloh, that's a far larger location."

"The message was not really about the location, General," Othniel gently reminded the old man, "he is asking you to spread the command through the cities of Judah."

"Yes, of course. You're quite right," Caleb answered, "Can you see to that for me?" Caleb requested. Othniel quickly agreed and while he didn't say it, military organisation was no longer one of Caleb's core strengths.

The celebrations came to an abrupt end as Othniel raced back to Anab and quickly rounded up one hundred young men to ride or run to all the cities of Judah and give the command. "Every man must present himself to the gates of the city of Shechem within the Tribe of Ephraim. The must be there no later than ten days from today."

A list of cities had been recorded years earlier on small smooth stones and kept in Caleb's quarters. They were arranged carefully by size corresponding to their distance from Anab. The smaller stones were closer, the largest the furthest. Each man was given several stones of similar size and told to deliver the news then return the stone to Caleb's storage. "Go, go, go," Othniel shouted. Within three days all the stones were safely returned and the great migration began.

Othniel prepared a camel specially for Caleb; a well-padded saddle with a sturdy wooden back rest to ensure the General rode with as little discomfort as possible. Othniel figured his camels could easily make the trip to Shechem in four days but in order to get Caleb there unexhausted he decided to spread it over six, which meant they arrived in Shechem one day before Joshua's deadline.

The next morning after arriving in Shechem, the trumpets for general assembly sounded early and immediately Othniel's mind told him he was back in a wilderness tent city. The sounds and smells of camp life, so abundant at that moment, had become quite foreign to the life he now lived. As he traipsed along, half asleep in the breaking dawn, he quietly thanked Yahweh for transforming his life so dramatically from his childhood years.

Othniel had seen Joshua off and on at Passover for most of the past thirty-five years since the war had ended, but the man addressing the crowd today only resembled a shadow of the former Commander of the mighty Army of Israel. However, despite his frail appearance, grey hair and the overuse of his trusty staff, his voice was strong and his words as blunt and cutting as ever.

"A few days ago," Joshua began, "I turned one hundred and six and as you can see, I'm old. I'm not going to live for much longer."

Several in the crowd shouted, "Never, never!"

"It's true," Joshua continued, "soon I will go the way of all before me and I'm very concerned for Yahweh's people, Israel. Will they continue to follow Him after I'm gone, after Caleb has gone and all that generation. So, Yahweh gave me a word to say to you today.

"Long ago your ancestors, including Terah, the father of Abraham and Nahor, lived beyond the Euphrates River, where they worshiped other gods. But Yahweh took your ancestor Abraham from the land beyond the Euphrates and led him into the land of Canaan. He has given him many descendants through his son Isaac. To Isaac He gave Jacob and Esau. To Esau He gave the mountains of Seir, while Jacob and his children went down into Egypt.

"Then Yahweh sent Moses and Aaron, and He brought terrible plagues on Egypt; and afterward He brought you out as a free people. But when your ancestors arrived at the Red Sea, the Egyptians chased after you with chariots. When your ancestors cried out to the Yahweh, He put darkness between you and the Egyptians. He brought the sea crashing down on the Egyptians, drowning all of them. With your very own eyes you saw what He did. You lived in the wilderness for forty years.

"Finally, Yahweh brought you into the land of the Amorites on the east side of the Jordan. They fought against you, but He destroyed them before you. He gave you victory over them and you took possession of their land. Balak, king of Moab, started a war against Israel. He even summoned Balaam to curse you, but Yahweh would not listen to him. Instead, He made Balaam bless you, and so He rescued you from Balak.

"When you crossed the Jordan River and came to Jericho, the men of Jericho fought against you, as did the Amorites, the Perizzites, the Canaanites, the Hittites, the Girgashites, the Hivites and the Jebusites. But Yahweh gave you victory over them. He sent terror ahead of you to drive out the two kings of the Amorites. It was not your swords or bows that brought you victory. Yahweh gave you land you had not worked for, and He gave you towns you did not build—the towns where you are now living. He gave you vineyards and olive groves for food, though you didn't plant them.

"So, fear Yahweh and serve Him wholeheartedly. Put away forever the idols your ancestors worshiped when they lived beyond the Euphrates River and in Egypt. Serve Yahweh only. But if you prefer not to serve Yahweh, then choose today whom you will serve. Do you prefer the gods your ancestors served beyond the Euphrates? Or perhaps the gods of the Amorites in whose land you now live?

"But as for me and my family, we will serve Yahweh." Joshua's words were blunt, fiery, despite his age. He meant every word and the message was clear. A response was urgent.

All the people assembled jumped to their feet and pumped their fist into the air as they cried out. "We would never abandon Yahweh and serve other gods. Yahweh our God is the one who rescued us and our ancestors from slavery in the land of Egypt. He was the one who performed mighty miracles before our very eyes. As we travelled through the wilderness among our enemies, He preserved us. Yes, it was Yahweh who drove out the Amorites and the other nations living here in this land where we now live. Let it be known that we too, Joshua, will serve Yahweh, for He alone is our God."

Joshua was unconvinced and shouted back, "You are not able to serve Yahweh, for He is a holy and jealous God. He will not forgive your rebellion and your sins. If you abandon Yahweh and serve other gods, He will turn against you and destroy you, even though He has been so good to you."

Othniel couldn't help but agree with Joshua. Most of the people only served Yahweh because of custom. They didn't really know Yahweh and hadn't learnt His ways. If someone were to come with a convincing argument they would be quickly persuaded. However, in this moment they were stirred up by Joshua's words and their response was resounding as they shouted, "No, we will serve Yahweh. He is our God!"

"Alright," Joshua shouted, feeling invigorated, more like his younger self. "You are witnesses of your own decision. Your declaration is clear. You have chosen to serve Yahweh."

"Yes," the multitude replied, "we are all witnesses to what we have spoken."

"All right then," Joshua said, "destroy all the idols among you, and turn your hearts completely to Yahweh, the God of Israel."

To which a chorus rang out, "Yes of course we will. We will serve Yahweh our God. We will obey Him alone."

Joshua gathered some scribes together and wrote out a covenant of their commitment to follow Yahweh and the people swore their agreement that same day at Shechem. He reiterated to them that each one present had committed themselves to follow the decrees and regulations of Yahweh.

Joshua recorded their commitment in the Book of God's Instructions. As a reminder of their agreement, he took a huge stone and rolled it beneath a large terebinth tree. Joshua called the people over and said, "This stone has heard everything we have said before Yahweh today. It will be a witness to testify against you if you go back on your word before God."

Othniel couldn't help noticing the irony of the location chosen by Joshua for the extracting of the people's commitment. Shechem was located directly in between Mount Ebal and Mount Gerizim. The two mountains Yahweh had instructed from which to pronounce the blessings and curses on the Land. The actual things that would occur if the people followed Yahweh or what would happen if they turned away.

Next morning Caleb called together all the heads of the Tribe of Judah. "This is a good opportunity," Caleb started, "since we're all together here, to speak of what happens after my pending death. I'm already too old to head up the Tribe of Judah so today we need to appoint a new leader, a younger man who has the strength and energy to lead." It was a sad acknowledgement but all present fully understood the reality of Caleb's words. There were no dissenting voices.

"In that case," Caleb continued, "I propose Othniel, my trusted lieutenant for all these years be hereby appointed today to the position of Elder of the Tribe of Judah." Othniel gulped, this was not his plan for the day. However, if Caleb wished it then he would obey. He would do as Yahweh purposed.

Again, there were no dissenting voices. Caleb turned to Othniel, gave him a great bear hug and said, "Thank you for your years of faithful service from a very young age. May you always walk in the ways of Yahweh and may He bless you with great wisdom to lead the mighty tribe of the sons of Judah."

Joshua 23:1-16, 24:1-28, Deuteronomy 27:12-13.

42

Caleb Dies

As Othniel concluded a land dispute, a function as the Elder of the Tribe of Judah, Charna, his now aging household slave burst into the room. "Master, come quickly, it's the General," she uttered breathlessly. Othniel dropped everything and followed his servant towards the open square of Anab.

A crowd of people huddling together around a patch of payment quickly made way as Othniel approached. The reason for the huddle became immediately apparent. His General, who had led the Tribe of Judah so gallantly for so many years now lay ungracefully on the cold stone pavement of the city square. Othniel, rushed forward and wailed, "Oh, Yahweh, not the General!"

Achsah was already there cradling his head. "What happened," Othniel demanded.

"As far as I can gather," Achsah answered, tears filling her eyes, "he was walking out to sit in the city gates like he always does when suddenly he fell down here and hasn't moved since."

Just at that moment, Caleb took a strong gasping breath of air and a much relieved Othniel said, "Oh, so he's not dead then."

"No, Achsah replied, "but he doesn't respond to anything. I tried to tickle him but he didn't even react to that."

The servants were ordered to make a stretcher of sheepskins, stretched and secured between two study poles. Others were dispatched to the nearby cities to inform all the sons of Caleb of their father's demise. Before long four strong men rolled Caleb onto the newly constructed frame and carried him into his house.

Achsah sat by her father holding his limp hand and Othniel sat on his other side doing the same. One by one each of his eight sons progressively appeared as the news spread. As they entered each one asked the same question, except the last. Immediately he entered the room someone quickly repeated the cause and prognosis.

That day and all that night the vigil continued as all of Caleb's sons and his only daughter and her husband, sat watching their patriarch's life ebb away. Othniel led prayers to Yahweh and recounted some of Caleb's mighty exploits, things the General had told him over the years of the mighty experiences of his life. From his time in Egypt as a slave, the plagues of Egypt, the first Passover and their deliverance from the Egyptian army through the parting of the Red Sea. His time

Caleb Dies

as a spy in Canaan and the rebellion that followed, the forty years in the wilderness then finally into the Promised Land. All the war he'd experienced and the giants he killed until finally he rested here in his inheritance. A lifetime committed to following Yahweh, a great father and teacher, always leading by example.

Sometime just as dawn was beginning to break over another day, the one hundred- and twenty-two-year-old turned his head towards Othniel opened his eyes wide and exhaled his last breath. The gentle giant of a man who had led Judah for so many years was dead.

Immediately it was certain Caleb's breathing had ceased several slaves were ordered to bring an abundance of water, together with several cloths. The men retreated to an outdoor courtyard to discuss the arrangements of informing the Tribe of Judah. Again, the stones were retrieved and one was given to each runner with careful instruction. 'Caleb was dead but no gathering was required or necessary as he is buried today on his inheritance near Anab. Othniel the Elder of Judah gives instruction that all Judah is to mourn Caleb's loss for the next thirty days.' The message was clear and the runners were dispatched with the instruction that immediately on their return they were to place their stone back in the container in the city square ready for their next use.

Meanwhile Achsah and several of her sisters-in-law carefully undressed Caleb and washed every part of his body in thorough preparation for the tomb. All the while about twenty middle aged women sat outside the house wailing and weeping, signifying the passing of a mighty man. The women inside covered Caleb's body with a very liberal coating of myrrh and several other very fragrant herbs then wrapped his body in a clean linen shroud. With the aid of several servants Caleb was lovingly, although perhaps slightly unceremoniously, placed onto the same stretcher that had been used to carry him to his bed the day previous.

About midday the great General's body was ready for his grave. After sending off the runners Caleb's sons had notified all the residents of their respective cities who now obediently assembled at the gates of Anab. Four sturdy men, faithful slaves of Caleb, hoisted his stretcher onto their shoulders and set off for the family tomb. Immediately behind them followed the same twenty women mourners who continued their faithful wailing. Next walked Achsah, supporting her elderly mother Maachch together with all her brothers' wives.

As the procession left the city gates the gathered crowd joined in. Women first, each one wailing like they'd just lost their own firstborn infant, despite the majority perhaps never having ever held a conversation with the man. Next the men joined the throng, Caleb's sons first. Unlike the women they all followed in complete silence, no one uttered a word but, as in Othniel's case, thoughts were rampant.

Down the hillside below Anab they went, around the lower valley and into the gorge of Achsah's upper and lower springs. Along one side of the stream between the springs were rocky cliffs supporting several quite large caves. One such cave had been used as a burial site for centuries. When Caleb arrived in

Anab he had ordered his slaves to clean out all the old bones and burn them. Once he was certain the place was clean, he declared this would be '*his*' family's tomb.

A path along the stream to the cave.

The pallbearers carried the body into the cave while the crowd remained outside. The women's noise became almost deafening as the four carriers carefully lifted Caleb's body from his stretcher onto a rocky ledge. Leaving the body to nature's course, the men retreated to the daylight displaying the empty stretcher where-upon the burial service concluded. The wailing ceased, the tears abated and all the residents returned to their home to attend to their evening chores. A mighty man was no longer a stabilising force throughout the tribe of Judah.

The thirty days of mourning ensued. All festivities were cancelled, solemn subdued clothing was required nor was any man allowed to shave or trim his beard or cut his hair. Apart from the outward adornments normal life continued.

As the days passed Othniel kept himself busy, firstly with managing his crops then with judging a seemingly endless line of family disputes. The majority of which related to inheritance or land grievances. The more interesting cases involved applying the Law of Yahweh to matters of bodily harm or theft. An eye for an eye, a tooth for a tooth.

Despite his busy days, Othniel felt Caleb's loss tremendously. Having an ear of wisdom to listen or advise on complex matters and decisions. For all of his sixty-two years Caleb had always been there. Even when his own father was alive it was Caleb who taught him the important things of life. He taught him how to fight, how to always outwit the enemy, how to enjoy life and especially the value of following Yahweh. Othniel sat in his quiet place and thanked Yahweh for placing Caleb beside him through his life. He asked for wisdom to be able to do the same for the young men he had influence over today.

One year passed quickly and now came the time to bury Caleb. At the time of his death, he had been laid in his grave in the family cave of the dead. However, because space in the cave was limited the shelf where his body had decayed had to be cleared for a future body.

Caleb Dies

Several days ago, a couple of servants had been dispatched to check that only a skeleton remained. Today the family had gathered at the mouth of the cave and the same two servants were instructed to retrieve the bones and bring them out on a large linen shroud for the family to pack. This was work for women while the men watched on.

Each bone was separated from the skeleton and stacked neatly in the centre of the shroud until eventually all the bones made a tidy compact pile about a metre (three feet) long by half a metre wide and high. The bones were then securely tied and wrapped within the shroud. The family stood and watched, saying their final goodbyes as the same two servants carried the pack of bones and placed them carefully on a pile of several others at the back of the cave. The shelf where Caleb's body had decayed was swept clean ready for its next occupant.

The women, Achsah included, who had handled the bones went off to the lower spring to wash and bath in water to cleanse their bodies. In accordance with the Torah, the Laws of Yahweh, they would remain unclean for seven days. A situation most women were well accustomed with as the same requirement was made each menstrual month.

It was only two years later when a messenger arrived with the news Othniel was dreading; Joshua had died. He was one hundred and ten years old. As with Caleb, Joshua had already been buried by the time the news reached him. His family had lain his body in his family tomb at the edge of Joshua's inheritance on the North side of Mount Gaash in the mountains of his Tribe, Ephraim.

Throughout all the cities of Israel thirty days of mourning were decreed and again, no hair cutting, no bright clothes nor any festivities. Othniel felt the loss deeply. He had been well acquainted with Joshua and understood his ways well but he'd never been close to him. He was however a father in Israel and someone appointed by Yahweh who could determine matters hard to judge. Nobody had been appointed as his replacement and this concerned Othniel greatly.

Eleazar the High Priest had also died not long after Caleb and his son Phinehas, about Othniel's age, was now High Priest. While Phinehas could be relied on to continue the traditions of the Tabernacle, he was not an adjudicator.

It seemed that every year yet another elder in Israel, and in Judah in particular, died and Othniel himself, although only sixty-six years old, was fast becoming one of the older men in Israel and in Judah in particular. His role as Elder of the Tribe only served to cement the fact that he was now at the top of the generational tree.

Judges 2:8-10.

43

Turning Away

It was a barmy evening and Othniel had been busy finalising his olive harvest. His son Hathath did the bulk of the supervision but Othniel liked to keep involved and today had been his involved day. Now he sat relaxing, drinking some wine and reflecting on not a lot, as he waited for his evening meal. Life was good in the Land.

From his rooftop Othniel had a great view of the central square in the town's centre. The area was used for assembly and market stalls, where several locals and travelling groups sold their produce, trinkets and such like. The square was also used by travellers who, on arrival, would sit together with their animals in the hope that someone would invite them in. Mostly this happened but if not, the square was a secure place to pitch a tent and spend a night.

Othniel watched as a man and his wife arrived with several donkeys and unloaded near the centre of the square. These visitors didn't seem interested in being taken in as they immediately set up their tents, fed their donkeys and went about preparing an evening meal. Othniel's observance was simply through curiosity, he found people watching interesting. Suddenly however, tonight his mild curiosity turned to shock, then horror.

After the visitor had fed his donkeys, he had unloaded a pack of stones from one of the donkeys then arranged the stones to form a small shrine. Once complete, he arranged several small wooden images around its top then lit a small fire. When the fire had taken hold, he called his wife and they both kneeled before the shrine. The man poured a flammable substance onto the fire which Othniel rightly assumed was incense. As the incense smoke swirled and rose the kneeling couple bowed forward until their heads were on the ground, repeating it three times.

Othniel was stunned. This man, presumably an Israelite, had wandered into his village and was blatantly serving foreign gods. The first commandment rang loudly in his ears; "I am the LORD your God, who rescued you from the land of Egypt, the place of your slavery. You must not have any other god but me." Rage filed Othniel's spirit as he leapt to his feet, rushed down his steps and across to the square.

"What, in the name of Yahweh, do you think you're doing?" Othniel shouted. Without waiting for a reply, he picked up the man's god images and threw them into the fire. He then began tossing the stones forming the shrine out across the square. The man jumped forward to rescue his wooden gods and defend his actions but Othniel shoved him to the ground.

A crowd quickly gathered as shouting in the midst of their tranquil city on a balmy summer evening was certainly not the norm. Othniel still in a rage turned his attention to the visitor. He rushed towards him, grabbed his garment just below his jaw and threw the man against a nearby ox cart. Still holding firm, he roared at the man, "Who are you and which city are you from?"

The startled man turned white as a sheet, never in his life had anyone treated him like this. Anab, he noted to himself was far from a friendly host. "I'm from the city of Nob of the Tribe of Judah," the man croaked.

"And this woman, I'm assuming is your wife, where is she from?" Othniel continued.

The man was a little more hesitant to answer that question, fearing the worst he said, "She is a Jebusite from the city of Jebus (later renamed Jerusalem by King David). It's very near our city and we trade with them. Many in my area have taken wives from there."

Othniel grunted and let go of the man who collapsed to the ground. "How old are you?" Othniel asked.

"Twenty-four," the man replied, relieved at the change of subject.

"Have you never heard of the Laws of Yahweh that Moses gave to us?" Othniel continued.

"Of course," the man answered.

"In that case, why are you worshiping these bits of wood?"

The man cheered up considerably and explained, "It was my wife that taught me. She has worshiped Baal all her life and everything has been good for her. Baal even saved her city from an attack by Israel during the invasion war."

Again, Othniel's rage soared as he heard the man's explanation. "This is exactly why Yahweh told us to never marry foreign wives," Othniel shouted. "Also, Baal never protected the city of Jebus, it's just that we've never made a serious attack on it yet. Someday however we will," Othniel added.

Othniel turned to the spectator crowd and asked, "Who else among you here saw this man and his wife bowing in worship to their foul images?" Several people put up their hands. "And are you prepared to testify to that fact even against this man's life?" Othniel queried. A couple of hands dropped down but the rest assured him that they too were outraged at the man's heinous act.

Othniel turned to a nearby young man asking, "Can you ride a camel?"

"Of course, sir" the man replied, regardless of competence.

"Quick, take two of mine and ride swiftly to Hebron and bring back a priest, someone who can read the Ten Commandments to us. Be back here by first light tomorrow and don't forget the Torah scroll."

As the young man set off on his appointed mission Othniel ordered some slaves to quickly adjust one of the oxen pens to make it secure from human escape. He then commanded others to bring some new rope and tie these traitors' feet and hands and throw them into the confines of the secured pen.

The young man and his wife pleaded for leniency assuring Othniel they would never worship Baal again. But to no avail and two very frightened people were thrown into a well-used oxen pen to spend a rather uncomfortable night. "Your judgement will be announced tomorrow, after the Law is read," Othniel advised as he locked them in.

Next morning the young man returned from Hebron early with two priests and a scribe who was charged with caring for the Torah scroll. Othniel called together all the city of Anab and commanded the prisoners be brought out. A sleep deprived couple stood to one side with Othniel in the centre. The witnesses from the previous evening were called to stand on his right side along with the priest. Othniel called the scribe to come forward to read the first commandment Moses had been given.

The scribe rolled the scroll to the page and began reading loudly to the people; "I am the LORD your God, who rescued you from the land of Egypt, the place of your slavery. You must not have any other god but me."

As he finished Othniel thanked the scribe then asked, "And what does the Torah say the penalty is to be for those that break this law?"

Again, the scribe rolled the scroll and found the section that dealt with penalties and read; "Suppose someone secretly entices you—even your brother, your son or daughter, your beloved wife, or your closest friend—and says, 'Let us go worship other gods'—gods that neither you nor your ancestors have known. They might suggest that you worship the gods of peoples who live nearby or who come from the ends of the earth. But do not give in or listen. Have no pity, and do not spare or protect them. You must put them to death! Strike the first blow yourself, and then all the people must join in. Stone the guilty ones to death because they have tried to draw you away from the LORD your God, who rescued you from the land of Egypt, the place of slavery." Again, Othniel thanked the scribe and asked him to take a seat.

Othniel addressed the group of witnesses and ask, "Did you see this man and his wife bow down and worship their images of Baal in our city square last night?" All the witnesses agreed and clearly affirmed they saw the evil act. "Did you also hear the man later say that his wife, a Jebusite, had enticed him to turn to Baal and worship him?" Again, the witnesses strongly agreed.

Othniel turned to the priests and said, "Can you please confirm that the Law requires at least two witnesses before a death sentence can be carried out?" The priests confirmed that yes that definitely is correct. "Then," Othniel continued, "can you confirm that today we have heard from more than two witnesses that this man and his wife did in fact carry out this despicable act?" The priest again quickly confirmed.

Othniel turned to address the prisoners and the gathered crowd. "It has been confirmed by many witnesses that you did worship a foreign god in our midst. We also heard that the Law of Yahweh prohibits such worship. We also heard from the Torah, the Law of Yahweh, given to us by Moses, that the penalty for worship of foreign gods is death by stoning. It is very clear that we have no other option but to carry out this sentence otherwise we too will come under the wrath of Yahweh for condoning the act.

"Carry them outside this great city and stone them until they're dead," Othniel commanded. The young couple protested loudly weeping and howling their regret as they were carried out and dumped into a large open area outside the city gates. The gathered crowd, around a thousand, and each picked up several stones as some young men quickly untied the visitors then dived for cover. As soon as the young men cleared a volley of a thousand rocks slammed into the young couple who fell silently to the ground and into the darkness of death.

Othniel felt the relief that the judgement of the visitors brought but he remained troubled by the young man's words that many in his city of Nob followed Baal. Next morning Othniel said goodbye to his beautiful but aging wife and set off on his trusty camel to see for himself the extent of the turning away from Yahweh throughout the land.

He rode off alone and two days later he arrived in the city of Nob. His quick inquiries confirmed the young man's words. Baal worship was rife in the city. A large image of the false god graced their city courtyard. Despite many invitations to stay the night Othniel declined and spent the night in an open field.

Was it just Nob or were there others? Next morning Othniel set off to visit as many cities in Israel as possible, to determine the extent of this turning away. Over the next month Othniel travelled to the very Northern tip of the border of the Land. He crossed the Jordan and travelled through all the eastern tribes then back along the Great Sea and finally to the confines of Anab.

What he saw disturbed him greatly, how quickly so many had turned away for Yahweh. Far from it just being the city of Nob many cities throughout the land had turned to public, unashamed idol worship. What angered him even more was the deafening absence of any dissenting voices. Several he met agreed with him but then quickly added, "What can we do about it?"

Othniel knew what to do however. He went up onto his rooftop and prayed and fasted for forty days and forty nights. Every day he cried out to Yahweh, repenting on behalf of his people who were so quickly rejecting Him. Asking Yahweh what could be done? How could this false worship be stopped? Yahweh didn't answer Othniel directly but he did receive an overwhelming sense of peace. He knew that Yahweh had heard his prayers and that he, Othniel, had acted righteously in dealing with the matter in his city of Anab.

Deuteronomy 13:6-10, Judges 3:5-7

44

Cushan-Rishathaim

Hashem was up early as he wanted to get his few sheep out onto a new pasture he'd spotted the day previous. Living in the valley of Dan, the city of Laish was a region of hot summers and well-watered pastures. Sheep breeding thrived in such an environment. This year, however, the rains had failed and good grass was a rare commodity.

Before setting off Hashem made his way in the breaking dawn to the square of the sleeping city, the only other early riser was a young rooster who crowed proudly in the distance. Hashem, a natural loner, enjoyed the serenity of this time of day. Arriving at the large solid silver image named the god of Laish, tended so lavishly by their very own Levite priest Micah, Hashem made a small offering of incense and bowed prostrate before the gleaning silver image. "Oh, please keep me safe, bring me to good pastures today and make it rain soon," he muttered.

Satisfied his day would be blessed, he tucked his wooden Baal image in his belt and set off to his sheep. Hashem counted out his twenty-three ewes and set off for the city gates. Since he was first to leave the city that day the unguarded gates were still securely lock – from the inside. Not that this secluded valley was in imminent danger but just to keep out stragglers and particularly wild animals. Lions and bears were common in the mountains and Hashem had close encounters with them on several occasions.

The glow of a rising sun was becoming strong behind Mount Hermon as Hashem pulled the gate open wide, whistling a merry tune as he led his flock out. Suddenly a razor-sharp sword smashed into Hashem's neck and he fell to the ground oblivious of the cause, embraced in the darkness of death. His attacker, having achieved his goal of capturing the city gates without alarm, beckoned for his companions to relinquish their hideouts and join him on a march into the city square. Within minutes close to five thousand heavily armed soldiers stood silently in the middle of Laish waiting for the city to awaken.

Cushan-Rishathaim was the king of Mesopotamia to the North of the land of Israel. He ruled from the region of Aram (located in present-day Syria about where the modern-day city of Aleppo now stands). His territory stretched from the Lebanon mountains eastward across the Euphrates, to parts of the Khabur River valley in North-Western Mesopotamia, (to the border of present-day Iraq.)

Although Cushan-Rishathaim wasn't a compassionate man his goal wasn't to slaughter and possess. He was focused on spoil and tribute. After hearing that the great commander of Israel, Joshua, had died he saw the land of Israel as unprotected. And indeed, it truly was, as Yahweh had lifted His hand from most of the land because of the wide-scale idolatry that had rapidly sprung up.

Cushan-Rishathaim had ordered his troops, about twenty thousand strong, to move down into Israel and take these unprotected cities by stealth. The death of Hashem this day simply provided his troops the means of gaining the city without a fight.

Back in Laish it didn't take too long for the assembled troops to be noticed. It was a maid going about her morning chores that saw them first. She screamed and ran to her master who in turn ran to the house of the city elder, slamming on his door in the dawn light. Immer, the Elder of the Tribe of Dan angrily opened his door to settle the commotion, but just as he opened his mouth to speak, he noticed the obvious reason and no words flowed – thousands of heavily armed foreign troops stood motionless in his city centre not more than fifty metres (one hundred and fifty feet) from his front door. Without a word he left his door open and disappeared inside, returning less than minutes later more suitably dressed. His long disused sword hung clumsily to one side.

Immer marched over to the troops demanding to know who they were and exactly what they were doing in his city? Three burley men jumped forward, grabbed him with zero resistance, removed his sword, then marched him to their Commander in the centre of the gathered army.

Through a translator the Commander explained, "That if all his wishes were carried out then nobody in the city would be harmed. They hadn't come for death but for spoil and tribute. His men would search every house and take whatever they fancied, there were no rules; fair maidens included. After we have emptied the city to our betterment then we'll leave," the Commander continued. "However, every year some of our men will be back to collect a payment of one thousand shekels of sliver. Is that clear?"

Immer wanted to shout, 'heck no!' but with so many armed men breathing down his neck what could he say. Finally, he spoke for the first time and said, "It must be the will of our gods. There's nothing I can do." Any thought or mention of Yahweh never entered his mind, so far had his transition become.

Immediately the Commander shouted, "Thank you for your cooperation, your life will be spared." He then turned to his men shouting commands only understood by them. A mighty roar went up and the soldiers disbursed in every direction, forcibly entering house after house.

Much screaming and shouting ensued but to no avail, the Commander's wishes were carried out. By the end of the day the entire city had been stripped of everything of value. Not one weapon of war remained. Every young virgin was removed as was all silver and gold, most clothing and much of their food storage. Dozens of oxen carts, previously owned by the city, stood laden with treasures. As darkness fell the laden army moved out of a grieving and very subdued Laish.

Cushan-Rishathaim

Surprisingly the large silver image that graced the city square remained, the invaders afraid to remove the people's gods. Several men gathered Hashem's body and considering him the traitor who allowed the attack, carried him to the nearest cliff and tossed his body over.

Seeing the ease of attack and lack of consequences for the uplifting of so much spoil from Laish, Cushan-Rishathaim ordered his men to slowly make their way South deeper into the Land of Israel. "Take as much spoil as you want for your wages, and order tribute for me," he directed.

Over the next eight years almost half the cities in the northern part of Israel and all the cities of the Eastern Tribes had been overrun by this ruthless tyrant Cushan-Rishathaim without a major battle.

Othniel walked towards the city gates one morning. His heart was heavy at the thought of how quickly the people of Israel had turned away from Yahweh after all the blessings He'd poured out on them for the past forty-seven years. How quickly His strong arm had been forgotten. All His miracles in bringing His people out of Egypt and guiding them through the desert for forty years. Why had the fathers not passed this on to the next generation? He thanked Yahweh for men like Caleb who had sowed an understanding of Yahweh into his entire life.

As Othniel got to the gates a very exhausted runner approached. "Please tell me where I can find Othniel, the Elder of Judah," he gasped.

"That would be me," Othniel replied as he commanded one of his nearby servants to provide water to the lad.

After consuming a couple of gourds of water the young man's speech strengthened as he said, "Father Othniel, the city of Nob has been overrun by the troops of Cushan-Rishathaim, King of Mesopotamia. He gained entry to the city by stealth then took everything, most of our clothes and food. All our weapons are gone and all our silver and gold plus he took all our virgins. What's more, he demands we pay him a tribute of one thousand shekels of silver each year. The Elders of our city sent me here to ask for your help," he concluded.

Othniel thought for a while as he reflected on the young man from Nob that had visited Anab some time back. He also considered his own visit to Nob a few weeks later and his abhorrence at their worship of the wooden god, Baal. Eventually Othniel said, "I have a message to take back to your Elders. Go pray to your gods for help, don't come to me. You have rejected Yahweh and He has lifted His support."

The young man stood staring at Othniel. This wasn't the level of support he'd expected from the leader of his Tribe. His city Elders had told him to ask for military assistance to deliver their city. "What are you waiting for?" Othniel shouted. "Get going with the message, NOW!" Sensing he'd outlived his welcome the young boy took to his heels and ran for Nob.

Othniel, however, abandoned all thought of work for the day. Judah was under attack. He had to talk to Yahweh. He

Cushan-Rishathaim

walked up onto his rooftop, fell prostrate and remained there until darkness fell that evening.

Judges 3:7-8

45

The Call

Othniel's thoughts troubled him, at seventy-five the thought of going to war had little appeal. And if they did go to war, on what basis could they expect Yahweh's help as the whole nation had turned to idol worship. Surely He'd just tell them to 'go, call on their chosen gods of wood.'

The desire to sleep eluded Othniel and he remained all night on his rooftop in the balmy air. Anger raged in his heart; how could anyone who had seen or heard of all the wonders and miracles that Yahweh had done possibly imagine that a carved piece of wood could ever do anything remotely similar, let along better. Whichever way he looked at it he couldn't find any logic or sense – a block of wood in preference to Yahweh – the living God.

Through the wee hours of the night Othniel's heart was drawn into a deep reflective mood. He felt his spirit drawing him to recount his upbringing, what had made him follow Yahweh so diligently. He reflected on his own father Kenaz

The Call

who, despite not having been born an Israelite, had developed a deep love for the Promised Land. A love that had been built into his heart by his adopted father Jephunneh. For as long as Othniel could remember, his father had told him how wonderful the Land was and how he had planned to possess a vineyard but that because of the curse brought about by those negative spies he would never see it. The consequence for his father of not speaking up when he knew his own brother, Caleb, was right, had cost him his inheritance.

Othniel recalled his resolve from a young age to speak up whenever he saw an injustice. He now repented before Yahweh because despite having seen the injustice of Baal worship eight years ago after the man from Nob was stoned, and his trip around Israel, he did nothing. He had prayed and fasted but that was all. He was the Elder of Judah, it was his job to speak up. He hadn't and now masses of Israelites were under bondage again even in the Promised Land! "Yahweh, I'm sorry," Othniel cried as genuine tears of repentance streamed freely.

As he sat in his gloom his thoughts were directed to his uncle and General, Caleb. He'd known Caleb for over sixty years, far longer than his own father who died when he was only nineteen. In all the time he'd known him he had never once seen Caleb doubt Yahweh, ever. In Caleb's words, 'If Yahweh has said it, then He will do it.' Caleb lived by that motto and every time he'd stepped out Yahweh had come through for him.

Othniel could feel his spirit stirring as he reflected on Caleb's methods. The first time he took him and his son Elah to train for war he'd given them both real, lethal weapons encouraging them both to kill the other. How at first it had seemed like a joke until the realisation dawned that unless he actually fought back he would be the one to die. Had Caleb not intervened that day one of them would have indeed died. The lesson; no holding back when under attack, there are no second chances in war nor in life.

Then Othniel pondered on the many days of battle he'd fought alongside Caleb as his lieutenant. Whatever he did, he did in the name of his God, Yahweh. And he did everything that Yahweh said. He always finished the job completely. If Yahweh decreed every living soul dead, then regardless of how he felt about killing women or children he did so because his fear of Yahweh was greater. Othniel knew that that same reasoning had been instilled in his own heart.

Yahweh, the mighty God of Israel required absolute obedience. However, that same God also focused all His protection and blessing on those who did His will completely. Othniel reflected on the blessings he'd received from Yahweh. His incredible wife, his large farmlands and two great sons to continue in his inheritance. Never once had the rains failed to come and always had his crops been plentiful.

His thoughts drifted to Ithamar the old scribe and priest of Hebron guarding the Torah. How he had taught Othniel the Laws of Yahweh. Unlike the young Levite that had read the Laws to him while still in the wilderness, when Ithamar read, he gave the Word life and meaning. He showed that everything Yahweh said was for a reason, sometimes because there was a blessing attached, other times it was for health or wellbeing and other times it was simply because He said so. Nothing with Yahweh was optional and everything was for a reason, regardless of his understanding of the reason.

As the dark of night began to give way to light his thoughts were directed back to the current state in Israel. Idol worship was rife and exactly as Yahweh had said repeatedly in His Law, He had bought an adversary against the nation. If this invading king was to be rid from the land, then the root cause had to be dealt with. The more he reflected on this the more certain Othniel became; If his people truly repented and turned back fully then Yahweh would support His people and get rid of this foreign invader. There would be war!

At that very moment a profound truth dropped into Othniel's heart. In his reasoning the previous evening he'd questioned how a people who had seen all Yahweh's might and miracles could turn away from Yahweh so quickly and easily? Now the truth was glaringly obvious as he had reflected on his life. He'd had Caleb, Ithamar and, to a lesser extent, his own father all sow into his life. They had all seen first-hand the great things that Yahweh had done and, not only had they told him about it, they had demonstrated their belief in Yahweh's continuing might through their living actions.

However, throughout the Land of Israel there were very few such fathers. So few that had, or that were willing to, pass on their knowledge and experience of Yahweh to the next generation. This was the reason for the falling away, there were not many fathers in Israel. All the fathers that had nurtured

Othniel were dead, therefore it was now his turn to step up and be a father to Israel. The enormity of that task hit him like a camel train, "Okay, Yahweh," Othniel spoke aloud, "but I can only do it with your help. Please show me how?"

As soon as Othniel had uttered those words he felt an overwhelming surge in his spirit and he knew, that he knew that he knew, the hand of Yahweh had come upon him.

Othniel descended from his rooftop, greeted his wife and called together the young men from the nearby cities. He selected eleven of them and after ensuring they could ride a camel, he gave them a mission. "Each of you are to take one of my camels and ride to the Elder of the Tribe I tell you of. Once you have found the Elder you must order him to discretely leave his village and meet me in Shiloh, at the Tabernacle there, in ten days from today. Hurry, do not loiter anywhere on the way, and come straight back here when you're done."

By noon all the camel riders had gone. Othniel went to the pool, washed his body thoroughly, washed his clothes and asked Yahweh to cleanse him for his inaction eight years ago when he had first seen the turning away. He had his servants prepare two oxen carts, secure enough to hold twenty female lambs. That night he slept in his own bed, a restful deep sleep, secure in the knowledge that all that he was about to do was the work of Yahweh.

Next morning at dawn he said goodbye to his faithful wife, mounted a donkey and rode off with the loaded oxen carts driven by his two sons. The going was slow and each night

The Call

involved a new city. Othniel's preference was to sleep in the open because of the idolatry in the cities but his sons were concerned for the sheep, "Too many lions about," they explained.

Despite the presence of so many idols Othniel told himself, 'Not long now.'

Five days later they rode into the city of Shiloh and straight to the door of the Tabernacle. Othniel commanded his sons to bring one of the oxen and three lambs as he strode off to find a priest. Previously the Tabernacle was bustling with activity, people coming and going with various offerings for cleansing, sin and a myriad of other reasons. Today, however, the place was almost deserted. The remains of the morning offering smouldered on the bronze altar, one or two servants stacked firewood in a neat pile behind the altar but there was not a priest to be seen.

"Where's the priest?" Othniel asked a servant.

"Oh, probably asleep in his abode over there," the servant answered pointing in the general direction. Non-Levites weren't usually allowed into the Tabernacle but without a soul around Othniel's anger raged. He marched over to the priest quarters and bust the door open. A startled overweight priest sat bolt upright in his chair.

"How dare you leave the house of Yahweh unattended," Othniel bellowed. Unaccustomed to such demands the priest jumped to his feet and asked what he could do, Sir. "Where is the High Priest?" Othniel asked. "I have a sin offering to present."

The priest scurried off and about half an hour later returned with a young man fully decked out in the clothes of the High Priest. While he did look the part, he was not Phinehas the High Priest Othniel knew. "Where's Phinehas," Othniel demanded.

"Oh, my apologies," the young man answered politely, "my name is Abishua. Phinehas, the High Priest, is my father but he has gone back to his city and has left me in charge. How can I help you?"

With the explanations complete Abishua sent a servant to summon several Levites to help with the pending offering. While they were waiting Abishua explained that things were incredibly quiet at the Tabernacle these days. Since the invasions had started, visits from the people had progressively slowed and since the last Passover had stopped completely. "They seem more intent on worshiping Baal then coming here to meet with Yahweh," Abishua explained sadly. "Apart from the morning and evening offering there's not much else to do."

"Well, I'm here to change all that," Othniel answered.

With a full quota assembled, Abishua had Othniel and his sons lay their hands on Othniel's ox and asked them to confess their sin. Othniel recounted his laxness in not speaking up about the Baal worship and asked Yahweh to forgive the sin of His people, of which he was a part. With the confessions done, Abishua sliced the animals throat while a couple of Levites captured the draining blood as it collapsed to the ground.

As the Levites set to work skinning and gutting the oxen Abishua took one of the bowls of blood and, after dipping a small brush into it, he flicked it once towards Othniel splattering him and his sons with the blood. He then sprinkled seven brush loads before Yahweh in front of the veil to the Holy place. With that complete the priest put some of the blood on the horns of the golden altar in the Holy place. He then poured all the remaining blood carefully at the base of the bronze altar. The ox was prepared, dissected and carried outside the Tabernacle by a few serving Levites, some distance away to be burned separately. All the fat, the two kidneys and the fatty lobe attached to the liver had been faithfully removed and the priest carefully placed them onto the now blazing altar which quickly consumed the fatty parts. "The ox burning in the flame outside is a substitute for you, Othniel, to pay a penalty for your sin," Abishua explained.

With the ox offered, the three lambs were presented as a guilt offering, as sacrifice of gratitude to Yahweh. Othniel and his sons each took their turn as their ram was slaughtered, its blood sprinkled and the bodies burnt. It was close to dusk when the proceedings drew to a close.

Later Othniel called Abishua aside and explained to him why he had come and that he had ordered the Elders from each tribe to meet him here in Shiloh in four days. He 'requested' that Phinehas be sent for, together with a large number of other priest and Levites. It was time to start the cleansing of Israel.

Judges 3:9, Leviticus 4:2-12, Leviticus 5:5-6.

46

Idols

Twelve men plus Phinehas the High Priest sat on the ground under a large open sided tent covering near the entrance of the Tabernacle. Before Othniel had time to explain what Yahweh had laid on his heart the other Elders began. This King, Cushan-Rishathaim is a plague from the very pit of Hades. Not only had he taken all their goods, weapons and young daughters, they had imposed a massive tribute on every city. And he sent his men every year without fail to collect his due.

On and on they went. Othniel tried to steer the conversation but their hurt and distress was obvious and this was their opportunity to vent. The immediate consensus was to call all Israel together and go to war. "Nobody pushes the people of Israel around like that!"

Eventually, with their anger vocalised, the talking slowed and Othniel stood and addressed his fellow elders. "My brothers", Othniel began, "the anguish our people are under is obvious to all. The reason I called you all here today is to answer the following question; Why has Yahweh allowed this to happen?"

Immediately Othniel mentioned the name of Yahweh a chorus of voices erupted. "Don't talk to me about Yahweh, we've cried out to Him for years and He doesn't answer," one said.

"He doesn't care for Israel anymore," another shouted.

"Since we've worship Baal properly," another said, "we've had peace in our cities. Provided we pay our tribute on time," he added.

"Enough," Othniel shouted. "Yahweh is the God of Israel. There is a reason why all this has come upon us. I have asked Phinehas to have his chief scribe read some sections from the Torah. I would ask, no actually," he corrected, "I insist you all sit quietly and listen. Our lives depend upon this."

The scribe stood and opened the scroll that lay on the table in front of him. He cleared his throat and began.

"I am the LORD your God, who rescued you from the land of Egypt, the place of your slavery. You must not have any other god but me." As he finished Othniel thanked the scribe then asked, "And what does the Torah say the penalty is to be for those that break this law?"

Again, the scribe rolled the scroll and found the section that dealt with penalties and read; "Suppose someone secretly entices you—even your brother, your son or daughter, your beloved wife, or your closest friend—and says, 'Let us go and worship other gods—gods that neither you nor your ancestors have known. They might suggest that you worship the gods of peoples who live nearby or who come from the ends of the earth. But do not give in or listen. Have no pity, and do not spare or protect them. You must put them to death! Strike the first blow yourself, and then all the people must join in. Stone the guilty ones to death because they have tried to draw you away from the LORD your God, who rescued you from the land of Egypt, the place of slavery."

"That is Yahweh's Law about foreign gods," Othniel stated. "Now will you please read the section on what Yahweh has said He will do if we turn away from Him?"

The scribe turned to a new section and again read emphatically.

"If you refuse to listen to Yahweh your God and to obey the commands and decrees He has given you, all His curses will pursue and overtake you until you are destroyed. These horrors will serve as a sign and warning among you and your descendants forever. If you do not serve Yahweh your God with joy and enthusiasm for the abundant benefits you have received, you will serve your enemies whom Yahweh will send against you. You will be left hungry, thirsty, naked, and lacking in everything. Yahweh will put an iron yoke on your neck, oppressing you harshly until He has destroyed you.

"Yahweh will bring a distant nation against you from the end of the earth, and it will swoop down on you like a vulture. It is a nation whose language you do not understand, a fierce and heartless nation that shows no respect for the old and no pity for the young. Its armies will devour your livestock and crops, and you will be destroyed. They will leave you no grain, new wine, olive oil, calves or lambs, and you will starve to death. They will attack your cities until all the fortified walls in your land—the walls you trusted to protect you—are knocked down. They will attack all the towns in the land the LORD your God has given you."

The scribe had barely finished when Othniel was on his feet fuming with anger, "What part of that last section my friend just read would you say describes our current situation," Othniel roared, his face flushed as he stomped around the circle glaring at each Elder. "Yahweh is the God of Israel! As we heard, that is His very first commandment. How dare any of you allow any member of your Tribe to bend their knee to a lump of wood they call Baal. Yahweh is our God; He is a living God. We must turn back to Him today!"

The men squirmed uncomfortably as Othniel's words hit home. "Fortunately, Yahweh is gracious, and forgiving," Othniel continued. "If we repent and put away these false gods and call on the name of Yahweh, He will return to us and He will deliver us from the hand of this evil invader. Unless we do that, we are all doomed to die. Have I made myself clear?" Othniel asked.

A couple of Elders quickly muttered in the affirmative and Othniel continued. "Right, since we all agree, here is what I want you to do. Each one of you are to call every man from your Tribe to assemble here within seven days from today. We will go through this same process with them and cleanse this nation.

"While they're getting here Phinehas will explain to you how and what to offer to Yahweh to cleanse yourselves. Now get to it. Go, go, go!" and he chased the men out of the tent, his anger at their sin spiralling into the physical.

Phinehas explained that each of the men had to offer a female lamb as a guilt offering and a male ox as a sin offering for all of you. Othniel listened while the Elders explained they didn't have any animals with them and could someone please give them one. "An offering without cost is meaningless," Othniel interrupted. "You'll have to buy an offering and as it happens, I brought along some spare ones."

The men were delighted at such an easy solution and quickly produced the ten shekels, the current going rate for a male lamb. "Actually, the price is one hundred shekels," Othniel stated calmly. After a raucous chorus claiming robbery, extortion and several unmentionables had subsided Othniel spoke calmly, "I want to make sure these offerings hurt. Why would you not be prepared to pay a high price to clear yourselves before Yahweh, the mighty God of Israel?"

After a short robust discussion each of the eleven men handed Othniel one hundred shekels each for a lamb and a further fifty shekels for their joint share in an ox for the sin offering. As the men walked off to the Tabernacle with their expensive offerings, Othniel quietly handed Phinehas, the High Priest, the one thousand six hundred shekels he'd recently

Idols

acquired. "A bonus offering to Yahweh," Othniel said with a smile.

During the intervening seven days after the call went out for all Israel to assemble urgently at Shiloh, Phinehas took the Elders aside and made them listen to the complete Law of Yahweh as given to Moses. Othniel demanded that every man bring their idols, their wooden Baal images and throw them in a pile outside the city gates. Much to his surprise, after hearing Othniel's words and listening to the full Law all the Elders and their supporting entourages reacted quickly to his demands. Their eagerness to avoid any further promised wrath of Yahweh plain for all to see. Once the pile was complete Othniel set it alight and declared Yahweh is the ONLY God.

Phinehas and the other priests walked the Elders through the required offerings for the cleansing of the Nation and by the time all Israel began to assemble on the sixth and seventh day the transformed Elders were all firmly of the same mind as Othniel. For many, it was the first time they'd heard the Torah read in over fifty years despite most being in their sixties and seventies.

On the eighth day, the Priest blew the trumpet early and all the men of every tribe of Israel assembled in the open space beyond the Tabernacle. Close to one million men and boys stood and listened while the same senior scribe read the relevant sections of the Law, gave the emphasis and explained the meaning.

Once the scribe had finished Othniel stood and addressed the people. "As you have heard, Yahweh is deeply displeased with Israel because we have so quickly turned after other gods. Repeat after me," he shouted, "Yahweh is the only living God. Yahweh is the God of Israel." Again, and again, he had the people repeat the affirmation, each time the words grew louder and the enthusiasm stronger.

Eventually Othniel stood and in his zeal for his God, Yahweh, shouted, "You have heard the Law. You deserve to die because of your Baal worship. Repent before Yahweh. Every man that has any type of image of any god, Baal or otherwise, I order you to bring it immediately and we'll make a great burning of them today."

A few hours later a massive pile of trinkets and wooden images stood just outside the city gates which Othniel quickly set alight. Again, he cried, "Great is Yahweh, the only great and mighty living God of Israel."

Next day Phinehas called the people together and explained the need for sacrifice and sin offerings for the people. He was about to offer Yahweh a red heifer offering for the sin of the nation. Any man who wished to bring his own sin offering was instructed to do so, the Tabernacle was open.

Othniel thanked Phinehas and urged everyone to seek Yahweh with all their heart and listen to the Law which the Levites would be reading every day. "But first," he shouted, "every one of you is to wash their bodies and clothes in a nearby stream today because, as from tomorrow, all Israel will have a three day fast and call on the name of Yahweh to deliver us from this evil king."

Later that day, Othniel sat with the same group of Elders and their trusted advisors. "We have to put an end to this man Cushan-Rishathaim who dares to come against the people of Yahweh. Any suggestions?" Various ideas were put forward but most were rejected as being too grandiose or impractical.

After much discussion Othniel said, "It's clear this King's governance over us must end today, whether he likes it or not. I suggest we simply send him a written message saying that 'The nation of Israel herewith rebels against your authority over us. We will no longer pay you any tribute or serve your wishes. Yahweh is our God and He will protect us.'"

The agreement with Othniel's simple plan was immediate and a scribe was called who recorded the message neatly. Later that afternoon a messenger rode off to the region of Aram with a rather small but potentially explosive letter tucked in his belt.

Over the next three days all Israel fasted and waited for a reply from their previous oppressor Cushan-Rishathaim, King of Mesopotamia. On the fourth day, at the completion of the fast, Israel gathered as one man and loudly declared the Yahweh was their God and also that day renewed a covenant to follow Him and Him alone, with all their heart from this day forward.

Deuteronomy 28:45-52,

47

Surprise Attack

Othniel didn't have to wait long for his reply from Cushan-Rishathaim. Only six days after he'd sent it the messenger returned. "Well, let me read his reply," Othniel demanded impatiently.

"Actually, he didn't give me one," the man replied. "After he read your note, he flew into an incredible rage, I thought he was going to kill me with his bare hands.

"When he'd calmed enough to speak, he just told me to stick around for a few hours and report what I witnessed. But he did add that he would show this Yahweh God who was in charge of Israel these days."

"Okay so you hung around, what did you see," Othniel demanded.

"He ordered the assembly of all his troop and ten thousand chariots. One of his Generals told me their army was close to a million trained soldiers. They were marching out of his city

Surprise Attack

towards Israel as I left. Their first victim they claim will be Othniel ben Kenaz."

Immediately on hearing the report the assembled Elders and their lieutenants flung their arms into the air in total despair. They roared insults at Othniel, "You idiot, Othniel, we're totally done for now!"

"Some leadership you've shown."

"We much prefer oppression and tribute than a gruesome death."

"Let's get home, gather our families and head for Moab."

Othniel's spirit stirred wildly within him as he heard their complaints. Not a one had even mentioned Yahweh. "Enough!" Othniel bellowed. "You're all a bunch of fools and every one of you deserves to die. Remember you bought this on yourselves by serving that piece of dead wood you called Baal. We all deserve to die because of that." Othniel strode around the group of Elders with glaring eyes and a face engulfed in rage.

"Just a few days ago, remember, we all repented before Yahweh and burnt those bits of wood. Yahweh is our God; He is our strength. He will save us. I know that because I've seen Him do so many, many times during my lifetime. Before we do anything else let's go and inquire of Yahweh," Othniel concluded. "And for-goodness-sake shut up with all this negative talk. This man Cushan-Rishathaim has dared to defy Yahweh claiming he's the one who rules Israel. Regardless of the size of his army he is an ant in the eyes of our God."

Othniel called Phinehas and said, "You guys wait here as Phinehas and I are going to consult Yahweh through the Urim and Thummim." As they walked off towards the Tabernacle Othniel stood well back from the tent enclosure containing the Holy Place and the Holy of Holies. Phinehas went off to a room at one side to dress in his full High Priest uniform including the Ephod containing the sacred stones of the Urim and Thummim.

While Othniel waited for the High Priest to return he lay prostrate before the Tabernacle. His reverence for Yahweh didn't allow him to stand as he quietly prayed in his heart calling on Yahweh to intervene and deliver his people. "Okay let's do this," a voice said. Othniel looked up at the voice to see Phinehas dressed completely in the High Priest garments with his son Abishua also dressed in his Serving Priest garments ready to assist. As Othniel stood to his feet suddenly a mighty awe overwhelmed him. He was about to have an encounter with the mighty living God of Israel.

Phinehas stood facing the entrance to the Holy Place directly in front of the veiled enclosure of the Holy of Holies which contained the Ark of the Covenant with its Mercy Seat above which Moses used so often to hear the literal words of Yahweh. Since Moses' time Yahweh's spoken word was rare but His revelation through the Urim and Thummim was more common. The process was a simple yes or no. If the Priest wearing the Ephod was asked a question, then one of them would glow brightly. If the Urim glowed then the answer was No, if the Thummim glowed the answer was Yes. The stronger the glow meant a more definitive answer. (*Author's note; This description of how the Urim and Thummim functioned is drawn from Hebrew beliefs and is used here with considerable poetic license. The Bible is very clear that the Urim and Thummim were used to consult God but nowhere does it define how they functioned. Please don't take the description here as definitive.*).

Abishua stood in front of his father, the High Priest, nearer the Holy Place but to his right-hand side. His purpose was to relay which stone glowed in response to the question. Othniel now stood about six paces behind the Priest but on his left, diagonally opposite Abishua. With everyone in place Phinehas said, "Okay, Othniel please ask Yahweh your questions. Remember to make them short and precise."

"Do we attack Cushan-Rishathaim?" Othniel began.

"Thummim says affirmative," Abishua announced.

"Do we wait until he sets the battle?" Othniel asked.

"Urim says No," Abishua replied.

"Do we make a rapid surprise attack?" Othniel asked.

"Yahweh says yes," Abishua answered. On and on the questions went until eventually Othniel had a very clear understanding of the mind of Yahweh on the matter and that victory was absolutely assured.

Othniel called all the people, still waiting at Shiloh, together. "Yahweh has been very clear in His answers," Othniel began. "Yahweh is going to fight for us against this evil king Cushan-Rishathaim." A mighty cheer went up from the listening throng. "We have to fight to restore our land," Othniel continued, this is not a gift but if we step forward to fight, Yahweh will fight with us. Victory is assured. He is coming from the North, so we march North at first light tomorrow and we'll surprise him just past the old city of Hazor. I know that Cushan-Rishathaim has confiscated most of your weapons but spend the afternoon fashioning anything that can be used lethally and be ready at first light. Axes make great weapons and I know most of you have one of those at least."

Othniel spent the rest of the day appointing Generals over Tribes, then having them assign their captains over thousands, hundreds and tens, a tradition instigated by Moses from Jethro's suggestion over a century ago. A count of weapons was made and it was discovered that there were only three thousand swords, spears or arrows to arm a million people. Cushan-Rishathaim's men had been thorough. These were allocated to those of senior rank to lead the battle. "The rest must rely on axes," Othniel stated. "Thank Yahweh. He is fighting for us!" he added.

For the next two days the Army of Israel, a motley bunch of now about six hundred thousand inexperienced poorly armed men, marched North toward the region of Hazor in accordance with Yahweh's instructions. Meanwhile Cushan-Rishathaim and his army of battle-hardened warriors and their mass of iron chariots marched South bent on bringing a rebellious Israel to heel. All-the-while the Angel of Yahweh moved invisibly ahead of Othniel and his people leading the way.

About mid-morning on the third day Othniel came to the brow of a range of hills which gave an amazing view down the valley to the Jordan River and the vast fertile plains of

Surprise Attack

Manasseh. Right on cue, just as Yahweh had said there was the vast army of Cushan-Rishathaim spread out all along the Jordan River preparing to cross. Othniel ordered his men to halt while they formed a plan.

Othniel called his Generals together and announced his plan. "We'll attack as they cross the Jordan," Othniel said. "We'll divide into four groups. Two groups will go wide, one to the North and one to the South to come round behind his army. The other two groups will attack from this side; again, one from the Northern side and one from the Southern side and we'll meet in the middle. We'll attack at night when I blow the shofar. Everyone is to shout, "Great is Yahweh," as they rush towards the enemy."

With all questions settled the two groups assigned to the Eastern flanks on the other side of the Jordan set off and much to their surprise not a man of the million strong enemy army noticed – no alarm was raised nor any warning sounded. It was like they had become invisible. Likewise, Othniel's two remaining groups took up their positions on the West side of the Jordan. Othniel remained in his command position which gave him the best view of the whole battlefield.

As darkness invaded the day the moon rose in all its splendour. This was the time Cushan-Rishathaim was waiting for and he gave the order for his troops to begin to cross the Jordan; a process expected to take a couple of days. His Chariots were useless around water and this made him vulnerable, the cover of darkness, he believed would give him the required protection.

Othniel watched and waited and quietly marvelled at the accuracy of the word of Yahweh. Victory was assured. Once Cushan-Rishathaim's crossing was well underway, impossible to halt or rapidly reverse Othniel stood calmly and blew the shofar long and hard. Immediately thousands of the troops of Israel leapt from their hidings and wielding their farm axes high they rushed the enemy from all four directions screaming at the peak of their lungs, "Great is Yahweh."

Cushan-Rishathaim's army, armed to the teeth, panicked. Most of their horses and chariots were being used in the water to ferry men and supplies rendering them useless for immediate war. Despite the bright moon the enemy seemed unable to distinguish friend from foe and began slaughtering every man in sight. The unfortunate fact that these were their comrades completely eluded them as terror and panic ensued.

By the time Othniel's troops actually arrived at the fight, there was very little actual fighting left for them to do. Abandoned weapons, however, were in abundance so the men of Israel discarded their farm axes and helped themselves to the recently deserted ones. Onward they pushed, finishing off the injured and occasional standing man.

On the Eastern flank Othniel's troops pushed forward and quickly united at the rear working their way forward towards the Jordan again finishing off the injured and occasional standing man. Before long they encountered the almost deserted command post of the great king Cushan-Rishathaim. His focus was towards the Jordan believing that to be the only source of the attack, he'd completely ignored his rear. Four men of Judah crept forward and leapt onto his stationary chariot and immediately overpowered the great king and his two nearby armour-bearers.

After others slaughtered the armour-bearers the men bound the great king hand to foot with rope and threw him back in his chariot. "Can you drive a chariot?" one of the commanders asked his young lieutenant.

Despite having never actually seen a chariot until that day he quickly replied with a proud smile, "Yes, of course," any chance to drive the chariot of one of the greatest kings of his time was not to be missed. Several hours later a somewhat flustered young lieutenant and a couple of his hearty companions had successfully navigated the seven kilometres (five miles) around the battlefield, the Jordan ford and up the hill to Othniel.

Seeing the once mighty king lying forlorn in his impressive golden chariot Othniel declared the battle over and sounded the retreat. As his troops regrouped again on the Western side of the Jordan, the remaining enemy troops abandoned all and headed for the hills and home. "Hang this troubler of Israel on the nearest tree," Othniel ordered. "And as you're doing it remind him that Yahweh is in charge of Israel. Great is Yahweh!"

Judges 3:10

48

Spoil and Passover

Othniel enjoyed ordering a couple of his young lieutenants to blow both the silver trumpets at the very first break of day, calling the congregation together. The many times he'd been awakened early from sweet dreams by the same sound during his time in the wilderness and the years of war were countless. Naturally this reason wasn't a factor in the early start this day. There was much to be done he told himself as deep down a tinge of sweet revenge simmered.

Othniel addressed his bleary men, "Yesterday Yahweh gave us a great victory. The cold body of the great troubler of Israel now lies under a non-descript tree near the river beyond us. All the tents and belongings of his vast army lie deserted on the other side. Today we'll receive Yahweh's reward and gather the spoil. All that you have lost because of that man over the past eight years will be returned today. Take what is yours, don't be greedy and share with your brothers. Remember the tithe to Yahweh."

Spoil and Passover

With his short speech over his now very awake Army raced down for the spoil. All day the men searched the deserted tents and belongings. The dead were stripped of clothing together with anything of value were thrown into a large pile for burning. Every man knew exactly what these troops had helped themselves to as they invaded their cities. They carefully counted the clothes, weapons, silver shekels and things of value. Just as Othniel had said, Yahweh was returning everything they'd lost and more. By the end of the day every man's possessions had been fully restored.

As the men pressed on through the huge expanse that only yesterday had been home to a million men they came across a large area that was enclosed in a wall made of ox skins, posts and pegs similar to the one that had surrounded the Tabernacle. As they searched for a way in one of the men heard a whimper, a faint cry of a woman coming from inside. "Go and get Othniel," he ordered his man.

By the time Othniel arrived the men had completed their search for the entrance. Finding only the one they stood near it weapons at the ready as Othniel approached. They quickly briefed him and formed an attack plan, certain that area was some sort of stronghold where they kept their women which they assumed would still be well guarded.

"Go," Othniel shouted and about two hundred heavily armed men rushed the sturdy curtain wall and gate. As the wall fell and the men invaded the sound of women screaming in fear became deafening. Finding no guards or protectors the invaders quickly realised the need to slaughter had vanished. A large group of young women had herded themselves into the centre of the compound, screaming and pleading for mercy.

Othniel ordered his men to stand down but remain on guard. "There may be attackers hidden among them," he advised. Othniel and a couple of others walked closer to examine the young women. Most were reasonably dressed and seem to have been fed and cared for but why were they enclosed like this? This thought troubled him and he shared his concerns with a lieutenant.

One of the women near Othniel on hearing what he'd said suddenly shouted excitedly, "They speak Hebrew!" A subdued and uncertain cheer went up from the women in response as they knew Israel wasn't the only nation in the region to speak Hebrew.

Now it was Othniel's time to be amazed. He approached the young woman who'd shouted and asked, "Who are you and what are you doing here?" Becoming more comfortable of Othniel's familiar dialect the women relaxed.

"We're all Hebrew women," she explained. "We were captured by Cushan-Rishathaim's men when they invaded our villages. They made us join this army, not to fight but," she paused, then lowering her gaze she added, "for his men." She didn't need to explain further. Othniel had encountered women held for this reason before. The commander used them for the gratification of his Generals and as rewards to those that fought well.

"So, all of you are Hebrews?" Othniel asked.

"Yes, every one of us," then woman replied.

"Put your weapons away," Othniel ordered his men. He then ordered his men to go through and ascertain which city each woman had come from, who's descendant they were? After that make sure they are fed and dressed well. Take them to the River Jordan and allow then to wash, discreetly away from the men, then bring them up to our camp on the other side. "Your nightmare is over, girls," Othniel shouted.

Later that day, after calling all to assembly, Othniel addressed his Army. "Yahweh has blessed us with so much spoil," he started. "So much spoil that we'll need at least three more days to finish the job. There is more good news. This morning Yahweh returned the daughters which this wicked king took from your families." He then ordered his men to bring out the several hundred women they'd recovered earlier in the day. "These women are all daughters of Israel. They were captured by Cushan-Rishathaim's men when he raided your cities. If you have lost a daughter or are from a city that has, please come forward now and claim them." A mighty cheer went up from the whole Army. To recover their daughters was indeed a blessing from Yahweh.

Within an hour every single young woman had been reunited with a family member. And even more remarkable was that there was not a man who didn't find the person they had lost. Every young virgin taken so violently had been returned and reunited with their loved ones. Othniel order that their relatives were to accompany them back to their villages leaving at first light next day.

By the end of the fourth day the camp had been cleared. The bodies of more than one hundred thousand men still smouldered to one side. All the horses had been hamstrung and let loose, in accordance with the Law of Yahweh. Thousands of sheep, cattle, donkeys and camels had been herded and despite every man taking his share for his loss still thousands remained – a portion for Yahweh, Othniel ordered. Just as Othniel had told his troops, 'All that you have lost because of Cushan-Rishathaim over the past eight years will be returned.' To a man, everything was restored, even his daughters.

"Tomorrow we begin our march back to Shiloh where we will celebrate before Yahweh, then you can return to your homes," Othniel advised.

It was the ninth day of the month Nisan when the triumphant Army settled into the Shiloh hills. Next day Othniel ordered all the men to celebrate the Passover by each taking a lamb from the spoil. "Keep it for four days and have the Levites take it's blood on the fourteenth day of Nisan," Phinehas advised all the people. "Roast the Passover lamb, eat it and celebrate heartily at the very beginning of the fifteenth day, after the evening of the fourteenth. Eat it to Yahweh as He is the one who gave us such a great victory. Remember, the fifteenth day is a holy day, a Sabbath day of rest."

A very grateful nation ate that Passover before Yahweh and thanked Him for His abundant blessing. Othniel and Phinehas were quick to remind the people that His blessings are always conditional. This blessing was because each man, as one nation, had repented and burnt their strange gods and turned back to

Yahweh. "All had been recovered this time, but you had better not test Yahweh ever again," Othniel advised.

After the Sabbath day of Unleavened Bread all the men stayed together enjoying the abundance of spoil, the food and the wine while they ate only unleavened bread for the six days until the final Sabbath, holy day.

During the six days Othniel counted out the surplus spoil, dividing it according to the number of cities of the Levites. He then commissioned several men to each deliver the spoil to their allocated city. Everything left over he dedicated to the house of Yahweh at Shiloh.

While Othniel was busy with the spoil Phinehas arranged for the Levite scribes to circulate among the people and read them the Torah, the Laws of Yahweh. They cautioned the people to keep walking in His ways. "You have all seen first-hand what happens," he advised, "when you turn aside. We've been fortunate this time but Yahweh may not be so merciful next time."

After the eighth day Othniel dismissed the people, warning them to continue to follow Yahweh only. "Serve Him with all your heart and have no other gods," Othniel warned. All the men left and returned to live in peace with their families. Their possessions restored – life was good.

Othniel returned with his sons to Anab to be with his beautiful wife and enjoy the blessings of His God. Yet again he had seen first-hand the incredible faithfulness of the God he served. Everything that the wicked king had taken had been completely and exactly restored, not one thing was unaccounted for.

Judges 3:10.

49

The Judge

There was little to do within his olive grove in the Spring time. The weather was mild, it was time to relax. Since returning from Shiloh that was about all he'd done. He figured that at seventy-three years old it was time to sit back and enjoy his inheritance.

He sat on the rooftop in the evening air enjoying a goblet of wine as he watched the usual evening activities in the nearby city Square. Tonight, was particularly busy as several visitors had arrived and taken up positions waiting for lodging invitations. Othniel was just tossing up whether to order one of his house servants to extend an invitation when one randomly appeared at his rooftop haven.

"Mr. Othniel," the slave began, "there are people at the door asking for you, sir." Leaving his sanctuary Othniel descended his stairway to his front entrance. 'People,' it transpires, was a definition used very loosely by the slave. Outside his door this evening were about fifty men, women and children each one seeking an audience with the great Othniel ben Kenaz of the Tribe of Judah.

Othniel was taken aback by the welcome. "What's all this about?" he asked. After much discussion it was established that because Joshua was dead and that Othniel had led the Army of Israel to such an astounding victory therefore he was now the undisputed leader of Israel. Othniel readily accepted he had led the Army in war but as for a leader in peacetime, that was an entirely different matter.

"Why do you need a leader, anyway?" Othniel asked.

The answer was clear; "To determine judgement on the matters that our Tribal leaders cannot settle." That need was for certain and had always been the function of Moses then Joshua, but he was no match for those great men. After much discussion Othniel finally said, "I'll pray to Yahweh and give you an answer in the morning."

As he retreated to his rooftop, he gave strict orders he was not to be disturbed, on any account – even if the house was on fire. Once back in his private place he laid out his case before Yahweh. Explaining, or at least attempting to, that he wasn't qualified to lead Israel. War was something he knew but answering hard questions on behalf of Yahweh was a whole new level.

At some late hour, having heard nothing like a voice from Yahweh he fell asleep. Any idea of what he was going to tell these visitors tomorrow eluded him. Othniel slept soundly that night, very soundly in fact; a deep sleep from Yahweh came upon him and he dreamed so vivid it was like He was physically there.

In his dream he was walking through the mountains of Israel, far beyond the borders of Judah when he came across a massive flock of sheep and goats. Such a massive flock, much larger than anything he'd ever seen. The sheep happily grazed on the green fields which seemed to go on forever. Strange he thought, he couldn't see a single shepherd, not a man or a woman was anywhere to be found as he walked through the sheep. Suddenly he noticed two young lions stalking their prey, dividing off a group and devouring them instantly. Next thing to the other side an attack came, this time from wild dogs while bears came from the North and mauled many.

Othniel looked on for a time horrified at what he saw. As he watched his spirit stirred, "This is not right," he shouted in his dream. "Nobody is caring for the flock and it's being devoured right and left." As he spoke, he rushed the bears who immediately scampered, likewise with the dogs and the lions. As he chased off the attackers those destroyed re-joined the others and a very contented flock resumed their grazing under Othniel's watchful eye.

Instantly he was awake, the reality of the dream still pounding in his mind. Immediately he knew the dream was from Yahweh, that was his answer, he was to shepherd the flock of Israel. Why? Simply because there was no one else.

Othniel raced down stairs to his house and woke his sleeping wife and excitedly explained Yahweh had spoken to him in a dream. At first Achsah didn't exactly share his excitement, continued sleep was her clear preference. However, as she listened, she understood Yahweh had indeed spoken. In all his seventy-three years he'd never met anyone Yahweh had spoken to outside of the Priesthood, Moses and Joshua. "What an honour," he said.

It was just at that moment that the reality of what Yahweh had spoken hit home. He explained to Achsah the detail of the dream and before he was finished, she interrupted saying. "If Yahweh wants you to judge Israel, I will support you in any way I can."

"Thank you," Othniel replied, "I'm certainly going to need your help. I have people here to present their cases tomorrow but I don't see why the people should come to me. We should travel in a circuit each year throughout Israel and meet them where they are. But I can only do that if you come too?" "Of course, my husband," Achsah answered. "Now let's get some sleep so you're fresh for your hearings tomorrow."

Refreshed, Othniel held court for the next few weeks in the open square in Anab. To his surprise even the most complex cases had a simple solution after hearing all the evidence. Many dealt with land issues or inheritance while others dealt with the place children of other wives had in a family. Othniel knew Yahweh was guiding his decisions as every time after a short reflection the answer would always be clear to him.

Othniel called together a group of young runners to travel to every city in Israel saying that all Israel is to gather without fail at Shiloh each year for the Passover in the month of Nissan and also for the Feast of Tabernacles in the month of Tishrei. Between those months each year please don't travel to Anab to have your cases heard because he was going to travel to them. Outside those months, if the case was urgent come to Anab but if it could wait then he'd hear it when he arrived.

Since it was already about a month past the Passover Othniel decided a shortened version of a circuit would be best for this year but from then on, every year he and Achsah would hit the road and visit every main city in Israel.

Much to Othniel's surprise he enjoyed the travel, meeting people and listening to their problems. Yahweh stood with him and while he did hear some heart-breaking situations, a definitive answer always brought joy.

The first year's circuit ended quickly and once again the Passover was calling. Othniel and Achsah mounted their camels as their servants drove the donkey cart with the necessary lambs. One perfect one for the Passover and several for food for the journey or perhaps to give away.

Immediately the festivities were ended the couple set off on their extended tour. Setting off from Shiloh they made their way back to the start point at Bethel. From there they headed over to Shechem, on to Megiddo then around Mt Tabor which was on the shore of the sea of Chinnereth (the Galilee). From there they journeyed South and crossed the Jordan to Jabesh Gilead and on to Mizpah and Heshbon. After Heshbon they crossed back over the Jordan near Gilgal then headed up to

Shiloh for the Feast of Tabernacles (Sukkot). After the feast, they would journey up through the mountains towards Jebus. Then via Bethlehem-Ephrathah and Hebron and finally back to Anab to much deserved rest and relaxation.

Each year as they travelled Othniel would ensure at least one scribe from the Levites of Hebron would accompany them. Their purpose was to read the Torah scrolls aloud in the Square of each city they visited, for all to hear. Several other Levites would accompany the scribes to help answer any questions the people had about the Torah. They mingled among the crowd, giving the meaning of the text being read, ensuring Yahweh's Laws were clearly understood.

This they did together consistently for the next thirty years. Throughout all that time the people feared Yahweh and followed His Law exactly. The name of foreign gods such as Baal became extremely rare in Israel for as long as Othniel lived.

Judges 3:9-11.

50

Death

Othniel had turned one hundred three years ago and while he did tire, he still abounded with energy, each year completing his circuit with ease. Achsah now ninety-nine would also celebrate her centenary in a few months. Unlike her husband, this year she had found the going tough. Sitting for hours on a restless camel shook her entire body but she endured it to be with the man she loved; he did the work of Yahweh.

Arriving at Shiloh for the Feast of Tabernacles she slumped from her camel as a servant made her comfortable and arranged the stick and brush booth that would be her home for the ten-day festival. The journey from Heshbon had been gruelling. Normally the camels would cover the distance in two days but this time the scorching sun and her general condition meant travelling only in the cool of the early morning. The afternoons were spent sleeping, relaxing and regaining the courage to do the same thing the next day.

Othniel was worried, Achsah's decline had been sudden. At the start of the circuit she was bright and bouncy, forever his stay and strength. It was about the time they crossed the Jordan to travel East that he first noticed her spark had waned. He watched as the servants tended her and his concern peaked that evening when she refused all food.

Throughout the ten days of the Feast Othniel busied himself with meeting and judging urgent matters, anything to distract him from his wife's condition. Finally, things ended and the time came to travel and disband. "I can't get on that camel again," Achsah complained. Othniel quickly agreed, what if she fell from the animal? That would be immediate death. He had his servants prepare a donkey cart, making a comfortable bed for his wife to sit on, supported for the journey home.

There would be no stops for judgements this time. Overnight stops yes, but no week-long stays. Ephrathah and Hebron would have to come to Anab this year.

Four nights later they rode into Hebron for their final night's stay, home beckoned. Riding in a cart had bode well with Achsah and she was bright and cheery as she alighted in Hebron that night and walked unaided to their lodgings. As was usual, Othniel's arrival never went unnoticed. All the city Elders were assembled for the evening meal where food and wine were in abundance. Much to Othniel's delight Achsah joined him, forever the faithful wife, her appetite had returned, she was bright and her usual relaxed self.

Death

Othniel slept well that night, his wife was on the mend and next day they'd be home. In a few months they'd celebrate her one-hundred years, life was good again.

Othniel woke early, keen to get home before the scorching heat of the late autumn invaded the day. "Wake up, my dear," Othniel called, "I can hear the birds calling for the dawn to come." Achsah didn't answer so Othniel dressed and, deciding to let her sleep some more, went out to organise his servants. Satisfied with progress he returned to his sleeping quarters to collect his wife.

The room was now flooded with daylight from the rapidly breaking dawn. Immediately Othniel could see something wasn't right. He rushed over to his wife who lay motionless on her bed and grabbed her in his arms. Her cold lifeless body flopped against him as the full realisation hit him hard. The love of his life for the past eighty-five years was dead – "Oh, Yahweh, why, why, why?" he wailed loudly. Immediately the room filled with people, their hosts and a myriad of servants all desperate to understand the reason for such a desperate call from the leader of Israel.

Othniel's daughter Rachael, who lived nearby within the city, was quickly summoned. She and her father, after allowing themselves to mourn a little, took care of the body, washing her and wrapping her in clean linen, ready for the tomb.

A messenger was dispatched to tell Othniel's two sons and all the people of Anab the news of Achsah's death. Othniel was heading directly to the burial cave between the upper and lower springs. All who wished to come should meet there.

Shortly after mid-day Othniel and his entourage arrived at the cave where every citizen of Anab had already gathered. Hathath and Meonothai rushed over to see their mother for the final time and to mourn with their father and sister.

Othniel wept uncontrollably as the servants carried the love of his life, placing her in the cold depths of the cave, her body forever engulfed in death. The deafening noise of the gathered crowd echoed down the massive canyon that held the cave, their loss genuine. Achsah had touched so many hearts and every person in the city of Anab had a story to tell of what she'd done for them personally.

The mourning done, Othniel and his family returned to Anab, another circuit complete but not how he'd envisaged it. Rachel decided to stay on for a few weeks and help her father settle. Her own children now grown and each with their own families, she had the time. Although why she'd bothered quickly became the question. First thing the next morning after committing his wife's body to the grave Othniel was up at the crack of dawn and into his olive grove.

Despite his son's insistence that everything was well under control Othniel was determine to keep busy, anything to keep his mind occupied on things that weren't to do with Achsah. All that winter he supervised the pressing and even insisted on delivering the tithe himself to Hebron and even as far as Debir.

Death

Passover neared and both Hathath and Meonothai strongly suggested he sit this one out but he'd have none of it. Five days before Passover he mounted his trusted camel and set off with his team to Shiloh and the Feast of Passover. As soon as the feast had ended, he set off just as he'd done for the past thirty years on his circuit around the cities of Israel. "Nothing will hinder me from doing the work of Yahweh," he announced. "For as long as I have breath in my body, I intend to serve Him."

The next ten years after Achsah died passed quickly, while Othniel continued his determined service to Yahweh. His wiry frame somehow provided the strength for him to abound throughout his annual circuit. He never failed to pass a judgement and every year the scribes taught the people, and the fear of Yahweh was strong in the land.

Othniel had been back in Anab for a few weeks and today he'd arrange to go with his son Meonothai to held herd his sheep from up near the upper spring and bring them in for shearing. Othniel enjoyed visiting the springs., It was a connection to his wife and the fond memory of her enticing her father to give her that massive land track still amused him.

Othniel marched off with a bright heart towards his camel. Just as he bent to untie the animals tether though, he fell headlong to the ground. Before he'd even hit cold pavement his life had gone and there he lay overcome by death as his anxious son rushed to his aid.

Later that day Othniel's body was carefully laid in the family cave, the same one that held the bones of his wife Achsah and his uncle and mentor Caleb. Runners were quickly sent throughout the land and all Israel mourned for the next forty days for the loss of their passionate leader who had led Israel for the past forty years.

Othniel was one hundred and thirteen years old when he died. He'd live through twenty years in the wilderness, five years of war conquering the land and eighty-eight years living in his inheritance. For thirty-seven years he'd lived in Anab beside Caleb but in total he'd know the man for sixty-two years. He'd always regarded Caleb as his father despite the love for his natural father, Kenaz, who had died so tragically when Othniel was just nineteen.

Next to Yahweh was his love for his most beautiful bride who he'd been married to for seventy-eight years. His three children, his countless grandchildren and great-grandchildren he counted as a bonus from Yahweh.

History simply records the life of this great man, a true father of Israel, in three short Bible verses; Judges 3:9-11

"But when the people of Israel cried out to Yahweh for help, Yahweh raised up a rescuer to save them. His name was Othniel, the son of Caleb's younger brother, Kenaz. The Spirit of Yahweh came upon him, and he became Israel's judge. He went to war against King Cushan-Rishathaim of Aram, and Yahweh gave Othniel victory over him. So, there was peace in the land for forty years. Then Othniel son of Kenaz died." (NLT)

Clearly, it's not the length of the obituary that counts but perhaps the abundant untold detail of how and why.

Why Are Fathers Few?

Through this book we saw fathers mentor sons.

- Jethro was a father to Moses.
- Jephunneh was a father to Kenaz.
- Kenaz was a father to Othniel.
- Caleb was a father to Othniel.
- Othniel was a father to Israel.

One simple fact is clear; men become fathers; they're not born that way.

In the natural, when a man produces a descendant, he is named as the father of that child. He is so named because the child carries his genes, his DNA. Every person alive today has a father and regardless of that person's relationship with him, the fact remains that a man played a part in their conception.

A dictionary definition of 'father' is to beget, or to be the founder, producer, or author of. Therefore, to be a father one must originate or produce offspring, or some other original object or service.

However here is the question; just because a man produces progeny does that make him a father? If, for example, after the birth he plays no further part in the life of the child, is he a father to that child? Well, yes from the sense that the child's origin is because of him. But no, when it comes to being a father to the life of the child. There is a monumental difference between originating something and nurturing the development of that thing.

A mother, because she carries the child and physically gives birth to it, forms a strong bond with it usually even before it is born. It is unusual, although not unheard of, for a woman to abandon her child. Predominantly, she will do anything to protect and nurture it, providing a safe and secure environment for it to grow and develop. Mother's love will ensure her child is fed, clothed and cared for in a loving way to cause it to grow strong and prosper. This will even happen regardless of the presence of a father. A mother naturally provides the care, the love and nurturing. Why then is a father necessary?

In the secular environment of today's world that question is often answered with a resounding 'not necessary'. Fathers have been relegated a secondary role in the child's upbringing. To be fair a lot of men have been very quick to accept this secondary part, but that does not make it right. The function of a father in a home has primarily been consigned to that of provider. His principal responsibility is to provide bread for the table, a roof overhead, clothing and transport. And of course, for the modern man his fair share of the day-to-day care.

Now of course I'm generalising and it's certainly not my intention to knock the role of women in society. It's quite okay for a woman to have a great career and be the principal earner in the household. What I'm talking about are the roles or functions men and women traditionally play in raising a child. Each has a task in rearing the descendant which is specific to each parent. If, for example, both parents spent their entire time providing food and shelter where would the nurturing come from?

In one sense both the mother and the father can provide all the cares needed by their child. But there are some things that come easier, or more naturally, to either gender. Generally speaking, a mother's love is protective and a father's love relates to wellbeing. He's interested to ensure the family line continues, that a legacy continues. A mother wants her child to flourish – to live long and prosper.

So what is the difference between a man who just wants to sire a child, to continue his genetic line and a man who wants to raise a child to produce a legacy?

1 John 2:14 sheds some light on this question: *"I have written to you, fathers, because you know Him who has been from the beginning, I have written to you, young men, because you are strong, and the word of God abides in you, and you have overcome the evil one."* (NKJV)

There has to be a dad for the birth of a child. But many dads never step into the role of being a Father. The difference between being a dad and being a Father is what this book attempts to demonstrate, with a practical example of Othniel. The man had a natural dad, Kenaz, but Caleb became his father. Caleb was the man who sowed continually into his life to mature him to such an extent that God was able to use him to lead the Nation of Israel, win wars and provide peace in the Promised Land for forty years.

Caleb had to step to the front and look ahead. He had to see beyond today. True fathers see the PLAN OF GOD, and propagate it.

To become a father, it's imperative you have vision. Fathers must be an example of maturity, integrity, honesty, and character. Fathers must realize they set the standard. Hopefully this book demonstrates in a practical way how Caleb, because of these attributes, caused Othniel to emulate him.

It's entirely possible to fill ourselves up with a lot of teaching through good books, great podcasts, YouTube videos and posts on social networks, but the individuals we're feeding ourselves from would not be our spiritual fathers. They are just teachers and these are not enough to build character into your life.

Lest you think I'm building some kind of case with just one verse of the Bible, take a moment and look at the lifestyle Jesus modelled during His earthly life. He taught and healed the multitudes, but He only discipled a dozen men. You could say that in order to spread His Gospel message — apart from dying on the Cross and redeeming mankind, which was His focus — He spread His message throughout the known world by pouring Himself into just twelve guys for His three years of ministry. They then took it to geographical places Jesus didn't physically go to during His life. He multiplied Himself in these men, in a manner of speaking.

Imagine if I was a house painter with many years of experience and, perhaps, I wanted to model evangelical Christian forms of discipleship in my business. To achieve this, would I hire a young man, pay him a small wage and ask him to observe me painting for six months? If he just watched me from his seated position in my van for this time, he could probably explain some correct concepts about house painting to a friend. But if I want to make an apprentice of this young man, I'd have to get him out of the van, give him absolutely every tool I had, and help him learn every aspect of actually painting. He'd have to get dirty, deal with his fears, take responsibility and so on.

Jesus warned His apprentices to watch out for the "leaven of the Pharisees." The leaven was the doctrine-focused spiritual fervency that naturally extracted them from truly loving people. Jesus didn't come to belittle them or suggest that scriptural knowledge and moral living was bad, but He came to fulfil, enlarge and expand what true spiritual formation was. He came to model a holistic life where doctrine, theology, knowledge and morality were coupled with love, mercy, faith and action.

Jesus tells us in John 14:6-11; "*I am the way, the truth, and the life. No one comes to the Father except through Me. If you had known Me, you would have known My Father also; and from now on you know Him and have seen Him.*" (NKJV)

It is through Jesus that we get to know the heart of our heavenly Father. Through Him we get to understand the very nature and attributes of who God is, what He does and how to serve Him and please Him.

Today too many Christians believe that coming to Jesus, being cleansed of sin, is the end game. Let me be clear; Without Jesus there is no salvation, no eternal life, no cleansing of sin. There is no other way to salvation than through Jesus. However, being saved is only the very start of our journey. Jesus desires us to know our Father.

Being born again is a physical thing. Ezekiel 36:26, describes the process; *"And I will give you a new heart, and I will put a new spirit in you. I will take out your stony, stubborn heart and give you a tender, responsive heart."* (NLT). Once we're born-again we no longer live according to the principles of this world. We live in the Father's Kingdom as we're told in Colossians 1:13; *"He has delivered us from the domain of darkness and transferred us to the kingdom of his beloved Son."* (NLT)

God did not stop there however, as we're told in Ephesians 1:5; *"God decided in advance to adopt us into his own family by bringing us to himself through Jesus Christ. This is what he wanted to do, and it gave him great pleasure."* (NLT). Being born-again means being born into the Father's family. He regards us as children, not in the loose sense we regard adoption today, but in the very real way it was done in ancient Israel, in the same way Kenaz became a son of Jephunneh in this book. Romans 8:17 explains our position further; *"And if children, then heirs; heirs of God, and joint-heirs with Christ; if so be that we suffer with him, that we may be also glorified together."* (NKJV) We are joint heirs along with our Lord and Saviour Jesus. Why, because we're in God's family.

Since God is then our Father, once we're born-again we must walk by the power of the Holy Spirit and get to know Him. It is a process which takes time but if we do that then every day we'll learn something more. We'll take another step in becoming like our Father.

The question I ask is this; Is that what we're seeing in the Church, the body of Christ today? We started this book with the verse in 1 Corinthians 4:15; *"For though you might have ten thousand instructors in Christ, yet you do not have many fathers; for in Christ Jesus, I have begotten you through the gospel."* (NKJV)

What are you passing on through your life? Knowledge or example? That's only a question you can answer. The Apostle Paul was concerned even in his time that there were not many fathers in the Church. Things have certainly changed since then but sadly is it for the better? Become an Othniel, get near to men and women of God, people who know the Father and walk a life in the power of the Spirit pleasing to God, surrendered to doing His will every day of your short life on this earth.

In closing there's something the world is very good at that has crept strongly into the church – not learning from the past. Fathers understand the past because they remember what it was like. Ask an old-timer about WW2 and they'll give you an entirely different answer than what you'll find in any book. It's the same with recent events in Church history.

When Israel became a Nation in 1948 in direct fulfilment of Bible prophecy, great excitement rose about the nearness of the end of the age. Much Bible-based teaching centred around being ready for His imminent appearing. Along with this however, some popular preachers became involved in speculation, date setting an such-like which failed to mature since it was man's plan and not God's. The unfortunate result is that today the entire subject is avoided like the plague in most churches. Years can go by without the return of Jesus being mentioned. Neither position is right but fathers know that teaching the truth without speculation is the required position.

Many will recall the move of the Holy Spirit that began in the seventies. The power of the Spirit became manifest, healing and miracles abounded. However, unfortunately, strange spirits also crept in with people overcome by laughter, drunk-like behaviour, angels began to be worshipped and much worse. The fruits being manifest were not the fruit of the Holy Spirit; self-control for example. Again, this was dealt with by abandoning the concept and today very little of the Spirit's power is manifest in most churches. To avoid the pitfalls, often the work of the Holy Spirit is ignored completely.

The list goes on when we consider the word of faith movement, the prosperity gospel, the new apostolic reformation, the watering down of the Gospel to avoid causing offense, avoiding preaching sin or Hell, forsaking of regular church meetings where the saints only come together collectively once a week on a Sunday and then for only exactly an hour and a half.

Where are we headed? The fathers among us need to wake up and speak up. Not to lead and steer the ship necessarily but to impart their knowledge learned through experience.

Just in case you're thinking this lack of fathers relates only to recent church history here's how someone explained the moving of the Church through the past two thousand years.

'The early church was what they were, they genuinely lived-out their experience of walking with God. The Church later became centred in Greece where it became a philosophy. From there it went to Rome and became an institution. After Rome it went to Europe and became our culture. Then, finally, it went to America and became a business.'

Spiritual fathers have seen it before and when faced with a situation they know what to do. Why, because they're old? No, because they're walked a life by the power of the Holy Spirit and they know and understand their God and Father.

Daniel puts it this way, Daniel 11:32; (part of verse) *"but the people who know their God shall be strong, and carry out great exploits."* (NKJV)

We're in the last days, don't be caught short.

Author's Note

This book is a work of fiction but the majority of the events detailed actually happened and I've given the scriptural references for you to check. My intent with this book is to demonstrate how even a simple life with all its ups and downs can achieve righteousness acceptable to God Most High. We must be clear however, that the only way righteousness is possible is if you surrender your life completely to the Lord Jesus Christ by acknowledging you are a sinner and through repentance asking Him to be the Lord of your life. If you do this He will redeem your soul and restore it back to the relationship God intended for you at creation. Jesus will make you fully righteous, placing you in perfect right standing with God for all eternity. You will be spared from the wrath of God soon coming upon this entire earth and be rewarded with eternal life, living and reigning with Jesus for ever. What amazing grace.

It is impossible to achieve this life by human endeavours. The Bible tells us that man's very best efforts are but filthy rags, totally unacceptable to Him. The Bible also tells us in Acts 4:12 that *"There is salvation in no one else! God has given no other name under heaven by which we must be saved."* [NLT] That name is Jesus Christ, who died in our stead as a blood sacrifice for our sinful state. This is the same Jesus who rose from the dead on the third day, thereby breaking the power of sin and death. Jesus has ascended to Heaven and currently sits at the right hand of the Father God. The Holy Spirit of God is given to those redeemed by Jesus to enable them to understand His word in the Bible and empower them to live a righteous life until Jesus returns. Jesus Christ is returning physically very soon to snatch away all those that are true to Him while God pours out His wrath on the unrighteous remaining on this earth.

Where will you stand when He returns or when you are called to your life's end? Will you stand with the righteous or the unrighteous? There are only two possible states, righteous or unrighteous and only the righteous obtain eternal life. There is no other way to that eternal life except through Jesus Christ.

Perhaps you've never actually accepted Jesus as your Lord and Saviour and don't like the sound of being subject to God's wrath, especially when the alternative is not onerous. If that's you, I would like you to stop for a moment and intentionally recite this prayer aloud, to confess with your mouth.

"Dear Lord Jesus,

I admit that I am a sinner, in need of you and your forgiveness. I turn now from my sinful past and make you the Lord, the King, the Boss of my life. I believe with all my heart and confess with my mouth that you are the Lord Jesus Christ and that you died on the Cross in my stead for all my sins, you were buried and rose again to life. I thank you for the Father's gift of eternal life through faith and I believe in you alone. I surrender every part of my life to you Lord Jesus, forever and ever. Thank you for the gift of your Holy Spirit which I receive from you now."

Just merely saying those words doesn't bring salvation. It is only when you truly make Jesus the Lord of your life that you become born-again, thereby receiving eternal life. The words must come from your heart. Only then are you guaranteed to be spared from God's judgement through Jesus.

God bless you if you've just genuinely prayed that prayer, you have now begun your journey with God. I recommend you find a church, if you don't already have one, pray and read your Bible every day and talk to your Pastor about getting baptised. Praise the Lord!

If you have been helped by this please also drop me an email and let me know as it's encouraging to hear of God's work in others.

God bless.

About the Author

Robert (Bob) Cottle has been a scholar of the Bible for over 50 years having read, studied and analysed God's word extensively during his lifetime. The discipline of reading his Bible was instilled in him at a young age. At first, this was a burdensome chore and later it developed into a perfunctory habit. As the years progressed, however, the habit matured into a pleasurable pastime exploring the detail of the God he loves and serves.

Bob has been actively involved in church life from a young age having served as a lay preacher for a number of years and also as a church elder for a time.

Married for 38 years, Bob and his wife Julie live in Nelson, New Zealand, and have three adult children and two grandchild – to date. In his secular life, Bob trained and worked in professional engineering then later in senior business management but is now retired from full-time employment and enjoys writing Christian books.

Bob is blessed with a natural aptitude to portray verbal and/or written word pictures. In retirement he has focused his abundant free time to the study and understanding of God's Word in the Bible which combined with his previous writing skills has enabled him to develop and author his interesting books.

This is his fourth book to be commercially published, Bob is confident with the subject matter particularly given his extensive knowledge of the Bible. His desire is to pass on a little of this understanding for the aid of fellow Christians for the furtherance of God's work.

Feel free to follow or contact Robert (Bob) on;

🅕 Robert J Cottle Author,

𝕏 @bobcottle,

✉ robertjcottle@gmail.com

Other books by Robert J Cottle

- The Bible, True, Relevant or a Fairy Tale. (Non-fiction)

- Fifty Shades of White, one man's quest for righteousness. (A novel, fiction)

- The Gospel of the Kingdom, not the Gospel of the Church. (Non-fiction)

- Not Many Fathers, why Othniel became a Judge. (A novel, fiction.)

- Eschatology 101, What the Bible says about the end of time. (Non-fiction)

www.ingramcontent.com/pod-product-compliance
Lightning Source LLC
Chambersburg PA
CBHW071213080526
44587CB00013BA/1356